Praise for *Any Happy Returns*

Peter Oppenheimer is a distinguished practitioner of the art and science of stock market analysis. This volume instills his wisdom in cogent and clear terms. I don't know how well anyone can explain markets or even explain respectively their movements, but no one should even try without mastering this volume's important lessons.

—Lawrence Summers, former United States
Secretary of the Treasury.

Following his excellent The Long Good Buy, Peter Oppenheimer, in this new and very stimulating book continues and deepens his brilliant analysis of the financial market cycles, linking these with major trends but also with the geopolitical, technological, and other business and societal transformations. The author signals and identifies the emergence of the "Post-Modern Cycle" and its potential far reaching effects.

—José Manuel Barroso, former president of the European
Commission and prime minister of Portugal.

Business and financial cycles matter. Peter Oppenheimer understands them well. But there are times when a combination of social, economic, political and technological factors makes the past a particularly unreliable guide. Peter introduces the idea of the post-modern cycle, reflecting some deep structural changes in our world. This book is an opportunity for us to liberate ourselves from the tyranny of the present, to think big and long term, and to reap the rewards.

—Sir Alexander William Younger, former Chief of MI6.

By skilfully interweaving the future and the past and incorporating history, culture and politics into his economic analysis, Peter Oppenheimer has written a book that is thought-provoking, insightful, and original.

—Professor Noreena Hertz, Institute for Global Prosperity,
University College London.

Peter Oppenheimer has written a thoughtful and insightful book. He draws our attention to the role that cycles play in helping us not only understand where we are in them, but also to forecast what is likely to follow.

—Kofi Adjepong-Boateng CBE, Research Associate, Centre for
Financial History, University of Cambridge.

Peter's comprehensive analysis of Financial Market Super Cycles (longer-term trends), within which many cycles evolve, provides many new and invaluable insights. It is an eloquently written book that uses data-driven evidence, charts, and trends to succinctly convey and reinforce the underlying message. A must read for financial market investors, practitioners, academics, and regulators.

—Narayan Naik, Professor of Finance at the London Business School.

Praise for *The Long Good Buy*
(published in 2020*)

Oppenheimer offers brilliant insights, sage advice and entertaining anecdotes. Anyone wishing to understand how financial markets behave - and misbehave - should read this book now.

> —Stephen D. King, economist and author of
> Grave New World: The End of Globalisation, the Return of History.

Peter has always been one of the masters of dissecting financial markets performance into an understandable narrative, and in this book, he pulls together much of his great thinking and style from his career, and it should be useful for anyone trying to understand what drives markets, especially equities.

> —Lord Jim O' Neill, Chair, Chatham House.

A deeply insightful analysis of market cycles and their drivers that really does add to our practical understanding of what moves markets and long-term investment returns.

> —Keith Skeoch, CEO, Standard Life Aberdeen.

This book eloquently blends the author's vast experience with behavioural finance insights to document and understand financial booms and busts. The book should be a basic reading for any student of finance.

> —Elias Papaioannou, Professor of Economics,
> London Business School.

This is an excellent book, capturing the insights of a leading market practitioner within the structured analytical framework he has developed over many years. It offers a lively and unique perspective on how markets work and where they are headed.

> —Huw Pill, Senior Lecturer, Harvard Business School.

---

* Some roles have since changed.

"The Long Good Buy" is an excellent introduction to understanding the cycles, trends and crises in financial markets over the past 100 years. Its purpose is to help investors assess risk and the probabilities of different outcomes. It is lucidly written in a simple logical way, requires no mathematical expertise and draws on an amazing collection of historical data and research. For me it is the best and most comprehensive introduction to the subject that exists.

—Lord Brian Griffiths, Chairman - Centre for Enterprise, Markets and Ethics, Oxford.

Any Happy Returns

Any Happy Returns

Structural Changes and Super Cycles in Markets

Peter C. Oppenheimer

WILEY

Registered Office(s)
John Wiley & Sons, Inc., 111 River Street, Hoboken, NJ 07030, USA
John Wiley & Sons Ltd, The Atrium, Southern Gate, Chichester, West Sussex, PO19 8SQ, UK

Editorial Office
The Atrium, Southern Gate, Chichester, West Sussex, PO19 8SQ, UK

For details of our global editorial offices, customer services, and more information about Wiley products visit us at www.wiley.com.

Wiley also publishes its books in a variety of electronic formats and by print-on-demand. Some content that appears in standard print versions of this book may not be available in other formats.

Designations used by companies to distinguish their products are often claimed as trademarks. All brand names and product names used in this book are trade names, service marks, trademarks or registered trademarks of their respective owners. The publisher is not associated with any product or vendor mentioned in this book.

Disclaimer
The views stated herein do not necessarily reflect the views of Goldman Sachs.

Library of Congress Cataloging-in-Publication Data:

Names: Oppenheimer, Peter C., author. | John Wiley & Sons, publisher.
Title: Any happy returns : structural changes and super cycles in markets /
    Peter C. Oppenheimer.
Description: Hoboken, NJ : Wiley, 2024. | Includes index.
Identifiers: LCCN 2023039325 (print) | LCCN 2023039326 (ebook) | ISBN
    9781394210350 (cloth) | ISBN 9781394210367 (adobe pdf) | ISBN
    9781394210374 (epub)
Subjects: LCSH: Business cycles. | Business cycles—History. | Economic
    development. | Investments. | Finance.
Classification: LCC HB3722 .O655 2024 (print) | LCC HB3722 (ebook) | DDC
    338.5/42—dc23/eng/20231002
LC record available at https://lccn.loc.gov/2023039325
LC ebook record available at https://lccn.loc.gov/2023039326

Cover Design and Illustration: Goldman Sachs

Set in 10/12 STIX Two Text by Straive, Chennai, India

SKY10068653_022924

*To my dear parents,
Neville and Deanna*

Contents

Preface

I thought of that while riding my bicycle.

—Albert Einstein

My previous book, *The Long Good Buy* was about economic and financial market cycles and the factors that affect them. This book is designed to be complementary; part history and part forward-looking, it focuses on longer-term structural changes in economic and financial markets, and the differing secular trends in which cycles evolve. It is aimed at students, market practitioners and anyone interested in the history and factors that drive longer-term patterns and trends in economies and financial markets.

Within financial markets, there is a patten of both short-term cycles and longer-term super cycles, or secular trends, within which the shorter-term cycles evolve. The shorter cycles largely relate to business cycles. Since 1850, there have been 35 recessions in the US economy (according to the National Bureau of Economic Research) and 29 equity bear markets (falls of 20% or more in the main equity index).

Over the period since the end of World War II (WWII), there have been 13 recessions in the US economy and 12 equity bear markets.

Equity markets tend to anticipate economic cycles. Since WWII, the equity market peak has come, on average, about seven months before a recession, and the market has reached a trough also, on average, about seven months before an economic recovery.

In addition to business cycles and fluctuations in economic factors, such as economic activity and interest rates, a variety of other factors have a considerable influence on markets and can drive longer-term trends. These can range from geopolitics, technological and institutional changes to shifts in government policies and changing fashions and trends in society. Structural breaks in these factors can create longer-term secular trends or super cycles that can last for extended periods, during which business and market cycles evolve. For example, an extended period of low inflation could encompass several business cycles. Equally, periods of strong economic growth, or stagnation, have prevailed for a long time even when they have been temporarily impacted by short-lived recessions. These long trends are often associated with specific market conditions and opportunities, and it is these that I have attempted to explore in this book.

Since WWII, there have been six super cycles in equity markets. Half of these super cycles were secular bull markets, that is, periods with very high returns and rising valuations, and half can be described as 'Fat and Flat', that is, periods with lower returns over a long period but with a wide trading range.

As an introduction, Chapter 1 looks at the history of thought around cycles in social and political views, economies and financial markets, and the impact that psychology and human behaviour can have on these cycles.

The main body of the book is then split into three parts:

I. **Structural Trends and Market Super Cycles** – a history of cycles and super cycles.

II. **Analysing Post-War Super Cycles** – a discussion of each of the post-WWII super cycles and the conditions that drove them.

III. **The Post-Modern Cycle** – a look at how the next cycle is likely to unfold, what its key characteristics will be, and how it will be influenced and defined by two factors: artificial intelligence (AI) and decarbonisation, the first defining the virtual world and the second very much shaping the real world.

Part I: Structural Trends and Market Super Cycles

Chapter 2 focuses on an explanation of cycles in financial markets and the tendency for patterns to repeat themselves across four phases – Despair, Hope, Growth and Optimism – and their drivers.

Chapter 3 describes the long-term history of super cycles in key economic variables: GDP, inflation, interest rates, debt, inequality and financial markets.

Part II: Analysing Post-War Super Cycles

Chapter 4 discusses the drivers of the 1949–1968 super cycle. I look at the impact of international agreements, the backdrop of strong economic growth, technological innovation, low real interest rates and a boom in world trade, consumption and credit, as well as demographics.

Chapter 5 looks at the 1968–1982 era of inflation and low returns, and the impact of high interest rates and low growth, social unrest and strikes, collapsing world trade, high government debt and lower corporate profit margins.

Chapter 6 is a description of what I call the Modern Cycle – a period characterised by the 'Great Moderation', disinflation and lower cost of capital, as well as the impact of supply-side reforms. I discuss the impact of the end of the Soviet Union on geopolitical risk, and the emergence of globalisation and increased international cooperation, as well as the effect of rapid growth in China and India.

Chapter 7 covers 2000–2009, and focuses on the bubbles and troubles that dominated the first decade of the new millennium, from the fallout of the technology bubble to the financial crisis of 2008.

Chapter 8 looks at the unique conditions that dominated the 2009–2020 post-financial-crisis cycle and the impact of zero interest rate policies on market returns.

Chapter 9 discusses the consequences of the pandemic, and in particular its impact on policy, and the transition from a deflationary to a reflationary narrative for economic and market returns.

Part III: The Post-Modern Cycle

Chapter 10 describes the emergence of what I call the Post-Modern Cycle, and the implications of a period of rising cost of capital, slower trend growth, a shift from globalisation to regionalisation, a rise in the cost of labour and commodities, increased government debt, higher infrastructure spending, ageing demographics and higher geopolitical tension.

Chapter 11 discusses how technology and AI are likely to shape market returns in the Post-Modern Cycle.

Chapter 12 focuses on traditional industries and the opportunities that are likely to come from decarbonisation and increased infrastructure spending in the Post-Modern Cycle.

Finally, Chapter 13 provides a summary and conclusions.

Acknowledgements

I would like to thank Goldman Sachs, and in particular Jan Hatzius, Chief Economist and Head of Global Investment Research, for their support and encouragement in writing this book. Much of the work in it reflects the input of my team in the macro research department and would not have been possible without the ideas, effort and support of my colleagues at Goldman Sachs – both within the research department and across the firm. My gratitude also goes to my long-standing colleagues in equity strategy over 20 years, David Kostin in New York and Tim Moe in Singapore.

I am especially grateful to Guillaume Jaisson at Goldman Sachs for his significant input, ideas and tireless support and help in putting together this book, and to Loretta Sunnucks for editing the manuscript and for her sage advice and input throughout the process. I couldn't have done it without them. I would also like to thank and acknowledge the rest of my team for their input and feedback: Marcus von Scheele and our previous interns Parthivi Bansal and Nicola Ricci for their support and for preparing the charts, as well as

Lilia Peytavin, Cecilia Mariotti, Andrea Ferrario and my assistant, Lauren Hutchinson. Thanks also to Nicola Doll for her work on the cover design, and to Paul Smith and Brian Moroney for their help and comments.

In particular, I would like to acknowledge and give special thanks for the significant contribution and invaluable advice of my close colleagues Christian Mueller-Glissmann and Sharon Bell, with whom I have worked since 2009 and 1996, respectively. Christian has greatly strengthened my understanding of markets across asset classes and has developed many of the frameworks reflected in this book. Sharon has been central not only to the ideas in this book, but also to my thinking about markets broadly and to the work we have produced together over the past three decades. I have learned so much from her and owe her a huge debt of gratitude.

Thanks also to those who read drafts of the manuscript and have made suggestions to improve it. I have been particularly fortunate to learn and benefit from the wisdom of José Manuel Barroso, former President of the European Union, and Sir Alex Younger, former Head of MI6. Both have given me invaluable insights into the impact of geopolitics and how to weigh up risks and opportunities in the context of global tensions. I am very grateful to Professor Noreena Hertz (UCL), for her comments and thoughts, and to my friend and former colleague at HSBC, Stephen King, for his detailed feedback, support and guidance over many years. My gratitude also goes to Lawrence Summers, former U.S. Secretary of the Treasury, for his encouragement. Professor Narayan Naik (London Business School), Kofi Adjepong-Boateng CBE (Centre for Financial History at Cambridge University) and Dr Sushil Wadhwani (former member of the Bank of England's Monetary Policy Committee) also gave me valuable feedback.

Finally, I would like to thank my very old friend Professor Anthony Kessel for having the patience to teach me how to understand statistics while at university!

My gratitude also goes to Gemma Valler, Stacey Rivera and Sarah Lewis, and all the team at Wiley, for their help and encouragement.

I would like to extend my sincere thanks to the many colleagues, clients and friends who have taught, aided and guided me over my career since it began in 1985. There are too many to mention individually, but their support means so much to me. Finally, my deep thanks go to my inspiring partner Jo for her wisdom and guidance, and to our wonderful children, Jake and Mia, for being so special and, well, . . . for being them.

About the Author

Peter C. Oppenheimer has nearly 40 years of experience working as a macro research analyst. He is Chief Global Equity Strategist and Head of Macro Research in Europe within Global Investment Research at Goldman Sachs. Prior to working at Goldman Sachs, he worked as chief investment strategist at HSBC and in a variety of other research roles at James Capel, Hambros Bank and Greenwells, where he started his career in 1985. Peter is a trustee at both the Development Committee for the National Institute of Economic & Social Research and The Anna Freud National Centre for Children and Families. He enjoys cycling and painting.

Chapter 1
An Introduction to Cycles and Secular Trends

The farther backward you can look, the farther forward you can see.

—Winston Churchill

I n *The Long Good Buy: Analysing Cycles in Markets*, I focused on the tendency for financial market cycles to repeat themselves over time. Most of these market cycles are driven by, or at least a function of, business cycles. Cycles are important, and trying to predict where we are in a cycle and what happens next is a key focus for investors. That said, equally, financial cycles can help predict economic cycles. As Claudio Borio[1] says: 'The main thesis is that macroeconomics without the financial cycle is like Hamlet without the Prince'.[2] In the environment that has prevailed for at least three decades now, just as in the one that prevailed in the pre-World War II (WWII) years, it is simply not possible to understand business

---

[1] Head of the Monetary and Economic Department at the Bank of International Settlements (BIS).
[2] Borio, C. (2014). The financial cycle and macroeconomics: What have we learnt? *Journal of Banking & Finance*, **45**, pp. 182–198.

fluctuations and the policy challenges associated with them without understanding financial cycles.

Although financial cycles are a persistent feature of economies and markets, they often exist within longer-term trends or 'super cycles', in which dominant drivers generate strong patterns of returns that can overshadow the shorter-term impact of the business cycles. Although shorter-term cycles are important, getting the bigger secular trend right can significantly enhance returns for investors over the longer run. For example, over an extended period of low inflation there could be several business cycles. Equally, periods of strong economic growth, or stagnation, have prevailed for a long time – even when they have been temporarily impacted by short-lived recessions. These long trends are often associated with specific market conditions and opportunities. Most investors spend their time and resources trying to understand the next development or inflection point in the cycle. However, the longer-term structural developments and inflection points are often more important, albeit much more readily neglected.

The Long Good Buy was published just at the start of the first UK lockdown during the Covid-19 pandemic. The consensus view before Covid-19 emerged was that global growth would be strong. Few people at the time were focused on supply chains or the potential for inflation to re-emerge as a serious threat. The notion that geopolitical tensions would trigger a war in Europe would have seemed far-fetched. These events in isolation would have been impossible to forecast. However, a confluence of social, political and policy developments suggests that we are in the early stages of an important inflection point: many of the factors that drive the shape and style of financial market returns are changing.

After this introductory chapter, the main body of the book is split into three parts. Part I is a discussion of the differences between cycles and structural trends. Part II presents a history of post-WWII super cycles and their distinctive drivers. Part III discusses the emerging super cycle and its potential characteristics. I describe this new era as the Post-Modern Cycle because it is likely to exhibit some of the characteristics of the traditional cycles of the post-WWII period, with higher volatility and weaker returns, but also to share some elements of the Modern Cycles of low volatility and rising valuations that have dominated the post-1980 period.

Repeating Cycles

One of the intriguing characteristics of cycles, at least in financial markets, is that they appear to repeat themselves over time – despite significantly different economic, political and policy environments. In a recent paper, authors Andrew Filardo, Marco Lombardi and Marek Raczko noted that, over the past 120 years, the United States has gone through the Gold Standard period, when inflation was low, and the 1970s, when inflation was high and volatile. Likewise, over this long historical period, the price stability credentials of central banks have shifted, and fiscal and regulatory policies have varied considerably.[3]

Cycles appear everywhere in our understanding of the physical sciences and the natural world. They range from astronomical, geological and climate cycles to the cycles in biology and sleep. The concept that conditions tend to repeat themselves is obvious not only in the natural world but also in human nature and societies, and, therefore, economies and financial markets. The complexity of and interconnectivity between societal priorities, politics, international relations and economic conditions mean that these cycles often exist in epochs, or extended periods, that are a function of structural trends and can create radically different outcomes for financial markets.

The recognition of cycles and trends in man-made systems, from politics to social attitudes, fashion and the economy, has a

---

[3] Filardo, A., Lombardi, M. and Raczko, M. (2019). Measuring financial cycle time. Bank of England Staff Working Paper No. 776.

long history.[4] The Ancient Greeks were interested in political cycles. Plato talks about the *kyklos* (or cycle) in *Republic*, Books VIII and IX in relation to different forms of government and the transitions between them. Aristotle also writes about cycles of government and the steps that can be taken to alter them in *Politics*, Book V.[5] Polybius (200–c. 118 BC) developed a theory of the cycle of government called *anacyclosis* that relates to the lifecycle of democracy, aristocracy and monarchy, and the forms that these can take (ochlocracy, oligarchy and tyranny). This concept is also referred to in the writings of Cicero and Machiavelli.

The Romans understood the importance of longer-term generational cycles, described as the *saeculum*. This was viewed as a period that generally defined a person's lifespan, or that of a complete renewal of a human population. For example, it could be a period first defined by a monumental event, say a war, to the point when everyone who had experienced the event first-hand had died. The Chinese developed the concept of dynastic cycles, in which history is dominated by waves of succession from empires or dynasties founded by strong leaders who are followed by rulers unable to maintain the same level of effectiveness, thus leading to the eventual decline of the dynasty.

The Social and Political Cycle

Although many factors have an impact on financial market cycles, macro factors, such as interest rates and growth, are key. In addition, longer-term trends in financial returns are influenced by social and political cycles, which can exhibit major structural shifts that spill over into business cycles and financial market returns.

---

[4] The belief that economic development and prosperity move in long-term cycles or waves was also developed in Marxist literature during the nineteenth century. Such work focused on fluctuations in profits as the central cause of cycles in economies. See Basu, D. (2016). Long waves of capitalist development: An empirical investigation. University of Massachusetts Amherst, Department of Economics Working Paper No. 2016-15.

[5] Aristotle (1944). *Aristotle in 23 Volumes*, Book V, section 1311b, translated by H. Rackham. London: Heinemann (Cambridge, MA: Harvard University Press).

Interest in the multi-dimensional influences of society, economies and political systems, and the ways in which these factors influence each other, has evolved over time. During the Enlightenment, scholars focused on what they generally perceived to be a 'natural order', and developed categories that described a series of fixed stages of cultural evolution and social development. In the nineteenth century, perceptions of cultural evolution and the way in which society evolved were heavily influenced by the theory of biological evolution developed by Charles Darwin in *On the Origin of Species* (1859). A theory of social evolution emerged in which society was seen as akin to an organism, and this biological analogy became popular among anthropologists and sociologists as a way of understanding development.

The perception of social development as a cyclical phenomenon gained prominence around this time, as social cycle theory in the field of sociology challenged the concept of a unilateral world view in which development was thought to be a constant. Instead, the cyclical approach views developments in society as a tendency for patterns to repeat themselves in cycles. Theories of multilinear cultural evolution also developed in anthropology. Such theories posited that human culture and society evolve in their own way by adapting to the environment at any time, just as political cycles and economies do. The work of anthropologists such as Franz Boas, Alfred Kroeber, Ruth Benedict and Margaret Mead turned attention away from generalisations about culture, focusing instead on understanding cultural processes within different societies. Seen along this more multilinear dimension, societal developments are a function of context and can change over time; for that reason, they repeat themselves if similar conditions prevail, just as economies or even financial markets do. For example, periods of economic stress are often associated with social unrest and political change in immensely different environments over time.

In the twentieth century, historians became more interested in cycles. Oswald Spengler (1880–1936), in *The Decline of the West* (1918–1922), used the analogy from biology that each civilisation passes through a lifecycle as it moves between birth and decline/ decay over long periods of approximately 1,000 years. British historian, economist and social reformer Arnold J. Toynbee came to similar conclusions, and in 1934 he published the first of his 12-volume work *A Study of History* in which he embraced the cyclical theory.

George Modelski, a key researcher in the Long Cycle Theory in politics, describes the connection between economic cycles, war cycles and the political aspects of world leadership in *Long Cycles in Word Politics* (1987).[6] His work suggests that there have been five long cycles in politics since the 1500s that loosely correlate with the economic cycles described in Kondratieff's waves. These very-long-run political cycles are based around periods of hegemonic rule. The first was in Portugal in the sixteenth century, and this was followed by the Netherlands in the seventeenth century, then Britain (first during the eighteenth century and again in the nineteenth century), with the United States taking over the mantle in the post-WWII period.[7] These long periods also had an impact on economic activity and, consequently, on financial markets. Most of these studies, it should be said, were European- or 'Western-based' and ignored major periods of development in other parts of the world; the 'silk road' trade, for example, a 6,400 km trade route that expanded economic growth and facilitated cultural and religious interactions between the second century BCE and the fifteenth century CE, is often missing from the early-cycle analysis, as are the Arab Muslim influence in the seventh century and that of the Mongols in the thirteenth century.

---

[6] There are similar concepts in politics. Schlesinger's work on US politics demonstrated the shifts through a liberal–conservative cycle, reflecting a 'self-generating' drive that then repeats itself, while Huntington's work identified periodic 'creedal passions' that drive the political process and shifts in the approach to policy. Political success becomes closely intertwined with the economic and social cycles. One type of party will generally govern when there are specific circumstances but change when the circumstances change. A governing party may be associated with prosperous times, or recessions. The success of this party often reflects these broader economic and social changes. See Rose, R. and Urwin, D. W. (1970). Persistence and change in Western party systems since 1945. *Political Studies*, 18(3), pp. 287–319.

[7] Thompson, K. W., Modelski, G. and Thompson, W. R. (1990). Long cycles in world politics. *The American Historical Review*, 95(2), pp. 456–457.

The struggle for power on the international stage also leads to cycles, or long-term trends, that are influenced by changing approaches to geopolitics and foreign policy. Arthur M. Schlesinger (Junior and Senior) argue in Cycle Theory, in the context of US history, that the United States alternates between periods of Liberal attitudes and increased democracy, in which society focuses on problems and resolving them, and periods of Conservative dominance, with a greater focus on individual rights, with each phase leading to the other.[8] They assert that Liberal phases lead to activism burnout, whereas Conservative phases lead to Liberal phases after long periods of unresolved problems. Klingberg also describes cycles in the realm of foreign policy as alternating between 'extroversion', periods of expansion of American influence, and 'introversion', when policy becomes more isolationist. In his 1952 paper, he described four 'introvert' periods averaging 21 years, and three 'extrovert' periods averaging 27 years.[9]

Just as social attitudes have an impact on and reflect economic conditions, so too does cultural expression in society. Oscar Wilde famously noted that 'life imitates art far more than art imitates life', and there is some evidence that social attitudes, reflected in artistic movements, reflect and often lead political and economic developments.[10] For example, Harold Zullow (1991) conducted a study of the lyrics of the top 40 US popular songs from 1955 to 1989, looking for evidence of 'rumination about bad events' and a 'pessimistic explanatory style'. He examined the cover stories of *Time* magazine over the same years to look for similar evidence and found that increased pessimistic ruminations in popular music predicted changes in the media's view of world events with a lag of 1–2 years. He also showed that there is a reasonable statistical relationship between popular music and consumer optimism (measured in surveys), as well as consumer expenditure patterns and economic

---

[8] Schlesinger, A. M. (1999). *The Cycles of American History*. Boston, MA: Houghton Mifflin.
[9] Klingberg, F. J. (1952). The historical alternation of moods in American foreign policy. *World Politics*, **4**(2), pp. 239–273.
[10] Wilde, O. (1889). *The Decay of Lying: A Dialogue*. London: Kegan Paul, Trench & Co.

growth (GNP). Pessimistic ruminations in popular songs and news magazines have tended to predict economic recession via decreased consumer optimism and spending.[11]

The Business Cycle

Interest in economic cycles, and their impact on financial markets and prices, developed mainly in the nineteenth century. The Kitchin cycle is based on a 40-month duration, driven by commodities and inventories. The Juglar cycle, developed to predict capital investment, has a duration of 7–11 years, while the Kuznets cycle predicted incomes and has a duration of 15–25 years. Groundbreaking theories on cycles were developed by Nikolai Kondratieff (1892–1938) in the 1920s. His work focused on the economic performance of the United States, England, France and Germany between 1790 and 1920. He identified long-term growth cycles that lasted between 50 and 60 years reflecting industrial production, commodity prices and interest rates, and argued that these were driven by cycles in technology.

Interest in cycles and trends increased following the Great Depression. Joseph Schumpeter developed his theories in *Business Cycles* (1939), shortly after Keynes's publication of *The General Theory of Employment, Interest, and Money* (1936). While Keynes focused on government policies, Schumpeter focused on the impact of companies and entrepreneurs. He argued that the longer Kondratieff cycles of around 50 years in duration were made up of overlapping shorter cycles, including Kitchin cycles (of around 3 years) and Juglar cycles (of around 9 years). He believed that the very long Kondratieff cycles were a result of creative destruction, a process whereby new technologies generate investment and economic growth, whereas older technologies decay. These technological

---

[11] Zullow, H. M. (1991). Pessimistic ruminations in popular songs and news magazines predict economic recession via decreased consumer optimism and spending. *Journal of Economic Psychology*, **12**(3), pp. 501–526.

innovations cause growth and a period of prosperity until the economy goes through a stagnation phase as the technologies are applied more broadly across the various sectors of the economy.

Schumpeter identified three long-term Kondratieff cycles. The first, from the 1780s to 1842, was associated with the first Industrial Revolution in Britain. The second, from 1842 to 1897, was driven by the innovation of the railroads and was the result of industrial countries using the new technologies in steamships and railways to benefit from opportunities in iron, coal and textiles. The third, from 1898 to the 1930s, was driven by electrification, and involved the development and commercialisation of electrical power, chemicals and automotive industries, which, at the time of his writing, he viewed as incomplete.

This approach to splitting cycles into long phases, or trends, suggests that, while there may be shorter-term fluctuations in economies and financial markets, there are also longer-term trends that may be driven by major innovations and, for that matter, developments in social attitudes, politics and geopolitics.

Super Cycles in Financial Markets

In terms of financial markets, the tendency towards both short-term cycles and longer-term trends reflects developments across the economy, politics, geopolitics and society. Irving Fisher (1933)[12] and John Maynard Keynes (1936)[13] examined the interaction between the real economy and the financial sector in the Great Depression. Arthur F. Burns and Wesley Mitchell (1946)[14] found evidence of the business cycle, while later academics argued that the financial cycle was a part of the business cycle, and that financial conditions

---

[12] Fisher, I. (1933). The debt-deflation theory of great depressions. *Econometrica*, **1**(4), pp. 337–357.
[13] Keynes, J. M. (1936). *The General Theory of Employment, Interest, and Money*. London: Palgrave Macmillan.
[14] Shaw, E. S. (1947). Burns and Mitchell on business cycles. *Journal of Political Economy*, **55**(4), pp. 281–298.

and private sector balance sheet health are both important triggers of a cycle and are factors that can amplify cycles.[15] Other research has demonstrated that waves of global liquidity can interact with domestic financial cycles, thereby creating excessive financial conditions in some cases.[16]

More recent studies suggest that measures of slack in the economy (or output gaps – the amount by which the actual output of an economy falls short of its potential output) can be explained partly by financial factors that play a large role in explaining fluctuations in economic output and potential growth, thereby implying a close link and feedback loop between financial and economic cycles.[17] A broader analysis of these longer-term cycles or regimes, however, shows that they are impacted by many factors. Political cycles, changes in social attitudes and priorities, demographics, technology and geopolitics all have an impact on each other. It is often the complex interplay between these drivers, as well as evolving social attitudes, that affect economies and financial returns over long periods of time and help to explain longer-term structural trends in markets, or super cycles.

Of course, this all raises the important question of whether financial market returns can be forecast or predicted. According to the efficient market hypothesis, the value of a market reflects all the information available about that stock or market at any given time; the market is efficient in pricing and so is always correctly priced unless or until something changes.[18] In this way, even if financial market returns are driven or influenced by long-term economic and political trends, these trends can't be anticipated because, if they

[15] Eckstein, O. and Sinai, A. (1986). The mechanisms of the business cycle in the postwar era. In R. J. Gordon (ed.), *The American Business Cycle: Continuity and Change*. Chicago, IL: University of Chicago Press, pp. 39–122.
[16] Bruno, V. and Shin, H. S. (2015). Cross-border banking and global liquidity. *Review of Economic Studies*, **82**(2), pp. 535–564.
[17] Borio, C., Disyatat, P. and Juselius, M. (2013). Rethinking potential output: Embedding information about the financial cycle. BIS Working Paper No. 404.
[18] Fama, E. F. (1970). Efficient capital markets: A review of theory and empirical work. *The Journal of Finance*, **25**(2), pp. 383–417.

could, they would already be reflected in prices. Others (e.g., Nobel economics laureate Robert Shiller) have shown that, although stock prices can be extremely volatile over the short term, their valuation, or price/earnings ratio, provides information that makes them somewhat predictable over long periods, suggesting that valuation at least provides something of a guide to future returns.[19]

Psychology and Financial Market Super Cycles

In addition to the relationships that exist between financial cycles and economic cycles, with bonds impacted by inflation expectations and equities by gross domestic product (GDP) growth, there are some patterns of human behaviour that reflect and sometimes amplify expected economic conditions. The way in which economics and fundamentals are perceived by investors is crucial to this mix. Academic work has increasingly shown that risk-taking appetite has been a key channel through which supportive policy (e.g., low interest rates) can impact cycles.[20] Willingness to take risk and periods of excessive caution (often after a period of weak returns) are factors that tend to amplify the impact of economic fundamentals on financial markets and contribute to cycles and repeated patterns. The weakness of economic forecasting models in understanding or taking account of human sentiment, especially in periods of extreme optimism or pessimism, is not a new finding. In his 1841 book *Extraordinary Popular Delusions and the Madness of Crowds*, Charles Mackay argues that 'Men [. . .] think in herds; it has been seen that they go mad in herds, while they only recover their senses slowly, one by one'.[21]

---

[19] Shiller, R. J. (1981). Do stock prices move too much to be justified by subsequent changes in dividends? *The American Economic Review*, **71**(3), pp. 421–436.

[20] Borio, C. (2013). On time, stocks and flows: Understanding the global macroeconomic challenges. *National Institute Economic Review*, **225**(1), pp. 3–13.

[21] Mackay, C. (1852). *Extraordinary Popular Delusions and the Madness of Crowds*, 2nd ed. London: Office of the National Illustrated Library.

The notion that individuals are rational and always use available information efficiently was not always the convention in economics. Keynes asserted that instability in financial markets was a function of psychological forces that can become dominant in times of uncertainty. According to Keynes, waves of optimism and pessimism affect markets, and animal spirits drive the desire to take risk. Other economists, such as Marvin Minsky (1975), have analysed these effects.[22]

A similar focus on crowd contagion, particularly when coupled with a powerful narrative, is described by Robert Shiller in his book *Irrational Exuberance* (2000).[23] Over long periods, if optimism builds, the impact on psychology and crowd behaviour can be significant, often leading to bubbles (that inevitably burst). Here, Shiller describes a bubble as 'a situation in which news of price increases spurs investor enthusiasm which spreads by psychological contagion from person to person, in the process amplifying stories that might justify the price increase and bring in a larger and larger class of investors, who, despite doubts about the real value of the investment, are drawn to it partly through envy of others' successes and partly through a gambler's excitement'. Throughout history, the impact of crowd behaviour and social influence is present in market cycles. Many high-profile celebrities and politicians became investors during the British Railway Mania of the 1840s. The Brontë sisters were among them, as were several leading thinkers and politicians, such as John Stuart Mill, Charles Darwin and Benjamin Disraeli.[24] They were in good company: King George I was an investor in the South Sea Bubble, as was Sir Isaac Newton, who reportedly lost £20,000 (equivalent to about £3 million in today's terms) when the market collapsed.[25]

---

[22] Minsky, H. P. (1975). *John Maynard Keynes*. New York: Columbia University Press.
[23] Shiller, R. J. (2000). *Irrational Exuberance*. Princeton, NJ: Princeton University Press.
[24] Odlyzko, A. (2010). Collective hallucinations and inefficient markets: The British Railway Mania of the 1840s. Available at SSRN: https://ssrn.com/abstract=1537338 or http://dx.doi.org/10.2139/ssrn.1537338.
[25] Evans, R. (2014, May 23). How (not) to invest like Sir Isaac Newton. *The Telegraph*.

This 'human' complication in forecasting was also featured in work on cycles by Charles P. Kindleberger, who argued that there was a tendency for herding in markets, with investors coordinating to buy assets when it would not normally be rational to do so, ultimately with the risk that financial bubbles develop.[26] He and other economists advanced the idea that psychological and sociological behaviour triggered emotional contagion and euphoria that can spread through crowds during booms, while also driving pessimism and extreme risk aversion that can cause, and exacerbate, a bust.[27]

Even outside of bubble periods, or in the depths of a crisis, individuals do not (as the traditional economic theories suggest) always act in rational, predictable ways. As prominent economist and psychologist George Loewenstein points out, 'whereas psychologists tend to view humans as fallible and sometimes even self-destructive, economists tend to view people as efficient maximisers of self-interest who make mistakes only when imperfectly informed about the consequences of their actions'. Understanding how humans process information and deal with risks and opportunities can go some way to explaining the existence of cycles in financial markets.[28]

Short-term shifts in sentiment can have a profound impact on financial markets at turning points in the market, but often these changes in attitude can last for long periods and are influenced by government policies.

Structural changes in industries and in economic factors, such as inflation and the cost of capital, can shift relationships between variables over time, and these structural changes constitute one of the main drivers of what we see as the conditions for the next cycle (discussed in Chapter 10). For example, the behaviour and performance of a stock-market cycle in an era of high inflation and interest

---

[26] Kindleberger, C. P. (1996). *Manias, Panics and Crashes*, 3rd ed. New York: Basic Books.
[27] Baddeley, M. (2010). Herding, social influence and economic decision-making: Socio-psychological and neuroscientific analyses. *Philosophical Transactions of the Royal Society, Series B*, **365**, pp. 281–290.
[28] Loewenstein, G., Scott, R. and Cohen, J. D. (2008). Neuroeconomics. *Annual Review of Psychology*, **59**, pp. 647–672.

rates could well be rather different from a cycle in a period of very low inflation and interest rates, and the way in which companies, investors and policymakers react to a given impulse may change over time as they adapt to the experiences of the past.

Long periods of high taxes and economic uncertainty resulted in low risk tolerance in the 1970s, for example, while the opposite was generally true from the mid-1980s and throughout the 1990s. I talk about these periods in Chapters 5 and 6. The period since the Global Financial Crisis (GFC) was influenced in large part by the experience that investors had of this crisis, as well as the extreme policy response that it evoked. The generation that experienced the Great Depression was generally more cautious than the so-called baby boomers of the post-WWII period, and was often termed the 'silent generation'. Equally, investors in the Japanese bubble of the late 1980s took a long time to shake off the fear of deflation. At the time of writing, the Japanese equity market remains about 20% below the level it peaked at in 1989.

Daniel Kahneman and Amos Tversky's work on prospect theory (first presented in 1979 and developed by them in 1992) had a significant impact on the understanding of psychology in social sciences. It describes how investors behave when faced with choices that involve probability. They argue that individuals make decisions based on expectations of loss or gains from their current position. So, given a choice of equal probability, most investors would choose to protect their existing wealth rather than risk the chance to increase wealth.[29] But this tendency to protect what you have rather than risk losing it for future gains seems to disappear in extreme situations when markets increase a great deal and a fear of missing out (or what has been dubbed FOMO) becomes a dominant driver of behaviour. This can be seen in relation to the run-up to the technology bubble in 2000 or the GFC of 2008.

Given that the GFC was largely unexpected, as was the recession that it caused, there has been an increased focus on the behavioural

---

[29] Kahneman, D. and Tversky, A. (1979). Prospect theory: An analysis of decision under risk. *Econometrica*, **47**(2), pp. 263–292.

drivers of financial markets: Hyman P. Minsky's (1975, 1986, 1992) work on financial instability has attracted more attention in the wake of the crisis.[30] His financial instability hypothesis is based on the idea that the economy causes bubbles and crashes. Periods of stability in the economy sow the seeds of the next bubble because they encourage investors to take on more risk. Eventually, the risk-taking causes a bubble that creates financial instability and panic. In this way, he argues that 'stability is destabilising'. I discuss in Chapter 6, for example, that policy actions taken after the Asian financial crisis of 1998, in the form of sharp cuts to interest rates, contributed to the conditions that led to the technology bubble. More recently, under different conditions, the huge monetary and fiscal support during the Covid-19 pandemic helped trigger a bubble in technology stocks in 2020 and 2021.

Since the GFC, interest in behavioural explanations and the psychology of markets has increased, contributing to a better understanding of how and why financial cycles develop and how they can often significantly exaggerate the developments of the economic and financial variables by which they are driven. Nobel Prize winners George A. Akerlof and Robert J. Shiller wrote that 'The crisis was not foreseen and is still not fully understood because there have been no principles in conventional economic theories regarding animal spirits'.[31] It is the impact of human behaviour and the way in which information is processed by humans that make the forecasting of markets so much more complicated than forecasting physical systems such as the weather.

In the case of economies and financial markets, there are significant feedback loops, or what George Soros describes as 'reflexivity', a concept that has its roots in the social sciences but is evident

---

[30] Minsky, H. P. (1975). *John Maynard Keynes*. New York: Columbia University Press. Minsky, H. P. (1986). *Stabilizing an Unstable Economy: A Twentieth Century Fund Report*. New Haven, CT: Yale University Press. Minsky, H. P. (1992). The Financial Instability Hypothesis. Jerome Levy Economics Institute Working Paper No. 74. Available at SSRN: https://ssrn.com/abstract=161024 or http://dx.doi.org/10.2139/ssrn.161024.
[31] Akerlof, G. A. and Shiller, R. J. (2010). *Animal Spirits: How Human Psychology Drives the Economy, and Why it Matters for Global Capitalism*. Princeton, NJ: Princeton University Press.

in financial markets.[32] A stock market that falls in anticipation of a recession, for example, might itself lead to a collapse in business confidence that alters the decisions of companies in terms of investment, thereby making the risks of a recession that much greater. Of course, falling markets also raise the cost of capital, which reduces future growth and hence becomes somewhat cyclical.

An additional complication is that the response of individuals to inputs, such as changes in interest rates, can vary over time, even when they are faced with similar conditions. In recent research, Ulrike Malmendier and Stefan Nagel (2016) argue that investors overweight their personal experiences when they form judgements about their expectations over time.[33] For example, perceptions about inflation may vary according to the conditions that you have been used to, and this might influence your decisions about the future more than would be suggested by relying on long-term historical relationships. This may explain why there are differences in inflation expectations among people of different age groups; rather than being rational and responding to a particular policy or trigger in a consistent and predictable way, investors may act quite differently depending on their own experience and psychology (Filardo et al., 2019).

Neuroeconomics, a relatively new field, provides further evidence of these types of varying reactions. This approach looks at how decision-making takes place in the brain and provides some insight into how individuals face choices that involve risk. Academics (George Lowenstein, Scott Rick and Jonathan D. Cohen) argue that people react to risks in two ways: in a dispassionate way and in an emotional way. This approach argues that we over-react to new risks, which may be low-probability events, but under-react to risks that are known to us, even though these are much more likely to occur. In this way, for example, a collapse in equities may

[32] Soros, G. (2014). Fallibility, reflexivity, and the human uncertainty principle. *Journal of Economic Methodology*, **20**(4), pp. 309–329.
[33] Malmendier, U. and Nagel, S. (2016). Learning from inflation experiences. *The Quarterly Journal of Economics*, **131**(1), pp. 53–87.

make people cautious of investing because they have faced a new risk, even though a new bear market is unlikely. At the same time, investors may be happy to buy equities towards the top of the market, despite regular warnings about higher valuations, because they have seen recent price rises and feel more confident to take the risk.

This would seem to be consistent with investor behaviour in the run-up to and following the GFC, as well as countless other booms and busts in history. Persistent rising returns in financial markets lead to optimism and the belief that the trend can continue. The required risk premium falls, and investors are lured into markets with the belief that risks are low and prospective returns will continue to be as strong as they have been in the past. In contrast, the proximity to large losses in the aftermath of the financial crisis pushed up the required risk premium – the expected future return that investors require to take on risk. As a result, the way in which companies and markets responded to sharp interest rate cuts was different in the post-GFC period relative to the period before. Having faced the experience of the financial crisis and the recession that followed, people collectively responded with greater caution than might have been the case previously. These swings in sentiment and confidence, partly informed by recent history, also drive financial market cycles.

As one recent study put it, 'there is increasing evidence that psychology plays a big role in economic developments. Results indicate that economy is highly driven by human psychologies, a result which is in conformity with the prediction of Keynes (1936) and Akerlof and Shiller (2009)'.[34] The renewed focus on psychology in understanding responses and behaviour around decisions is increasingly used in public policy. In 2008, Richard H. Thaler and Cass R. Sunstein published *Nudge: Improving Decisions about Health, Wealth, and Happiness*, which focused on behavioural economics. The book became a best seller and has had a

---

[34] Dhaoui, A., Bourouis, S. and Boyacioglu, M. A. (2013). The impact of investor psychology on stock markets: Evidence from France. *Journal of Academic Research in Economics*, 5(1), pp. 35–59.

widespread impact on policy. Thaler went on to win the Nobel Prize for Economics in 2017 for his work in the field.

So, despite all the political, economic and social changes that have occurred over the past decades, there have been repeated patterns in economies and financial markets. There are also important drivers of longer-term returns that determine the type of regime investors find themselves in – whether, for example, the market is driven by periods of rising (or falling) valuation, by profit growth, or by rising (or falling) equity risk premia.

I discuss, in Part I, the differences between cycles and structural trends.

Part I

Structural Trends and Market Super Cycles

Chapter 2
Equity Cycles and Their Drivers

Wave-like swings in the mind of the business world between errors of optimism and pessimism.

—Arthur Cecil Pigou

Historically, within financial markets there is a pattern of short-term cycles and longer-term super cycles, or secular trends, within which shorter-term cycles evolve. Although there are long-term shifts in the return profile of equities that depend on prevailing macroeconomic conditions (in particular, the trade-off between growth and interest rates), most equity markets show a tendency to move in cycles that relate to some degree to the prevailing business cycle. Because equity markets move in anticipation of future fundamentals, the expected prospects for growth and inflation tend to be reflected in current prices. These market moves can also affect valuation; if investors start to expect a recovery in future profits from a recession, for example, then the valuation of the equity market will rise in the period before the improvement emerges.

Across an investment cycle, there are typically both a bear market (a period when prices are falling) and a bull market (a period when stock prices are generally rising or are relatively stable in price returns). That said, no two cycles, or even secular super cycles, are the same. Some are much longer than others, and some are disrupted mid-way through, perhaps by a specific shock or event that takes the index back to the inflection point without completing a full cycle. Nonetheless, looking at history we can at least gain a sense of what an 'average' cycle looks like and how it evolves.

Looking at data from the early 1970s, although they differ in strength and length, these cyclical patterns seem to repeat themselves, albeit somewhat differently each time. Most of the cycles over the past 50 years can typically be split into four distinct phases, each driven by distinct factors. Most of these cycles also evolve within a longer-term super cycle or structural trend.

The Four Phases of the Equity Cycle

The division of the cycle into phases is simplified and illustrated in Exhibit 2.1. This is very much a stylised version of reality but it mirrors the tendency for markets to move in cycles, and shows

Exhibit 2.1   The four phases of the equity cycle

1 Despair

Bear market:
Price moves from peak to trough:
- Expectations are not met
- Period of worst returns
- Poor earnings growth

2 Hope

P/E multiple expands
- Expectations of a better future
- Period of highest return
- Poor earnings growth

4 Optimisim

P/E multiple grows faster than earnings
- Expectations are extrapolated
- Second best return
- Weak earnings growth

3 Growth

Earnings grow faster than the P/E multiple
- Reality catches up to expectations
- Second lowest return
- Highest level of earnings growth

Volatility increases

Volatility decreases

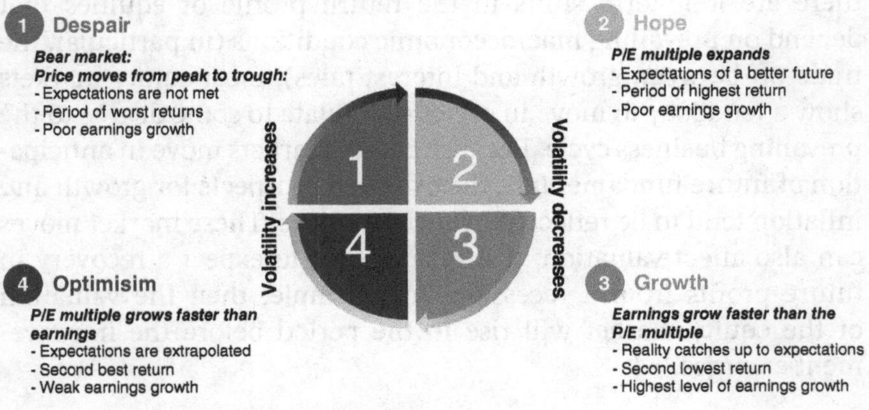

SOURCE: Goldman Sachs Global Investment Research

how distinct phases reflect the extent to which the index price performance is driven by actual profit growth when it emerges and/or by expectations of future profit growth, which we can measure as changes in valuation – such as the price/earnings ratio (P/E multiple), which rises as investors anticipate future improvements in profit growth and declines when they anticipate weaker growth.

1. Despair

The period when the market moves from its peak to its trough is also known as the bear market. This correction is mainly driven by falling valuations (P/E contraction), as the market anticipates and reacts to a deteriorating macroeconomic environment and its implications in terms of lower expected earnings. Usually, at this point, earnings have not yet fallen as the economy has typically not yet fallen into recession.

2. Hope

This is typically a short period, when the market rebounds from its trough valuation (P/E expansion). This occurs in anticipation of a forthcoming trough in the economic cycle, as well as future profit growth, and leads to a rise in valuation multiples. The end of this phase usually roughly coincides with the peak of the P/E multiple (maximum positive sentiment about future growth). This phase is critical for investors, since it is usually when the highest returns in the cycle are achieved. However, it tends to start when the actual macro data and profit results of the corporate sector remain depressed. Crucially, the main driver here is expectations: while this phase often coincides with weak data, it occurs when the second derivative (the rate of change) in the economic data starts to improve. So, the best time to buy into the equity market tends to be when economic conditions are weak and after the equity market has fallen, but when the first signs start to emerge that economic conditions are no longer deteriorating at a faster pace.

3. Growth

This is usually the longest period (on average, 45 months in the United States), when earnings growth is generated and drives returns.

4. Optimism

This is the final part of the cycle, when investors become increasingly confident, or perhaps even complacent, and where valuations tend to rise again and outstrip earnings growth, thereby setting the stage for the next market correction. This is the classic period characterised by a fear of missing out (FOMO) – where investors fear missing out more than they fear making losses. These periods are generally driven as much by sentiment and psychology as by actual fundamentals, and are usually associated with rising valuations in equity markets as investors become more confident.

The Drivers of the Four Phases

This framework demonstrates that the relationship between earnings growth and price performance changes systematically over the cycle. While earnings growth is what fuels equity market performance over the long run, most of the earnings growth is not paid for when it occurs but rather when it is correctly anticipated by investors in the Hope phase, and when investors become overly optimistic about the potential for future growth during the Optimism phase.

Exhibit 2.2 illustrates this for the United States using data since 1973. For each phase, it indicates the average length of the phase, the average price return and how it is distributed between multiple expansion and earnings growths. While the Growth phase sees most of the growth in earnings, the price return mainly occurs in the Hope and Optimism phases.

Exhibit 2.2 Decomposition of returns during US equity phases: average of cumulative nominal returns (annualised) for each S&P 500 cycle from 1973

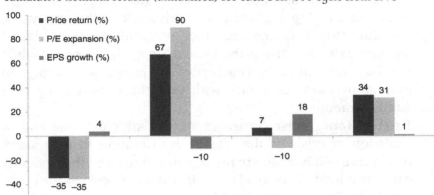

SOURCE: Goldman Sachs Global Investment Research

The phases are clearly linked to the economy. This allows for a more precise interpretation of the phases and helps to identify when we are moving from one phase to the next. Gross domestic product (GDP), or economic activity, tends to contract during the Despair and Hope phases as output falls behind potential. The economic trough occurs between the middle and end of the Hope phase. In the Growth phase, economic activity tends to expand and, eventually, output growth outpaces potential growth.

Using this simple framework, investors' forward-looking return requirements across the phases evolve as follows:

- **During the Despair phase,** investors become increasingly concerned about the prospects for future returns, and therefore require an increasingly high future expected return for holding equities. This reaction occurs against a backdrop of an increase in volatility, an increase in spare capacity (often described as the output gap[1]) and, typically, the start of a recession during this phase. This leads to lower equity valuations (P/E multiples) and a falling market, along with a rise in the equity risk premium (ERP). Taking data since 1973, this phase has lasted on average 14 months in the United States. It is a phase when earnings are still rising (modestly) but prices fall sharply, on average by more than 30%, with valuations contracting by a similar amount.

- **In the Hope phase**, investors start to anticipate the end of recession or crisis as the rate of deterioration in data slows (things are still bad but are not deteriorating), and this visibility caps the potential downside risk. Investors respond to the lower tail risk by increasingly accepting lower future expected returns (and higher valuations); the equity risk premium declines and valuations rise as the 'fear of missing out' often drives investor sentiment. Typically, at this stage policy support, often in the form of interest rate cuts, will also begin to embolden investors to start to discount a future recovery. While volatility is still high, it tends to fall towards the end of the Hope phase as activity data starts to stabilise, even at a low rate. In this phase, investors essentially pre-pay for the expected recovery in earnings during the Growth phase and valuations rise, as shown in Exhibit 2.2. While the Hope phase typically is the shortest of the phases (on average around 10 months), it tends to be the strongest part of the cycle on an annualised basis, with average returns of roughly 50% (around 70% annualised) and valuation expansion of roughly 70% (around 90% annualised).

- **In the beginning of the Growth phase**, investors have already been paid for expected future earnings growth during the Hope phase, but the growth has yet to materialise. The output gap typically peaks sometime during the Hope phase, alongside unemployment, but remains very high at the beginning

---

[1] The output gap is the amount by which the actual output of an economy falls short of its potential output.

of the Growth phase. Investors often pause, questioning long-run growth expectations very much in a 'wait and see' frame of mind. The result is that value in terms of expected future returns is rebuilt during the Growth phase as earnings growth outpaces returns, and volatility declines. On average, this phase of the cycle in the United States has lasted for almost 4 years (45 months), generating mid-single-digit returns per year, all backed by an annual increase in earnings of roughly 20%. Consequently, P/E multiples tend to contract by around 10% over this period.

- **Eventually, in the Optimism phase**, the built-up value becomes large enough to attract more investors who fear missing out; returns outpace earnings and expected future returns consequently decline. Towards the end of the phase, volatility picks up as the sustainability of the high returns is tested by the market. This phase lasts an average of 21 months but, once again, it experiences strong price appreciation of around 30% annualised, driven entirely by valuation expansion, while profits stagnate.

In conclusion, the actual earnings growth and price returns are surprisingly unsynchronised. Over an entire cycle, almost 100% of the earnings growth occurs during the Growth phase, while little is achieved in price performance. On the flip side, the strongest part of the cycle (in terms of performance) is the Hope phase, while profits are still falling. This emphasises the key point that investors tend to pay forward for expected growth in the future at a time when valuations are low. The Optimism phase is the second-strongest phase of the cycle. Exhibit 2.3 shows these results for the US equity market.

The discussion above is, of course, about averages over many decades and so provides a useful framework. But each cycle is slightly different: inflation dynamics may change from one period to another, or there could be stronger economic growth than in the past.

Exhibit 2.3 Valuations expand the most during the Hope and Optimism phases: S&P 500 cycles from 1973 (data in nominal terms)

	S&P 500			
	Despair	Hope	Growth	Optimism
Length (m)	14	9	45	22
Average of cumulative returns				
Total return (%)	–36	54	44	80
Price return (%)	–38	50	28	70
EPS growth (%)	5	–8	84	3
P/E expansion (%)	–39	66	–31	64
Average of cumulative returns, annualised				
Total return (%)	–32	73	10	38
Price return (%)	–35	67	7	34
EPS growth (%)	4	–10	18	1
P/E expansion (%)	–35	90	–10	31

SOURCE: Goldman Sachs Global Investment Research

The Cycle and Bear Markets

In the cycle framework described above, the Despair phase is the bear market period in which stocks decline. However, while the initial recovery from a bear market (the Hope phase) tends to be similar irrespective of the scale of the bear market, the Despair phase tends to vary in duration and severity according to what has driven it. For this reason, the risk of staying invested in a bear market is not equal on each occasion.

I split bear markets into three categories, each with their own distinct characteristics:

1. **Structural bear markets** are triggered by structural imbalances and financial bubbles. Very often there is a 'price' shock, such as deflation, and a banking crisis that follows. Structural bear markets on average see falls of roughly 50%, last over 3.5

years and take nearly 10 years to recover fully and surpass their initial level in real terms.

2. **Cyclical bear markets** are triggered by rising interest rates, impending recessions and falls in profits. They are a function of the economic cycle. Cyclical bear markets on average see falls of around 30%, last over 2 years and take roughly 4 years to return to the initial index level in nominal terms (61 months in real terms).

3. **Event-driven bear markets** are triggered by a one-off 'shock' that either does not lead to a domestic recession or temporarily knocks a cycle off course. Common triggers are wars, an oil price shock, emerging markets crisis or technical market dislocations. The principal driver of the bear market is higher risk premia rather than a rise in interest rates at the outset. Event-driven bear markets on average see falls of 30%, roughly the same as cyclical bear markets, but they last around 8 months and recover within just over a year in nominal terms (55 months in real terms).

Most structural bear markets are associated with financial bubbles that, when they burst, broadly cause problems as the private sector deleverages. Often the stresses spill over into the banking sector, deepening the economic downturn.

There are a few consistent hallmarks of financial bubbles that lead to structural bear markets. In particular:

1. Excessive price appreciation and extreme valuations
2. New valuation approaches justified
3. Increased market concentration
4. Frantic speculation and investor flows
5. Easy credit, low rates and rising leverage
6. Booming corporate activity
7. 'New Era' narrative and technological innovations
8. Late-cycle economic boom
9. The emergence of accounting scandals and irregularities

Good examples of structural bear markets are the collapse that was triggered by the 1929 crash, the downturn in Japan in 1989/90 and, most recently, the GFC. Each exhibited similar conditions of broad-based asset bubbles, euphoria, private sector leverage and, finally, a banking crisis. Meanwhile, the bear market during the Covid-19 pandemic was an example of an event-driven downturn. At the time it occurred, the economy was relatively balanced, with low and stable growth and inflation. True, the event itself was unusual and the initial shock to growth extreme, but the scale and breadth of policy support were such that the market hit was short-lived and the recovery rapid, like other event-driven bear markets in history.

Nevertheless, these averages are taken over many decades. If we isolate the bear markets since WWII, we find similar profiles in terms of the depth of bear markets, but generally shorter duration. This is an important observation because it suggests that the payoff for being invested when anticipating a recovery is less beneficial now than it may have been in the past.

Identifying the Transition from Bear Market to Bull Market

The Hope phase (the start of a new bull market) nearly always begins during recessions when the economy is weak, and news is bad. The Hope phase is the strongest (but shortest) phase. It is important for investors not to miss it. But how can they know whether any initial recovery from a bear market is not just a temporary rally in an ongoing downturn? Valuation, growth and interest rates are all key. The combinations of these drivers can also help to identify turning points.

Valuations and the Market Inflection

Valuations tend to fall as investors anticipate a recession. However, although a low valuation may be a necessary condition for a market recovery, alone it is not sufficient. Exhibit 2.4 shows the average

Exhibit 2.4   Valuations below the 30th percentile of historical averages are associated with positive forward returns (data since 1973, global equities)

Valuation percentile		Average forward return		Hit rate	
from	to	12m	24m	12m	24m
0%	10%	14%	21%	81%	90%
10%	20%	11%	30%	92%	98%
20%	30%	12%	38%	82%	95%
30%	40%	9%	15%	69%	82%
40%	50%	6%	16%	67%	73%
50%	60%	9%	17%	66%	73%
60%	70%	7%	13%	62%	76%
70%	80%	10%	16%	82%	79%
80%	90%	5%	16%	66%	71%
90%	100%	–2%	–2%	46%	50%
Unconditional average		8%	18%	73%	82%

NOTE: Percentile for World NTM P/E, LTM P/E, LTM P/B and LTM P/D (Inverse of dividend yield). Hit rate equals the percentage chance of positive return.
SOURCE: Goldman Sachs Global Investment Research

valuation percentile for several metrics for the global equity market. This aggregate measure includes 12-month forward P/E, 12-month trailing P/E, 12-month trailing price/book value (P/B) and 12-month trailing price/dividend (P/D, the inverse of dividend yield). Generally, valuations below the 30th percentile of historical averages are associated with positive returns, while extreme high valuations are followed by downturns.

This is important information as it suggests that, even if the market falls further from this point, or there is a risk of further economic deterioration, very depressed valuations can provide a good entry point for investors, particularly for those who have a time horizon of 6 months or more. Nonetheless, this is only a reliable indicator in isolation if valuations have fallen to extremes. Other fundamental factors, such as growth and policy, are also critical.

Growth and the Market Inflection

Equity markets tend to do better when growth is weak but improving, rather than when it is strong but slowing. Improving economic growth has a good relationship with returns over the previous year (as markets anticipate it), but it is not always a good predictor of future returns. Typically, the US equity market has begun to price a recession on average 7 months prior to the official start of the recession, based on the National Bureau of Economic Research's definition (Exhibit 2.5), with a trough prior to the end of the recession. The 2001 recession is the only one to have departed from this pattern. In that instance, the market continued to decline well after the economic recession ended, reaching a trough 8 months after

Exhibit 2.5   The US equity market has begun to price a recession on average 7 months prior to the official start of the recession

| Market peak | Months between market and recession inflection points | | |
	Market peak to recession start	Recession start to market trough	Market peak to trough
Jun-48	6	6	12
Jan-53	7	1	8
Aug-56	13	2	15
Aug-59	9	6	15
Nov-68	13	5	18
Jan-73	11	10	21
Feb-80	0	2	1
Nov-80	8	12	20
Jul-90	1	2	3
Mar-00	12	18	30
Oct-07	3	14	17
Feb-20	0	1	1
Average	7	7	13
Median	8	6	15
Max	13	18	30
Min	0	1	1

SOURCE: Goldman Sachs Global Investment Research

the recession ended and 30 months after its pre-recession peak. But this was largely a reflection of the scale of overvaluation that preceded it.

In this sense, market returns are countercyclical. For example, if we take the ranges of a cycle as it transitions from trough to growth, from growth to peak, and so on, it is the period from the weakest point as it improves (but is still weak) that typically generates the highest average monthly returns (50 to trough in Exhibit 2.6). Conversely, the weakest returns are when the economy slows from peak towards contraction (peak to 50 in Exhibit 2.6). Exhibit 2.6 shows this for S&P 500 average monthly returns during different phases of growth measured using the ISM manufacturing index. The ISM index is based on a national survey of purchasing managers in the United States, and it tracks changes in the manufacturing and non-manufacturing sectors of the economy. An ISM above 50 represents an expansion, while a reading under 50 represents a contraction,

Exhibit 2.6 The strongest returns occur when the economy is weak but improving

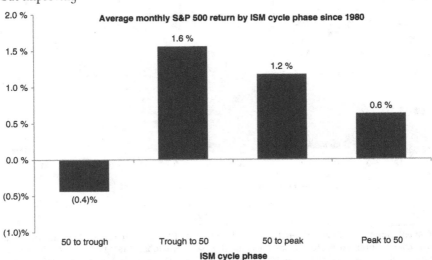

SOURCE: Goldman Sachs Global Investment Research

and a reading at 50 indicates no change. The further away from 50, the greater the level of change.

In line with this pattern, the equity market nearly always starts the Hope phase of the next bull market while corporate earnings are still deteriorating.

Most bear markets trough around 6–9 months before a recovery in corporate earnings per share (Exhibit 2.7), and roughly 3–6 months before any trough in growth momentum (using the rate of change in the ISM as a benchmark, see Exhibit 2.8).[2] Therefore, the Hope phase is associated with rising valuations; the price recovery happens *in anticipation* of a profit recovery. In real time,

Exhibit 2.7   The average bear market troughs around 9 months before a recovery in corporate earnings per share: United States, S&P 500 actual earnings

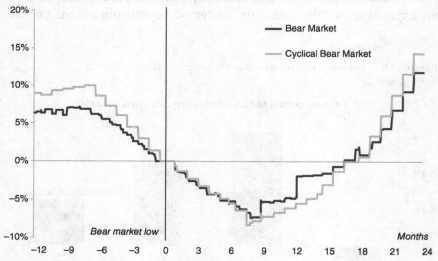

SOURCE: Goldman Sachs Global Investment Research

[2] Oppenheimer, P., Jaisson, G., Bell, S. and Peytavin, L. (2022). Bear repair: The bumpy road to recovery. Goldman Sachs Global Investment Research, Global Strategy Paper. Available at: https://publishing.gs.com/content/research/en/reports/2022/09/07/8ebbd20c-9099-4940-bff2-ed9c31aebfd9.html.

Exhibit 2.8   The average bear market troughs roughly 3–6 months before any trough in growth momentum: change in ISM relative to bear market low

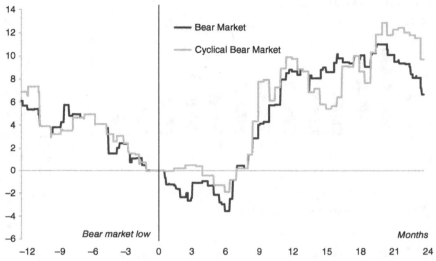

SOURCE: Goldman Sachs Global Investment Research

therefore, it is very difficult to know with any confidence whether a deterioration in economic activity is sufficiently priced for investors to start to think that the rate of deterioration is about to slow.

Does this mean that there is a particular level or rate of growth that investors should have in mind as an indicator of a potential inflection point during a bear market? The answer is yes, but only when growth hits extremes (much as we saw with valuation).

The PMI is another broadly followed survey of current economic conditions. It is a guide to the pace of growth and has the advantage of being more frequent and timelier than GDP. Like the ISM, a level below 50 is considered to reflect an economy in contraction, while above 50 it represents expansion. Significant weakness is typically followed by strong returns and significant strength is followed by weak returns; very weak data is positive for equities (as investors start to anticipate a recovery), and very strong data is often negative (as it is typically seen as close to the peak of the cycle).

Exhibit 2.9   The PMI needs to be at extremes (either high or low) to be useful as an indicator on its own: S&P 500 12-month forward returns, percentage positive return and ISM level

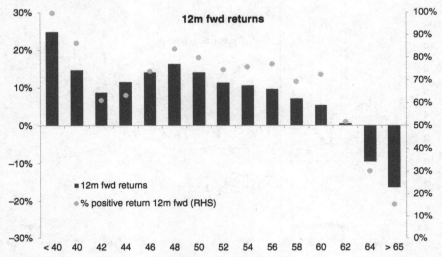

SOURCE: Goldman Sachs Global Investment Research

However, one needs to be cautious: weak economic momentum is often viewed as a sign that the economy will weaken further. So, the PMI needs to be at extremes (either high or low, see Exhibit 2.9) to be useful as an indicator on its own.

Combining Growth and Valuation as a Signal

While both valuation and growth play a part in the recovery process from bear markets, each, in isolation, is typically useful only at extremes. What, then, can we derive from a combination of valuation and growth signals?

Exhibit 2.10 combines the ISM with the valuation percentile mentioned earlier (a combination of P/E, P/B and P/D). Valuations below average and an ISM below 50 generally provide a reasonably good signal over 6 months. The value of combining these metrics is further enhanced when we look at 12-month forward returns.

Exhibit 2.10   When valuations are below the 50th percentile and the ISM is contracting (below 50), forward returns tend to be strong: ISM, S&P 500 valuation percentile and 12-month forward return (%)

Valuation		< 40	38–42	42–46	46–50	50–54	54–58	58–62	62–66	> 65
0%	20%	28%	30%	15%	24%	15%	7%	12%	1%	1%
20%	40%	22%	18%	10%	12%	15%	11%	0%	–12%	
40%	60%		7%	17%	13%	9%	10%	15%	–24%	–29%
60%	80%		47%	23%	17%	8%	9%	9%	–33%	–17%
80%	100%		–18%	–16%	14%	10%	11%	2%	7%	

SOURCE: Goldman Sachs Global Investment Research

In the Optimism phase, towards the peak of the cycle, strong growth trumps high valuations and the market tends to be strong. During the Despair phase, where valuations are below the 50th percentile but the ISM is contracting (below 50), forward returns over a 12-month horizon also tend to be strong.

Inflation, Interest Rates and the Market Inflection

In addition to low valuation, an easing of inflationary concerns and interest rates is typically a combination that tends to help the healing process.

As Exhibit 2.11 shows, the market usually falls in the run-up to the peak in headline inflation as concerns about the impact of higher interest rates mount. That said, after the peak, there is a little more variance depending on other conditions, although on average the market does recover, particularly over 6–12 months, and has a better chance of doing so if investors expect a soft rather than a hard landing.

Interest rates also play a part. On average, the market starts to recover just before 2-year US Treasury rates start to fall and typically not until the fed funds rate has peaked (Exhibit 2.12), and in many cases the markets continue to weaken after the initial rate cuts if growth is deteriorating rapidly at the time.

Exhibit 2.11   An easing of inflationary concerns and interest rates also typically tends to help the healing process: United States, CPI since the 1940s

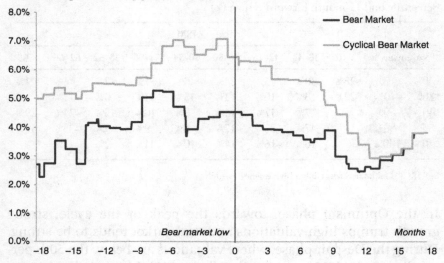

SOURCE: Goldman Sachs Global Investment Research

Exhibit 2.12   On average, the market does not recover until the fed funds rate has peaked: fed funds effective rate since the 1950s

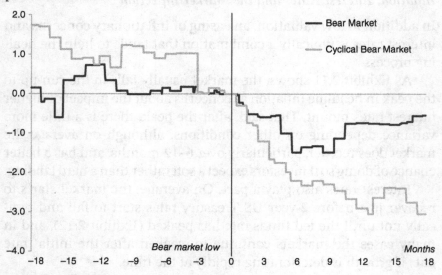

SOURCE: Goldman Sachs Global Investment Research

Exhibit 2.13 Accelerating real GDP is associated with positive returns irrespective of the direction in real rates, while decelerating growth coupled with rising real rates is by far the worst scenario: US real GDP growth and real 10-year Treasury yield, since mid-1970s

		Real 10-year Treasury yield			
		Falling	Stable	Rising	All
US real GDP growth	Accelerating	19%	16%	19%	18%
	Stable	14%	15%	12%	13%
	Decelerating	8%	0%	–4%	4%
	All	12%	11%	11%	11%

NOTE: GDP (Goldman Sachs US Current Activity Indicator) 3-month average vs 3-month average 12 months prior: accelerating >1%, stable between 1% and –1%, decelerating <–1%. Real 10-year change vs 12 months prior: rising >25 bp, stable between 25 bp and –25 bp, falling <25 bp.

SOURCE: Goldman Sachs Global Investment Research

Combining Growth and Interest Rates

As we have seen when combining valuation and growth momentum, it is really the confluence of factors rather than any single factor that best helps investors judge the trough in the market, or at least the probability of achieving a positive return when buying during a bear market. Growth momentum coupled with the change in real interest rates is another useful indicator. As Exhibit 2.13 shows, accelerating real GDP is associated with positive returns irrespective of the direction in real rates, while decelerating growth coupled with rising real rates is by far the worst scenario.

In the next chapter, I turn to the conditions and factors that drive longer-term secular trends, or super cycles.

Chapter 3
Super Cycles and Their Drivers

When patterns are broken, new worlds emerge.

—Tuli Kupferberg

C ycles, both in economic activity and in financial markets, tend to repeat their patterns and unfold within the boundaries of structural trends that can last for extremely long periods. History shows that economic activity and real incomes can be relatively flat, or even recede, for many decades, while other periods experience consistent growth and prosperity. Equally, within financial markets, there are long-term periods, or super cycles, where overall returns are subdued, while others exhibit a powerful trend of rising returns. When these longer-term trends or regimes change, the impact can be significant as investors are often unprepared for them; assumptions become entrenched and are often slow to adjust to a new reality.

I describe the longer-term periods of lower growth as 'Fat and Flat' markets: periods when point-to-point real returns are low but large swings or trading ranges exist. These are distinct from the long-lasting upswings that I describe as super cycles. The factors and conditions that drive these super cycles will be the topic of the next part of this book, with each chapter covering a different super cycle since World War II (WWII).

Before discussing the post-WWII super cycles and financial markets, it is worth putting recent developments into a longer-term context. With the benefit of some long-term data series compiled by academics, we can see that there have been major structural shifts in several key economic, political and social trends throughout history. It is these long-term structural conditions that have contributed to long-term secular shifts in the returns and leadership characteristics of financial market cycles.

Super Cycles in Economic Activity

Perhaps the best known and most widely used longer-term series of economic activity is based on the pioneering work of British economist Angus Maddison (1926–2010). Maddison's work has been continued by the Groningen Growth and Development Centre where he worked (in a project referred to as the Maddison Project Database). Moreover, many other long-term datasets have been developed since his original work, based on subsequent reconstructions of his analysis using historical archives (including the use of parish data, registers, poll tax returns, school and hospital records, and many other sources), and combining various datasets to create a better and deeper understanding of past economic and social trends and super cycles.[1] Work carried out by the Bank of England and other central banks complements these datasets, and is also illuminating.

---

[1] Broadberry, S. (2013). Accounting for the Great Divergence: Recent findings from historical national accounting. London School of Economics and CAGE, Economic History Working Paper No. 184. Broadberry, S., Campbell, B., Klein, A., Overton, M. and van Leeuwen, B. (2011). *British Economic Growth, 1270–1870: An Output-Based Approach*. Cambridge: Cambridge University Press. Malanima, P. (2011). The long decline of a leading economy: GDP in central and northern Italy, 1300–1913. *European Review of Economic History*, 15(2), pp. 169–219. van Zanden, J. L. and van Leeuwen, B. (2012). Persistent but not consistent: The growth of national income in Holland 1347–1807. *Explorations in Economic History*, 49(2), pp. 119–130. Schön, L. and Krantz, O. (2012). The Swedish economy in the early modern period: Constructing historical national accounts. *European Review of Economic History*, 16(4), pp. 529–549. Álvarez-Nogal, C. and De La Escosura, L. P. (2013). The rise and fall of Spain (1270–1850). *The Economic History Review*, 66(1), pp. 1–37. Costa, L. F., Palma, N. and Reis, J. (2013). The great escape? The contribution of the empire to Portugal's economic growth, 1500–1800. *European Review of Economic History*, 19(1), pp. 1–22.

Most estimates suggest that, between 2,000 and 1,000 years ago, global gross domestic product (GDP) fell, even as the population grew by around 15% in total. However, an astonishing change in economic activity and living standards has taken place over the past 1,000 years. Over this period, the world's population has increased nearly 30-fold to 8 billion people, and life expectancy has increased almost three-fold. World GDP and GDP per capita have risen 100-fold and 50-fold, respectively (see Exhibits 3.1 and 3.2).[2] Much of this extraordinary change has come in phases or super cycles rather than in a continuum.

While Maddison's original work suggested that the bulk of the improvements to economic activity and life expectancy started from 1820, more recent revisions suggest that, even before the acceleration of growth that occurred from the early nineteenth century, there were significant long-lasting trends of economic growth, or super cycles, that often endured for several decades. There were also long periods of contraction or structural decline.[3]

Exhibit 3.1 World real GDP has increased more than 100-fold since 1600: world real GDP and population (indexed to 100 in 1600, log scale)

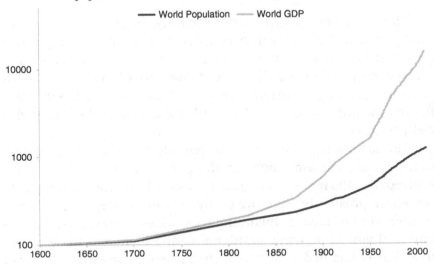

SOURCE: Maddison Database 2010

[2] Maddison, A. (2010). *The World Economy: A Millennial Perspective*. Paris: OECD.
[3] Bolt, J. and van Zanden, J. L. (2020). The Maddison Project. Maddison-Project Working Paper No. WP-15.

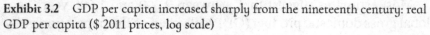

Exhibit 3.2   GDP per capita increased sharply from the nineteenth century: real GDP per capita ($ 2011 prices, log scale)

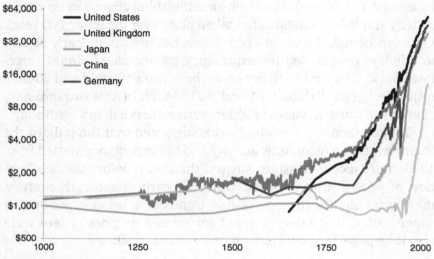

SOURCE: Maddison Project Database 2020

These earlier growth waves mainly began to emerge in Europe around the eleventh century, following earlier periods of much stronger growth in Asia. By the fourteenth century, Europe had overtaken China and the rest of Asia. Asia then entered a prolonged period of relative stagnation, with per capita income remaining roughly flat until the second half of the twentieth century.

The factors that explain these periods of growth and stagnation help to shed some light on the global super cycles that have evolved over the more recent past. Historically, periods of long-term economic prosperity were driven by significant step changes in a combination of factors, including technological advances, innovation in financial markets, immigration and increased trade. All of these have remained important factors in explaining super cycles in growth and financial markets in the twentieth century, as the next part of the book discusses.

In particular:

1. **Italy 1305–1420: 40% growth in per capita income.** Italian cities expanded and established major trade routes across Europe and Asia.[4] The Venetians opened important trading routes across Europe between Flanders, France, Germany and the Balkans, while China opened routes to ports on the Black Sea. As with other super cycles in history, as well as more recently, technological innovation played an important role. Venice relied heavily on advanced shipbuilding and breakthroughs in navigational technologies, including the use of the compass. The increased development and sophistication of its financial system and opening up of credit markets, combined with a strong administrative system, were all important factors.[5] Venice also became a major centre for learning and education, with famous professors such as Galileo Galilei, a pioneer of book publishing and innovation in several fields. (Venice's dominance in glass blowing, for example, made it a leader in the manufacture of spectacles.)[6]

   Portugal and Spain also developed rapidly during the so-called Golden Age of Discovery (1400s–1600s). As with other periods of economic expansion, exploration was central, as was openness to immigration. For example, Muslims continued to make up a large part of the population, and in the early fourteenth century more than 200,000 Jews lived in Portugal, making up about 20% of the total population.[7] Many of them played a key role in developing trade and science. Abraham Zacuto, for example, developed tables that were used as the principle for Portuguese navigation, including by Vasco da Gama on his trip to India. By the sixteenth century, Portugal had become the

---

[4] Fouquet, R. and Broadberry, S. (2015). Seven centuries of European economic growth and decline. *Journal of Economic Perspectives*, 29(4), pp. 227–244.

[5] Maddison, A. (2001). *The World Economy: A Millennial Perspective*. Paris: OECD.

[6] In 1301 the Giustizieri Vecchi, the superintendents of Venetian Arts granted permission to all craftsmen to make 'vitrei ab oculis ad legendum' (glass lenses for reading).

[7] The Jews were later expelled from Portugal in 1497 when Manuel I married Princess Isabella of Spain, who agreed to marry him if he expelled the Jews.

leader in trade around Europe and was key to the opening up of routes via the Atlantic Islands and to Africa. Portugal had strategic advantages given its location on the South Atlantic coast of Europe. Its success in deep-sea fishing contributed to its increasing nautical edge over rivals.

2. **Holland 1505–1595: 70% increase in per capita income.** The main drivers were again the rapid expansion of trade and the shift in economic output away from agriculture and towards commodities of higher value. Advances in shipping technology and building capacity were another key component of its success. By 1570, the Dutch merchant navy had a capacity as large as those of Germany, England and France combined. It also had advanced technology in canal building and benefited from increased power generation from its windmills. Later, during the seventeenth century, the Dutch Golden Age saw the trade, science and art of the Netherlands take their place among the most prominent in Europe. During this time, Dutch merchants and settlers, affiliated with the Dutch East India Company (VOC), the world's first publicly listed company, and the Dutch West India Company (GWC), established trading posts and colonies in the Americas, Africa and Asia, protected by the powerful Dutch navy.

3. **Sweden 1600–1650: 40% growth in per capita income** (success was driven by expanding trade routes through the Baltics).[8]

4. **Britain 1650–1700: over 50% growth in per capita income.** The end of the Civil War, the Glorious Revolution of 1688 and the establishment of a constitutional monarchy, as well as the rule of law, created an institutional framework that was supportive of growth. Britain managed to achieve a combination of population growth and growth in per capita GDP. Between 1720 and 1820, British exports increased more than sevenfold and its per capita income grew more than that of any other European country.[9]

---

[8] Schön, L. and Krantz, O. (2015). New Swedish historical national accounts since the 16th century in constant and current prices. Department of Economic History, Lund University, Lund Papers in Economic History No. 140.

[9] McCombie, J. S. L. and Maddison, A. (1983). Phases of capitalist development. *The Economic Journal*, **93**(370), pp. 428–429.

The Modern Era: Growth from the 1820s

Between these earlier super cycles of European growth from the eleventh century until 1820, real incomes had increased roughly threefold.[10] Since 1820, however, world economic development has been extraordinary (Exhibit 3.3). Income per capita has risen faster than population, and by 1998 it was 8.5 times higher than in 1820, while population had grown 5.6-fold.[11]

Up until the nineteenth century, a lower population often meant a higher income per head, as there were fewer mouths to feed. Declines in population – usually a function of climate change, bad harvests or disease – would typically boost prosperity for those who survived. In an economy that was not growing, where the total 'pie' remained the same size, the only way for one person (or country) to become richer was for someone else to become poorer. During the period known as the Black Death, for example, the plague killed almost half of the English population (which declined from over 8 million to 4 million in the 3 years after 1348). Those who survived became richer, as farmers were able to use only the most productive land (rather than resorting to less productive land to feed a larger population, as previously). The relationship between growth and population was developed by Thomas Malthus, in what became known as the Malthusian Law of Population, or Malthusianism. This theory posits that, while population growth is exponential, resources growth, including food growth, is linear; thus, if populations grew too much, this would trigger a collapse in living standards and, ultimately, a catastrophe. However, all of this was about to change from the early part of the nineteenth century, as technology and capitalism combined to generate much higher growth.

---

[10] Roser, M. (2013). Economic growth. Available at https://ourworldindata.org/economic-growth.
[11] Maddison, A. (2001). *The World Economy: A Millennial Perspective*. Paris: OECD.

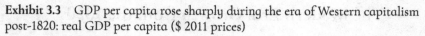

Exhibit 3.3   GDP per capita rose sharply during the era of Western capitalism post-1820: real GDP per capita ($ 2011 prices)

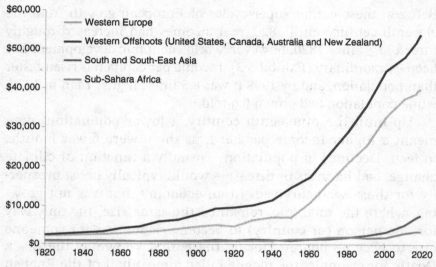

SOURCE: Maddison Project Database 2020

According to Maddison, the era of capitalist growth from the nineteenth century can be split into five distinct phases that are the result of specific 'system shocks':[12]

1. The Age of Capitalist Development: 1820–1870
2. The Old Liberal Order: 1870–1913
3. The War Years (beggar-thy-neighbour phase): 1913–1950
4. The Golden Age: 1950–1973
5. The Neo-Liberal Age: 1973–1998

Of these, the Golden Age generated the best period of growth, at least for Western Europe and the United States (see Exhibit 3.4). The post-1973 era generated the second-best (although the period from 1973 to 1983 was hampered by the oil shocks, which I discuss in detail in Chapter 5). The Old Liberal Order between 1870 and

[12] Maddison, A. (2001). *The World Economy: A Millennial Perspective*. Paris: OECD.

Exhibit 3.4 The Golden Age generated the best period of real growth in the West: global real GDP per capita, annualised growth rate

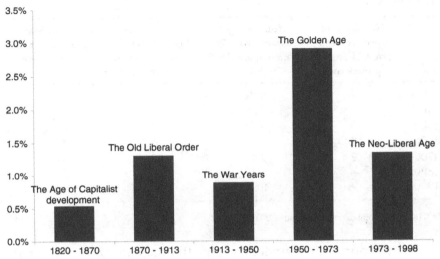

SOURCE: Maddison Database 2010

1913 saw the third-highest growth. The War Years were hampered by the collapse of trade and migration, while the early phase of capitalism from 1820 to 1870 saw the slowest growth, although this was mainly because robust growth was limited to European countries in a pre-globalised world. The 1900s overall saw significant increases in higher-growth years than other centuries (see Exhibit 3.5).

Other academic studies have identified similar patterns of long-term cycles, or super cycles. Deepankar Basu, for example, identifies an up-wave from 1949 to 1982 and a down-wave from 1968 to 1982.[13] The more recent super cycle between 1983 and 2008 comprises the upswing from 1983 to 2007 and the downswing post-2008. Interestingly, these correspond closely to the financial market super cycles that I discuss in Part II of this book.

---

[13] Basu, D. (2016). Long waves of capitalist development: An empirical investigation. University of Massachusetts Amherst, Department of Economics Working Paper No. 2016-15.

Exhibit 3.5   Years with annual GDP growth rates above +1.5% and below –1.5%: England/Great Britain, Italy, Holland, Sweden, Spain and Portugal are the countries considered

	No. phases of 4-year consecutive 1.5% annual growth rate	% Years in 4-year consecutive 1.5% annual growth rate	No. phases of 3-year consecutive –1.5% annual growth rate	% Years in 3-year consecutive –1.5% annual growth rate
1300s	1	1.1%	2	1.6%
1400s	1	1.0%	10	8.0%
1500s	3	2.3%	14	8.7%
1600s	2	1.3%	9	4.3%
1700s	2	1.3%	12	5.8%
1800s	8	5.3%	4	2.0%
1900s	38	40.0%	4	3.2%

SOURCE: McCombie and Maddison (1983)

For the purposes of understanding financial markets, the explosion of growth in the post-WWII period has been particularly striking (Exhibit 3.5). Again, there have been several recessions and cycles, but the overall trend has been especially strong relative to longer-term historical experience. Over the 50 years following 1950, the global population increased by 150%, while GDP rose by 600%. It is this remarkable period, post-WWII, that I turn to in more detail in the next part of the book.

Super Cycles in Inflation

From a financial markets perspective, two main variables matter most: growth and inflation. While there is evidence of long waves of economic growth and contraction, the data on inflation is also cyclical. Inflation, like economic growth, has not increased in a straight line but has passed through various structural episodes over time. Stephen King's recent book is an excellent discussion of the topic for those seeking more details.[14]

---

[14] King, S. D. (2023). *We Need to Talk About Inflation: 14 Urgent Lessons From the Last 2,000 Years.* New Haven, CT: Yale University Press.

Although much of what we think of as inflation is a recent phenomenon (from the twentieth century), there are clear periods of inflation and deflation throughout history, and many of these phases lasted for long periods of time. Indeed, inflation was already a problem in the Roman Empire between the middle of the second century AD and the end of the third century AD. Over this extended period, the price of wheat increased 200-fold. One of the key causes of higher prices was the debasement of metal coins – quite literally, reducing the precious metal content of coins. The practice encouraged private citizens to follow suit by cutting off the edges of coins.[15] This was also done during the Great Debasement in England, between 1544 and 1551, under the orders of Henry VIII.[16] It resulted in the volume of precious metals used in gold and silver coins being reduced or replaced entirely with cheaper metals, such as copper. Despite large sums already having been raised by the Dissolution of the Monasteries and higher taxes, the practice was adopted to offset the effects of significant overspending to pay for the King's personal lifestyle and to fund wars with France and Scotland. Over a century later, the problems experienced as a consequence of quantitative easing (QE) and the devaluation of sterling against gold led to an important innovation: the first Gold Standard, introduced by Sir Isaac Newton (who became Master of the Royal Mint) in 1717.[17]

Long-term data in England shows that periods of inflation and disinflation were quite common. A study by the Bank of England looking at the price of three essential products shows that the average price of bread in London in 1694 was 5.6 old pence (about 2.3 p) per 4 pounds in weight.[18] In 1894, the price was just 5.5 old pence, though it had risen to one shilling and five old pence (about 7 p) at the time of the Napoleonic Wars. In the last major inflationary wave

---

[15] MacFarlane, H. and Mortimer-Lee, P. (1994). Inflation over 300 years. Bank of England.

[16] Owen, J. (2012). Old Coppernose – quantitative easing, the medieval way. Royal Mint.

[17] Shirras, G. F. and Craig, J. H. (1945). Sir Isaac Newton and the currency. *The Economic Journal*, 55(218/219), pp. 217–241.

[18] MacFarlane, H. and Mortimer-Lee, P. (1994). Inflation over 300 years. Bank of England.

in the 1970s, prices rose very sharply. Bread prices tripled between 1974 and 1984 and had increased by a further 60% by 1993.[19]

The retail price of a ton of coal in London rose sharply between 1700 and 1830, by roughly 70% to 20 shillings, but then remained broadly unchanged over the following 70 years (1900). It then rose by about a third to 30 shillings during World War I (WWI), before later dropping back again to 20 shillings.

Inflation was one of the defining economic characteristics of the second half of the twentieth century (Exhibit 3.6). Many factors drove inflation over that period, and policy failure was one. In 1964, inflation measured a little more than 1% per year, roughly where it had been over the preceding 6 years. Inflation began

Exhibit 3.6   Inflation was one of the defining economic characteristics of the second half of the twentieth century: UK Consumer Price Index (indexed to 100 in 1694, log-scale)

SOURCE: Bank of England Millennium Dataset

---

[19] Thomas, R. and Dimsdale, N. (2017). A Millennium of UK Macroeconomic Data. Bank of England OBRA Dataset.

Exhibit 3.7 Inflation accelerated sharply during the twentieth century: US Consumer Price Index (log-scale)

SOURCE: Goldman Sachs Global Investment Research

ratcheting upwards in the mid-1960s (Exhibit 3.7) and reached more than 14% in 1980. It eventually declined to average just 3.5% in the latter half of the 1980s.[20] I will focus more on this period in Chapter 6.

Super Cycles in Interest Rates

The history of interest rates is no less amazing than that of growth – indeed, the two are linked. A data series from the Bank of England shows how global bond yields have generally trended downwards since the fourteenth century. Like the other key macro variables and drivers of financial assets, this has not been a straight line. There have been

---

[20] Bryan, M. (2013). The Great Inflation. Available at https://www.federalreservehistory.org/essays/great-inflation.

periods of rising interest rates, of course, but the trajectory has been one of dramatically lower interest rates over time. The rise in bond yields in the post-WWII period during the inflationary years of the 1970s is particularly striking, as is the remarkable decline since then.

There are many explanations for this long-term secular down-trend after the 1970s. Some have associated the long-term decline with an increase in the 'convenience yield'.[21] This is a concept that pointed to a growing imbalance between the global demand for safety and liquidity and its available supply.[22] Others have put it down to a global savings glut and argue that the Global Financial Crisis (GFC) and slow subsequent recovery suggested that the explanation was 'secular stagnation'.[23] Others attribute much of the phenomenon to demographics.[24]

For example, a series of crises since the mid-1990s increased the demand for safe assets. The Asian financial crisis of 1997, the Russian debt default of 1998 and the collapse of Long-Term Capital Management (LTCM) may have been early triggers. This was further supported by the impact of the collapse of the technology bubble and then the GFC of 2008. Other triggering factors often put forward include a shift in the rate of per-capita consumption linked to ageing demographics.

The further collapse in interest rates since the GFC of 2008 – and the pandemic of 2020 – left interest rates at the lowest levels in history (Exhibit 3.8). This has been a key driver in explaining two secular bull markets: (i) between 1982 (the inflationary peak in interest rates) and 2000 (the peak of the technology bubble); and (ii) the post-GFC era from 2009 to 2020, partly fuelled by the impact of QE.[25] I focus on these periods in Chapter 8.

[21] Bernanke, B., Bertaut, C. C., DeMarco, L. P. and Kamin, S. (2011). International capital flows and the returns to safe assets in the United States, 2003–2007. International Finance Discussion Paper No. 1014.

[22] Bernanke, B. S. (2005). The global saving glut and the U.S. current account deficit. Speech at the Sandridge Lecture, Virginia Association of Economics, Richmond, VA, March 10.

[23] Summers, L. H. (2014). U.S. economic prospects: Secular stagnation, hysteresis, and the zero lower bound. Business Economics, 49(2), pp. 65–73.

[24] Lunsford, K. G. and West, K. (2017). Some evidence on secular drivers of US safe real rates. Federal Reserve Bank of Cleveland Working Paper No. 17-23.

[25] Schmelzing, P. (2020). Eight centuries of global real interest rates, R-G, and the 'suprasecular' decline, 1311–2018. Bank of England Staff Working Paper No. 845.

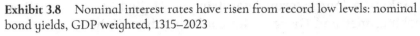

Exhibit 3.8   Nominal interest rates have risen from record low levels: nominal bond yields, GDP weighted, 1315–2023

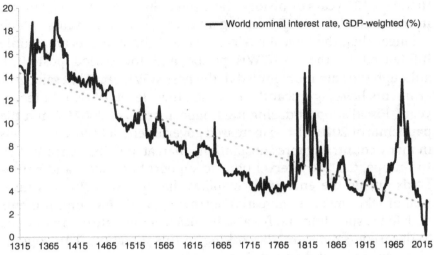

SOURCE: Bank of England

Super Cycles and Government Debt

Alongside growth, inflation and interest rates, there is evidence of super cycles in government debt. Again, while economic conditions have an impact on debt, long waves in debt levels show the crucial interplay between economic activity, inflation and government policy. Work by Poghosyan analysed data for government debt between 1960 and 2014, and identified 209 debt expansions and 207 debt contractions across 57 countries. Of these, 120 expansions and 118 contractions were in emerging economies, and 89 expansions and 89 contractions were in advanced economies. Once again, we can see a cyclical pattern. Debt expansions lasted an average of 7 years and contractions just over 6 years. In terms of scale, the median expansion was 14.5% of GDP and the median contraction was 10.7%.[26]

---

[26] Poghosyan, T. (2015). How do public debt cycles interact with financial cycles? IMF Working Paper No. 15(248).

Taking a longer-term dataset in the United States, Engelbert Stockhammer and Giorgos Gouzoulis' study of debt cycles shows that over 125 years of history, the United States experienced cycles in corporate debt to GDP lasting an average of 11–12 years, which is longer than the typical business cycle.[27] These results are mainly influenced by the pre-WWII period and the period post-1973, although they are more muted in the post-WWII era. That said, governments have significantly increased their levels of debt in recent years. Fiscal support during the financial crisis of 2007/08 and the pandemic of 2020/21 has increased government debt-to-GDP levels in many countries more substantially than at any time since WWII. In Europe, too, the interventions to support businesses and households during the energy price spikes that followed Russia's invasion of Ukraine have increased borrowing, and new commitments in defence spending and fiscal subsidies to accelerate commitments to decarbonisation are all working in this direction. This topic is discussed in more detail in Chapter 12.

Super Cycles in Inequality

History shows that inequality, like the other macroeconomic drivers described above, is also cyclical, although it moves slowly, in long-term trends.[28]

Using land and tax records, academics have been able to analyse wealth inequality over long periods, particularly in Europe. Research by Guido Alfani shows a large fall in wealth inequality between 1340 and 1440, after the Black Death. However, inequality increased again between 1440 and 1540. Estimates for England show that by 1524/25, inequality had returned to the same level as in 1327–1332, with 64% of wealth in the hands of the top 10%

[27] Stockhammer, E. and Gouzoulis, G. (2022). Debt–GDP cycles in historical perspective: The case of the USA (1889–2014). *Industrial and Corporate Change*, **32**(2), pp. 317–335.
[28] Szreter, S. (2021). The history of inequality: The deep-acting ideological and institutional influences. IFS Deaton Review of Inequalities.

(equivalent to a Gini coefficient of 0.76).[29] Research by Lindert offered a central estimate that about 83% of wealth was in the hands of the top 10% of England's population in 1670, implying further significant growth in inequality since around 1525.[30] Piketty estimates that by 1800, inequality had fallen below the levels of 1740.[31]

Then, the period post-1800 saw a sharp rise in inequality, as wealth concentration surpassed previous peaks by the early twentieth century. The wealth of the top 10% property holders reached more than 94% between 1900 and 1910, with the top 1% owning 70% of UK property (Exhibit 3.9). Wealth inequality fell

Exhibit 3.9   The concentration of property in Britain declined significantly in the twentieth century: share of property in Britain owned by top 1%, top 10%, middle 40% and bottom 50%

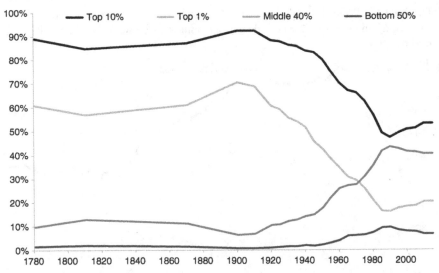

SOURCE: Piketty (2020)

[29] Alfani, G. (2021). Economic inequality in preindustrial times: Europe and beyond. *Journal of Economic Literature*, **59**(1), pp. 3–44.

[30] Lindert, P. H. (1986). Unequal English wealth since 1670. *Journal of Political Economy*, **94**(6), pp. 1127–1162.

[31] Piketty, T. (2020). *Capital and Ideology*. Translated by A. Goldhammer. Cambridge, MA: Harvard University Press.

between 1910 and 1990, with significant reversals after WWI, and then, after the advent of the welfare state, it declined significantly following WWII (Exhibit 3.10). By 1990, the top 1% had seen their share of wealth fall to 18%, while the lowest 50% held a 10% share of the nation's wealth. The data, however, shows that although wealth inequality has fallen, income inequality has been rising since 1980 (Exhibit 3.11), as a consequence of the supply-side and tax reforms put in place after the economic crisis of the 1970s (see Chapter 5). More recently, inequality has increased again in most countries, partly reflecting the unintended consequences of policies put in place to resolve the financial crisis, including the introduction of QE, which contributed to rising asset wealth.[32]

Exhibit 3.10   Wealth inequality in the UK declined significantly during the twentieth century: share of UK net personal wealth owned by the top 1% and top 10%

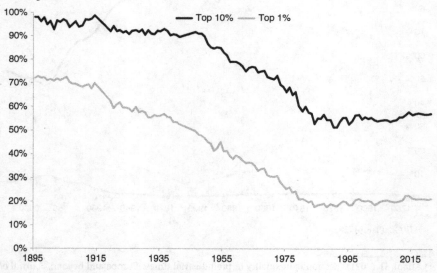

SOURCE: World Inequality Database

[32] Piketty, T. (2014). *Capital in the Twenty-First Century*. Translated by A. Goldhammer. Cambridge, MA: The Belknap Press of Harvard University Press.

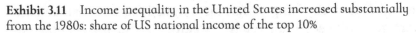

Exhibit 3.11   Income inequality in the United States increased substantially from the 1980s: share of US national income of the top 10%

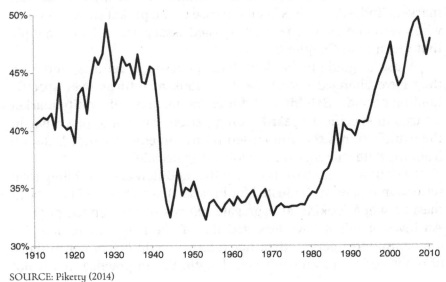

SOURCE: Piketty (2014)

Super Cycles in Financial Markets

Given the inter-relationships between economic cycles and trends in inflation, interest rates, inequality and government policy, it is not surprising that financial assets also experience long-term trends. Some academics define the financial cycle as the co-movement of medium-term cycles in credit and property prices; they find that financial cycles have lasted on average 16 years (since the 1960s), longer than the business cycle (which tends not to exceed 8 years), and with much greater volatility.[33]

Both equities and bonds tend to experience longer-term phases of high or low returns that are a function of the combination of economic and political conditions in which they exist. These periods

---

[33] Drehmann, M., Borio, C. and Tsatsaronis, K. (2012). Characterising the financial cycle: Don't lose sight of the medium term! BIS Working Paper No. 380.

often coincide with rising or falling wealth inequality, since asset owners generally see their relative wealth rise during secular bull markets. Indeed, this has been the case in the period since the GFC, when zero interest rate policies boosted asset price inflation, a topic that I turn to in Chapter 8.

A useful guide to the long-term patterns in returns, and how they have changed over time, is to look at returns over specific holding periods. Exhibit 3.12, for example, plots US equity market returns in specific 10-year holding periods over time (each bar in the exhibit shows the annualised return on equities after inflation from the date shown, over the following decade).

Over time, there have been significant differences in rolling total returns in real terms (adjusted for inflation), which would have been masked when looking at aggregate returns over extended periods. An investor might have expected that if she had held equities for a medium-term period, then her returns would be similar to those of other periods of an equivalent length. But in practice that is not

Exhibit 3.12 There have been significant differences in rolling total returns in real terms (adjusted for inflation): subsequent 10-year annualised real total returns

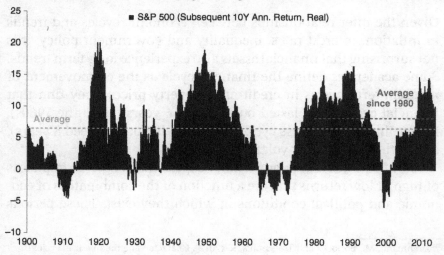

SOURCE: Goldman Sachs Global Investment Research

necessarily true. For example, returns on equities purchased at the start of major conflicts (e.g., WWI and WWII) were negative for extended periods, as it took a great deal of time to recover from the initial losses. Similarly, equities bought at the peak of the bull market in the late 1960s, with high valuations, before the spike in global inflation, also saw negative returns.

Similarly, periods of high inflation have been associated with lower real returns than periods of low inflation.

In an historical context, the period of the technology bubble and its collapse at the end of the 1990s is particularly striking. Equities bought at the top of the technology bubble in 2000 – and even through to 2003 – achieved over the subsequent decade some of the lowest real returns in US equities (along with the 1970s) in over 100 years. Equities bought during the period that followed have resulted in much stronger returns – in line with long-run averages. Meanwhile, investors who entered the stock market following the GFC enjoyed strong returns.

The 10-year holding periods with the highest returns typically occur in periods of strong economic growth; the booms of the 1920s and post-WWII reconstruction of the 1950s are good examples. Others are periods of low or falling interest rates, such as in the 1980s and 1990s, and periods following large bear markets, when valuations have reached low levels.

That said, although equities have performed better over longer-term holding periods and have performed well post-GFC in particular, it is the real returns in the bond market since the 1980s that have been truly remarkable compared with most periods in history (Exhibit 3.13). US Treasuries bought in the early 1980s, at the peak of the inflation cycle, have annualised real returns of over 10% for 10 years (and over 7% for 20 years). This means that if an investor had invested $1,000 in US government bonds in 1980, in real terms her investment would be worth around $6,000 at the time of writing (adjusted for inflation).

Even bonds bought in the early 1990s have annualised real returns of around 5% for 20 years – the kind of real returns that investors used to hope for in equities. These extraordinary returns suggest that investors had not fully priced in at the outset the likely

Exhibit 3.13   The real returns in the bond market since the 1980s have been truly remarkable compared with most periods in history: subsequent 10-year annualised real total returns

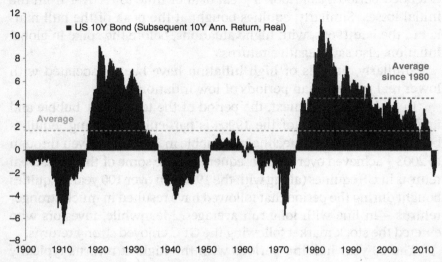

SOURCE: Goldman Sachs Global Investment Research

fall in inflation and interest rates, and emphasise the critical role that changing expectations play in the eventual returns that are achieved.

Looking at equities versus bonds also shows some interesting longer-term trends and secular periods. Recessions typically generate higher returns in bonds than equities (interest rates tend to come down but equities are usually more negatively impacted by falling growth expectations). But, over the longer run, the period from 1950 to 1968 saw a powerful secular trend of equity markets outperforming bonds (Exhibit 3.14). The reverse was true between 1982 and 1994 – while it was a positive period for financial assets in general, it was less good for equity markets, as bonds benefited from a sharp fall in inflation expectations.

1990–2000 saw a period of strong equity outperformance, driven by robust growth and the impact of globalisation, while the disinflationary era post-2000 through to 2010 once again saw bonds outperform equities. The GFC was good for both bonds and

Exhibit 3.14 US equities have materially outperformed bonds post-GFC and since the Covid-19 crisis: relative total return performance

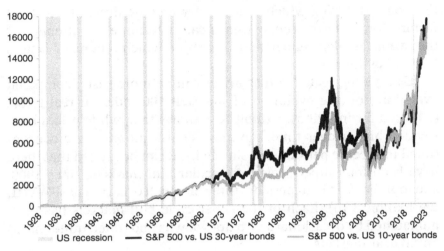

US recession — S&P 500 vs. US 30-year bonds — S&P 500 vs. US 10-year bonds

SOURCE: Goldman Sachs Global Investment Research

equities – supported by ultra-low interest rates – but benefited equities more, reflecting the emerging digital revolution and high profit growth, particularly in the United States.

So, it appears that most of the significant factors that influence financial markets go through long-term super cycles or secular trends, as well as shorter-term business cycles. Because financial markets are driven by changes in economic variables, assessments of risk and approaches to policy, it is not surprising that they also exhibit long-term trends during which returns are strong or weak depending on these other factors. In the next section, I look at each of the super cycles in equity markets since WWII and unpack their key drivers and influences.

Super Cycles in Equities

Most equity cycles revolve around economic cycles but, cutting across these, and often lasting longer than a single cycle, there can also be powerful and long-lasting secular trends. Generally, these are a function of structural shifts in both macroeconomic and political conditions. Just as the cycle tends to be broken down into distinct phases during which returns vary and are driven by distinct factors, longer-term secular trends can determine the strength of the overall market return, and determine which sectors or factors lead or lag the index.

Using a log scale (so that prices can be more easily compared over time) on the evolution of the S&P 500 index in real terms (adjusted for inflation), Exhibit 3.15 shows that, while prices have trended higher over time, the most significant gains are concentrated in specific periods. For simplicity, it can be argued that there have been four super cycles, or secular bull markets, since 1900, and four 'Fat and Flat' periods (three of which occurred post-WWII; see Exhibit 3.16). Each of the super cycle bull markets has been punctuated by occasional sharp drawdowns and (often quite sharp) 'mini' bear markets.

Exhibit 3.15   There have been four secular bull markets since 1900 and four 'Fat and Flat' periods: S&P 500 real price return

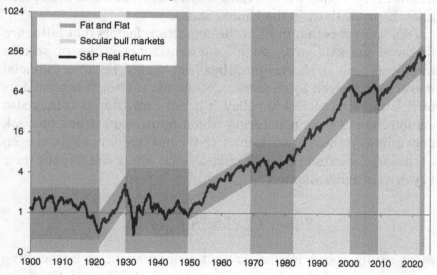

SOURCE: Goldman Sachs Global Investment Research

Exhibit 3.16 Post-WWII there have been three secular bull markets and three 'Fat and Flat' periods

Start	End	Years	Phase	Price return (nominal)		Total return (real)	
				Total	Annualised	Total	Annualised
Jun-1949	Nov-1968	19	Secular bull market	700%	11%	1109%	14%
Nov-1968	Aug-1982	14	Fat & Flat	-5%	0%	-39%	-4%
Aug-1982	Mar-2000	18	Secular bull market	1391%	17%	1356%	16%
Mar-2000	Mar-2009	9	Fat & Flat	-56%	-9%	-58%	-9%
Mar-2009	Feb-2020	11	Secular bull market	401%	16%	417%	16%
Feb-2020	Jun-2023	3	Fat & Flat	31%	8%	18%	5%

SOURCE: Goldman Sachs Global Investment Research

For example, the secular bull market of 1982–2000 was interrupted by the crash of 1987, the Savings and Loan crisis in the late 1980s, the bond crisis in 1994 (when 30-year US Treasury yields rose around 200 basis points in just 9 months) and the Asia crisis of 1998. But one can still consider these periods part of a secular super cycle in which a powerful structural bull market, driven by some favourable structural factors, remained uninterrupted over extended periods, even during the corrections. The three major structural upswings since the end of WWII have been as follows.

1. 1949–1968: Post-World War II Boom

This period was dominated by the powerful post-WWII economic boom and is often referred to as the Golden Age of Capitalism. It was supported by the United States' initiative to aid Europe economically through the Marshall Plan (or the European Recovery Plan), which helped to boost growth and reduce unemployment. Productivity growth was strong, particularly in Europe and East Asia, and the post-WWII 'baby boom' further strengthened demand.

2. 1982–2000: The Modern Cycle

Tackling inflation was one of the key drivers of this secular bull market post-1982. The inflationary era, which had been so damaging to financial markets, ended partly because of the so-called Volker credit crunch (a period known for the recession caused by the US Federal Reserve tightening cycle that started in 1977), which took US fed funds rates (policy rates) from around 10% to close to 20%. From that point, inflation started to fall globally and, coupled with a vigorous recovery in economic activity from a deep recession, and the collapse of the Berlin Wall in 1989, confidence – and asset valuations – started to rise. From August 1982 to December 1999, the compounded real return on the Dow Jones Industrial Average was 15% per year, well in excess of long-run average returns, or indeed the increase in earnings or book value over the period.[34] Much of this secular bull market there-fore reflected valuation expansion – a phenomenon that pushed up both equity and fixed-income (bond) returns at the same time.

3. 2009–2020: The Post-Financial-Crisis Cycle and Zero Interest Rates

The secular drivers of risk assets shifted materially in the period after the technology bubble burst in the late 1990s. Since the start of the current century, the dominant structural driver of finan-cial assets had been the combination of falling inflation expecta-tions and interest rates, which tended to push up equity and bond valuations.

The fortunes of equity markets changed in the aftermath of the financial crisis and the start of QE and zero rate policies. Having collapsed by 57% from its 2007 peak, the S&P 500 started a power-ful recovery that was to result in one of the longest bull markets in history. Part of the strength of the recovery, as with the bull market in the early 1990s, was a function of the scale of the declines in the economy and market that had preceded it. In the United States in particular, the collapse in the housing market had resulted in a huge loss of household wealth. With more than $1 trillion in sub-prime mortgages outstanding, the spread of losses throughout the economy and financial institutions was significant. At the same time, according to then Fed Chair Ben Bernanke, 'too-big-to-fail financial institutions were both a source (though by no means the only source) of the crisis and among the primary impediments to policymakers' efforts to contain it'.[35] Between 2007 and 2010, the median wealth of a household in the United States fell 44%, result-ing in levels dropping below those of 1969. Stock prices had also fallen sharply, leaving them relatively cheap and offering significant

---

[34] Ritter, J. R. and Warr, R. S. (2002). The decline of inflation and the bull market of 1982–1999. *The Journal of Financial and Quantitative Analysis*, **37**(1), pp. 29–61.

[35] Bernanke, B. S. (2010). Causes of the recent financial and economic crisis. Testimony before the Financial Crisis Inquiry Commission, Washington, D.C.

valuation expansion possibilities considering the start of QE and the resulting collapse in financial conditions.

What each of these super cycles has in common is a combination of low starting valuation, falling or low cost of capital and a low starting margin. Generally, strong economic growth and regulatory reforms also played a part in reducing the risk premium in equity markets; in the decades since 1980, a combination of supply-side reforms, technological change and globalisation has also pushed up margins. The post-GFC cycle extended most of these trends.

In addition to these super bull markets, there have been two major periods of 'Fat and Flat' super cycles; these are by and large weak cycles for equities in index terms, but with wide trading ranges.

1. 1968–1982: Inflation and Low Returns

The collapse of the global exchange rate system managed by the Bretton Woods Agreement, together with the policy mix of the late 1960s, was to a considerable extent responsible for the rise in inflation through the period. Geopolitical tensions leading to two major energy shocks and their related recessions resulted in weak profit growth. Increased regulation, labour unrest and higher taxes were also important drivers. The period resulted in aggregate nominal price returns in the S&P 500 of −5%, or an annualised price decline of 0.4%. This decade or more of poor returns extended into other asset markets. Bond markets saw even lower returns than equities, and only 'real assets' (which offered some protection against inflation) had positive returns.

2. 2000–2009: Bubbles and Troubles

In many ways this was the archetypal 'Fat and Flat' cycle. Overall returns for investors were poor, but the range of outcomes was very wide. The period started with the sudden collapse of the technology bubble, which burst on the cusp of the new millennium.

The bear market in equities was deep but cyclical. The price adjustment owed more to the realignment of equity valuations than a deep or prolonged recession. As markets troughed, they were buffeted again by the 9/11 terrorist attacks and the increased risk premium that investors demanded to reflect such an uncertain geopolitical environment. Ultimately, however, economies recovered, and the legacy of low interest rates contributed to rising private sector borrowing and the housing boom in the United States. When this housing boom finally burst in 2007, the collapse sent shock waves through the financial system; these were amplified by a banking crisis, triggering another severe bear market that finally troughed in 2009.

One other point to make about super cycles in financial markets (and in economies) is that they can vary considerably across geographies as well as across time. The long period of outperformance of the US equity market, relative to others, in the decade after the GFC is a good example, and one that I discuss in Chapter 8. Another point that is often overlooked is the long

Exhibit 3.17 The Nikkei 225 was stuck in a Fat and Flat trading range: S&P 500 and Nikkei 225 price performance (in local currency)

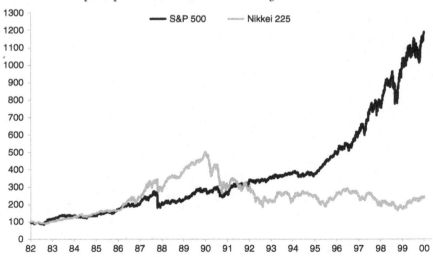

SOURCE: Goldman Sachs Global Investment Research

'Fat and Flat' cycle experienced in Japan after the collapse of its financial bubble at the end of the 1980s. While other major developed equity markets entered the 1982–2000 super cycle bull market, Japanese equities remained in a narrow trading range as they struggled as a consequence of sclerotic growth and deflationary risks. At the time of writing, notwithstanding its 20% rebound in the first half of 2023, the Japanese equity index remains roughly 20% below the level at which it peaked in 1989 (Exhibit 3.17).

Part II of this book describes each of these super cycles in turn and unpacks the conditions and drivers of equity markets.

Part II

Analysing Post-War Super Cycles

Chapter 4
1949–1968: Post-World War II Boom

A new optimism – filled with the promise of the future – prevailed.
—The Metropolitan Museum of Art

T he post-World War II (WWII) period was dominated by a powerful economic boom and is often referred to as the Golden Age of Capitalism. It was supported by the United States' initiative to aid Europe economically through the Marshall Plan (or the European Recovery Programme), which helped to boost growth and reduce unemployment. Productivity growth was strong, particularly in Europe and East Asia, and the post-WWII 'baby boom' further strengthened demand.

While the economic environment was conducive to strong returns in equity markets in this period, valuations also recovered from their post-WWII levels, aided by a secular decline in the equity risk premium as many of the risks to the global system faded.

Like most structural bull markets, this period reflected a combination of robust growth and low inflation. It also began with low valuations; as new international institutions and a rules-based global trading system emerged, the price/earnings ratio (P/E multiple) of the S&P recovered from 9× in 1949 to 22× in 1968.

Over the super cycle, S&P returns in real terms including dividends reached roughly 1,100%, or 14% at an annualised rate (Exhibit 4.1).

Exhibit 4.1   Over the super cycle, S&P returns in real terms including dividends reached roughly 1,100%, or 14% at an annualised rate

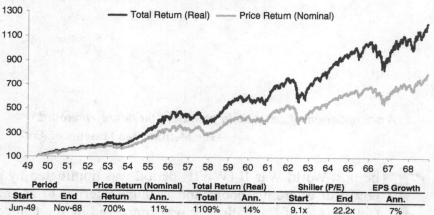

Period		Price Return (Nominal)		Total Return (Real)		Shiller (P/E)		EPS Growth
Start	End	Return	Ann.	Total	Ann.	Start	End	Ann.
Jun-49	Nov-68	700%	11%	1109%	14%	9.1x	22.2x	7%

NOTE: Shiller price/earnings (P/E) is a valuation measure. It is calculated by dividing the index price level by the average inflation-adjusted 10-year earnings per share (EPS).

SOURCE: Goldman Sachs Global Investment Research

Specifically, this boom period included:

1. International agreements and falling risk premia
2. Strong economic growth
3. Technological innovation
4. Low real interest rates
5. A boom in world trade
6. A baby boom
7. A consumer and credit boom

International Agreements and Falling Risk Premia

Following the economic devastation of the Great Depression and WWII, there was a concerted effort to build a new rules-based system of economic management and international trade. The memory of the Great Depression was a primary concern for policymakers, who were determined to avoid the failures of pre-war capitalism and prevent the expansion of communism. Initiatives were directed towards rebuilding infrastructure but also establishing an economic system that could fight recession and depression and minimise the risk of high unemployment.

In July 1944, the allied nations met at Bretton Woods, New Hampshire, to agree to a new monetary order aimed at avoiding a collapse of international trade, one of the factors that led to the Great Depression. The aim was to develop a new international system after WWII that would provide for post-war reconstruction. It reflected previous Gold Standards but took account of the problems that had led to the Great Depression and, in particular, the rigidity of the classic Gold Standard, which collapsed after World War I, resulting in competitive devaluations and restrictive trade policies. The result was an agreement to establish an International Monetary Fund and the World Bank Group, which came into existence in 1945 and would have the ability to lend reserve currency to countries with balance-of-payments deficits. The system was designed primarily by John Maynard Keynes (adviser to the British Treasury) and US Treasury Chief Economist Harry Dexter White.

Despite the successes at Bretton Woods, there were disagreements. Keynes wanted a Clearing Union that could intervene in a crisis by issuing a new international currency called the 'Bancor'. This currency would enable funds to be transferred from countries with a balance-of-payments surplus to those with a corresponding deficit, allowing them to trade without the need to deflate their own currencies if they had a deficit. The proposal put forward by White won the debate and was adopted; it focused on a Stabilisation

Fund based on a fixed pool of national currencies and gold. In the end, the White plan succeeded but it included the ability to ration the currency of a surplus nation to limit the size of imports from that country.

Twenty-nine countries initially signed the new system, which became fully functional in 1958 with the objective of maintaining their currencies fixed within a narrow 1% band against the dollar, which, in turn, was fixed to the price of gold, at $35 an ounce. The US Treasury had to adjust the supply of dollars to keep the price of gold fixed, and in this way maintain credibility in the ability to convert back into gold. The system broke down in 1971 following persistent US current account deficits that led to foreign-held dollars exceeding the stock of gold in the United States, undermining the ability to redeem dollars for gold at the fixed price. This failure was one of the factors that contributed to the volatility and economic stresses of the 1968–1982 period, which I discuss in Chapter 5.

Strong Economic Growth

In addition to the Bretton Woods initiative, growth-stimulating policies were adopted in the aftermath of WWII, improving the outlook for growth in the economy and the corporate sector. The most important of the global initiatives came from the Marshall Plan. While only in operation for 4 years from 1948, US aid – together with a similar type of aid to Japan – amounted to 40.5% of US exports in 1946–1949 and the United States spent over $13 billion on European reconstruction.

The Marshall Plan was complemented by other policies to stimulate growth in the United States and to halt the spread of Communism. The Employment Act of 1946 committed the government to 'promote maximum employment, production, and purchasing power', as well as increased coordination between monetary and fiscal policy. This Act became a key pillar in the dual mandate of the US Federal Reserve. It effectively focused on the combined economic goals of maximum employment and price stability – an ambition still articulated in policy statements in the recent past. In 2020, for example, Federal Board Chair Jerome H. Powell restated that 'In conducting monetary policy, we will remain highly focused on fostering as strong a labor market as possible for the benefit of all Americans. And we will steadfastly seek to achieve a 2 percent inflation rate over time'.[1]

As a result of these initiatives, the United States and other major economies experienced robust growth after WWII. Between 1948 and 1952, the Western European countries received significant aid to boost production and export capacity with the aim of widening the market for US products; consequently, both the United States and European countries benefited from higher growth. Supporting this, the creation of the European Payments Union kickstarted multilateral trade and boosted efficiency and resource allocation.[2]

In the United States, gross domestic product (GDP) had increased from $228 billion in 1945 to just under $1.7 trillion in 1975 (Exhibit 4.2). By 1975, the US economy represented 35% of total global industrial output and was over three times as large as that of Japan, the next-largest economy.[3] As with all the other super cycles, however, shorter-term cycles occurred during the secular upswing. The United States, for example, experienced five recessions between 1945 and 1970 (1948–49, 1953–54, 1957–58, 1960–61 and 1969–70).

---

[1] Powell, J. H. (2020). New economic challenges and the Fed's monetary policy review. Speech (via webcast) at Navigating the Decade Ahead: Implications for Monetary Policy, an economic policy symposium sponsored by the Federal Reserve Bank of Kansas City, Jackson Hole, WY, 27th August.
[2] United Nations (2017). Post-war reconstruction and development in the Golden Age of Capitalism. *World Economic and Social Survey 2017*, pp. 23–48.
[3] countryeconomy.com. Gross Domestic Product.

Exhibit 4.2   In the United States, GDP per capita surged after WWII: GDP per capita (1920 to 1976), adjusted for inflation and for differences in the cost of living between countries

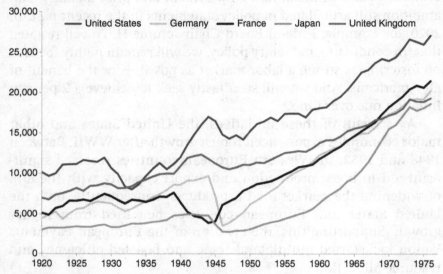

SOURCE: Our World in Data

Europe benefited as well, and enjoyed the fastest growth as a region in the world between 1950 and 1969, although Japan experienced the strongest growth as a single country.[4] In Europe, the European Coal and Steel Community was set up in 1951 (including France, Western Germany, Italy and Benelux), and in 1957 the Treaty of Rome established the European Economic Community (EEC) as a driver for closer cooperation. Both provided a further boost to regional growth. The Federal Republic of Germany saw economic growth of over 6% per year over this period.

The period from 1949 to 1968 also saw a much more stable economic environment (Exhibit 4.3), as unemployment rates fell by about one-third compared with the period from 1870 to 1913.[5]

---

[4] Statista (2023). Average annual growth in the economic output of Western European countries during the Golden Age from 1950 to 1970. Available at https://www.statista.com/statistics/730758/western-europe-economic-manufacturing-output-growth-golden-age/.

[5] Glyn, A., Hughes, A., Lipietz, A. and Singh, A. (1988). The rise and fall of the golden age. United Nations University WIDER Working Paper 43/1988.

Exhibit 4.3   The post-war decade saw a much more stable economic environment as unemployment rates fell: civilian unemployment rate for 16 years+

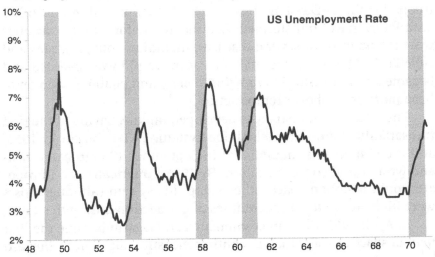

NOTE: Shading represents NBER recessions.
SOURCE: Goldman Sachs Global Investment Research

Technological Innovation

The post-WWII period was an era of profound change on both the technological and social fronts, and many innovations contributed to changing lifestyles and economic growth. Television became increasingly popular and, by 1953, colour television had emerged in the United States. The growth of the television industry revolutionised society by providing a new source of social influence and advertising, as well as an ability to watch events unfold in real time. Optical fibre and video recorders were developed, as well as transistors, which led to the miniaturisation of computers, while the introduction of magnetic-core memory increased the storage capacity of computers about eightfold. Battery-operated telephones emerged (the precursor to the mobile phone), and word processors.

Significant medical advances were made. Penicillin was first invented by Scottish scientist Alexander Fleming in 1928, but it was not mass produced until WWII. It was considered so important in the war that the United States prepared 2.3 million doses for allied troops for the D-Day landings.[6] Since WWII, penicillin and other antibiotics have transformed healthcare. Before long, vaccines were introduced for several diseases, including polio, measles and rubella. In May 1950, the oral contraceptive pill was invented and became a major factor in changing society and enabling women to have more control over reproduction.

The telecoms industry also developed rapidly. Laying of the first transatlantic submarine telephone system, TAT-1, began in 1955, and the system was inaugurated in September 1956 to carry east- and west-bound communication. By 1956, Americans and Europeans could telephone each other using this system (although costs were high, at $12 for three minutes of connection during the day).

In April 1961, Russian cosmonaut Yuri Gagarin became the first man in space and less than a month later, astronaut Alan B. Shepard became the first American in space. In July 1969 the Apollo 11 mission resulted in the first moon landing, triggering a new set of technological innovations, including memory foam, cordless vacuum cleaners and freeze-dried food, among other nutritional technologies.

Another innovation, perhaps less transformative economically, but significant from a social perspective, came in the recorded music industry. Until 1948 music was recorded on discs that measured 10 or 12 inches in diameter (also known as '78s' as they were played at 78 revolutions per minute); these discs were very brittle. Columbia Records introduced vinyl records that were less delicate and were played at 33⅓ revolutions; the upshot was a significant increase in storage. While the older 78s could accommodate around four minutes of recording time per side, the new 33s could hold 25 minutes per side. In 1949 the new format 45 REM records were released by RCA Victor. The first record pressed in this format was *Pee-Wee the Piccolo*, a children's story. But the new format soon became a major catalyst for pop music. Elvis Presley's first record, *That's all right,*

---

[6] The National WWII Museum (2013). *Thanks to Penicillin . . . He Will Come Home! The Challenge of Mass Production* [Lesson Plan from the Education Department].

was released in 1954 and in 1955 he was signed to RCA records. He had his first global hit that year with *Heartbreak Hotel*, which went to number 1 in the hit parade in four countries and reached the top ten in many others. In the same year, Bill Haley and the Comets released *Rock Around the Clock* and sold three million records. The new format of music consumption became central to the social development of the new 'teenage' cultural revolution that dramatically changed society over the following decades.

Low and Stable Real Interest Rates

Post-WWII reconstruction provided a critical spur to economic growth, but labour participation was another important contributor. Low and stable interest rates for an extended period also helped.[7]

Even though inflation and interest rates did rise over the period overall, there was a degree of financial repression. The United States accumulated huge debts in the build-up to WWII and, as a result, the Federal Reserve supported the Treasury by adopting a form of yield curve control that capped interest rates along the yield curve.[8] The caps were from 3.8% on Treasury bills and 2.5% on longer-term bonds. By 1947, US inflation was rising quickly and had surpassed 17% (CPI index), and by 1951 it had increased to above 20%. Consequently, the peg on short-term interest rates was lifted to prevent inflationary pressures from rising further, with the Federal Reserve Accord of 1951. Although yield curve control had ended by the early 1950s, a form of financial repression continued.[9] Inflation increased but nominal interest rates were low and real interest rates (nominal rates minus inflation) were lower still, or even negative, and remained low for over three decades after WWII (Exhibit 4.4). The United States managed to keep real interest rates for long-term debt below 1%.

---

[7] Rose, J. (2021). Yield curve control in the United States, 1942 to 1951. Available at https://www.chicagofed.org/publications/economic-perspectives/2021/2.

[8] Miller, A., Berlo, J. C., Wolf, B. J. and Roberts, J. L. (2018). *American Encounters: Art, History, and Cultural Identity*. Washington, D.C.: Washington University Libraries.

[9] Reinhart, C. M., Kirkegaard, J. F. and Sbrancia, M. B. (2011). Financial repression redux. Available at https://www.imf.org/external/pubs/ft/fandd/2011/06/pdf/reinhart.pdf.

Exhibit 4.4   Real interest rates were markedly negative on Treasury bills and 10-year bonds: nominal 10-year interest rate minus 10-year average inflation

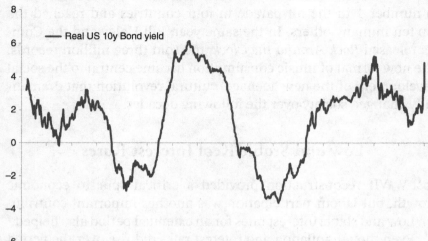

SOURCE: Goldman Sachs Global Investment Research

According to Carmen Reinhart, the use of interest rate ceilings on deposits, which resulted in even lower real rates on deposit savings than on Treasury yields, incentivised savers to hold government bonds. At the time, this was occurring in many advanced economies, aided by capital controls, and it helped delay the emergence of leakages from investors seeking higher yields.

Exceptionally low real interest rates also helped governments to pay down the significant debt they had built up through WWII. For example, in the United Kingdom, government debt fell from 216% of GDP in 1945 to 138% in 1955.

Other policy initiatives were directed at boosting growth. Tax reforms formed part of this. In the 1950s, for example, personal top-rate tax rates in the United States were over 90% and the top rate of corporate tax was more than 50%. In the 1960s, the administration of President John F. Kennedy cut rates dramatically, contributing to the consumer boom and sharp rises in equity prices.

A Boom in World Trade

The major industrial countries experienced exceptionally low levels of manufacturing exports at the start of WWII but ended the war with a period of significant trade growth.

The existence of the International Monetary Fund (IMF), the World Bank and the Bretton Woods monetary system helped to reduce uncertainty and volatility in global economies. These were complemented by new organisations aimed at boosting global trade: the General Agreement on Tariffs and Trade (GATT), created in 1948, and the United Nations Conference on Trade and Development (UNCTAD), founded in 1964. In that same year, the sixth round of GATT negotiations started, commonly called the Kennedy Round of multilateral trade negotiations. By 1967, these negotiations had resulted in cuts to trade tariffs by an average of 35–40% on many items, and they were widely described at the time as the most important trade and tariff negotiations ever held.

Trade increased across the Atlantic, but also with Asia. Trade from Japan to the United States, for example, increased at an annual rate of close to 20% through the 1950s and 1960s, and the volume of trade was eight times higher between 1950 and 1975 than during the period from 1913 to 1950.[10]

A Baby Boom

The post-WWII period resulted in a significant rise in the population of most developed economies (Exhibit 4.5). This 'baby boom' provided a major boost to demand.[11] Marriage and fertility rates rose, and the number of births increased significantly.

---

[10] Glyn, A., Hughes, A., Lipietz, A. and Singh, A. (1988). The rise and fall of the golden age. United Nations University WIDER Working Paper 43/1988.

[11] Anstey, V. (1943). *World Economic Survey, 1941–42* [Book Review]. *Economica*, **10**(38), pp. 212–214.

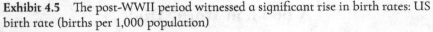

Exhibit 4.5 The post-WWII period witnessed a significant rise in birth rates: US birth rate (births per 1,000 population)

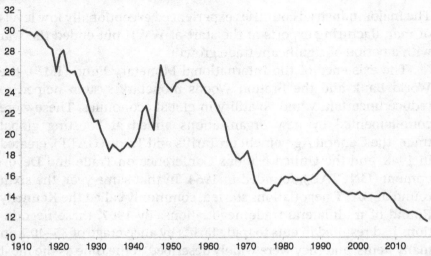

SOURCE: U.S. Department of Health & Human Services

Diane J. Macunovich described the boom, which occurred simultaneously across the Western World, as a 'birth quake'. In many cases, the number of babies born annually doubled within a few years. This was largely unexpected, as neither demographers nor social scientists had predicted the boom. Long-term population projections carried out in Europe in 1944 assumed that the lifestyle aspirations of the urban populations of Europe would spread to the poorer areas, resulting in downward pressure on fertility.[12]

The baby boom also brought about huge social change. There was a creative explosion in everything from film, painting, music and clothing to furniture design. An acceleration in house building led to a boom in more modern and cheaper furniture. New materials facilitated a fresh approach across the creative industries.

---

[12] Notestein, F. W. (1983). Frank Notestein on population growth and economic development. *Population and Development Review*, 9(2), pp. 345–360.

As the New York Metropolitan Museum of Modern Art put it, 'a new optimism – filled with the promise of the future – prevailed'. This optimism spilled over into consumer demand and equity returns.[13]

The Consumer and Credit Boom

Unemployment fell dramatically in the post-WWII years, increasing consumer confidence. The creation of the Welfare State in the United Kingdom and other social safety nets boosted optimism and encouraged consumers to borrow.[14] In the United Kingdom, for example, the post-WWII years saw the roll-out of the Beveridge Report on social security and the National Health Service (NHS) was established in 1948. Government spending on social security rose from 4.9% of GDP in 1939 to 8.3% in 1974. Taxes as a share of GDP increased from 21.6% in 1937 to 33.5% in 1951 and, by the late 1940s, a high-earning household would have a total tax burden of around 80%.[15] Set against this, however, was the growing ability of consumers to take on debt.

The consequence of this boom was a rise in consumer debt. US household debt rose from less than 40% of household income at the beginning of the 1950s to almost 140% of household income by the 2000s.

The shift towards higher household debt was boosted by innovations in credit markets. The idea of consumer credit was not new. Evidence on clay inscriptions shows that credit was used more than 5,000 years ago in ancient Mesopotamia, in transactions between merchants from Mesopotamia and Harappa, a neighbouring region.[16]

---

[13] Goss, J. (2022). *Design, 1950–75*. Essay – The Metropolitan Museum of Art.

[14] Vonyó, T. (2008). Post-war reconstruction and the Golden Age of economic growth. *European Review of Economic History*, **12**(2), pp. 221–241.

[15] Crafts, N. (2020). Rebuilding after the Second World War: What lessons for today? Warwick Economics Department, CAGE Research Centre.

[16] Frankel, R. S. (2021). When were credit cards invented: The history of credit cards. Available at https://www.forbes.com/advisor/credit-cards/history-of-credit-cards/.

Innovations in credit markets emerged rapidly in the 1950s, and a new range of unsecured instalment and revolving loans, as well as student loans, became more popular in the United States after WWII. These consumer loans were provided by the government (with student loans and government-sponsored mortgages), private companies including retailers, banks and credit card companies, as well as non-profit credit unions.

Perhaps the critical innovation, however, came with the introduction of credit cards. Department charge cards grew in popularity around this time, and in 1950 the Diners Club card became the first to gain widespread use as a general charge card. It was developed by Frank McNamara and Ralph Schneider after McNamara found that he had left his wallet at home when he came to pay for a bill at a restaurant.

American Express developed its first credit card in 1958, which allowed consumers to pay their bills monthly for an annual fee. The growth in credit, alongside other changes in society, generated a virtuous cycle of growth and optimism. In the United States in particular, the growth of suburbs meant that people became ever more reliant on cars to travel to their place of work, and demand for cars ballooned. By 1955 General Motors had become the first US corporation to earn more than $1 billion in revenue in a year, and it outsold the combined production of its main competitors. It was the largest company by revenue (in 2008, the stock had fallen in value back to its 1954 value).[17]

As car sales increased, so did demand for roads. In 1956 the US Congress authorised the construction of the interstate highway system. By 1960, about 10,000 miles of interstate highway had been built, which, in turn, opened up new opportunities for services along the highways (including restaurants, motels, gas stations and movie theatres; Exhibit 4.6). In the United States, out-of-town shopping centres started to emerge, and by 1964 there were more than 7,600 shopping centres across the country, many of them close to the fast-growing suburbs.

---

[17] *The Economic Times* (2008, July 1). General Motors's stock skids to 1950s level.

Exhibit 4.6   At the drive-in: vehicles fill a drive-in theatre while people on the screen stand near a new car, 1950s

SOURCE: Photo by New York Times Co./Hulton Archive/Getty Images. https://www.gettyimages
.com/detail/news-photo/vehicles-fill-a-drive-in-theater-while-people-on-the-screen-news-photo/
3076062

All-Consuming Consumerism

Consumerism became a lifestyle. Companies encouraged the use of 'planned obsolescence' – changing styles of clothes, and even cars, on an annual basis to make consumers want to buy more.[18] This trend was to have dramatic environmental consequences that only became a focus in later decades. These products were marketed as objects that would make people's lives easier, but the drive towards higher sales and profits was ever present. When asked about his views on good product design and aesthetics, a famous industrial designer quipped 'the most beautiful curve is a rising sales curve', encapsulating the allure of consumerism for companies.[19]

---

[18] Whiteley, N. (1987). Toward a throw-away culture. Consumerism, 'style obsolescence' and cultural theory in the 1950s and 1960s. *Oxford Art Journal*, **10**(2), pp. 3–27.
[19] Raymond Loewy Quotes – The Official Licensing Website of Raymond Loewy.

Low unemployment encouraged consumers to borrow to fund their growing aspirations.

Lifestyle advertising was stimulated further by the growth of television in the 1950s, providing advertisers with the opportunity to reach a much wider audience. The introduction of mass commercial television had a positive impact on retail sales. Related to this, Woojin Kim of the University of California, Berkeley, argues that the growth of sitcoms in the United States promoted the ideals of suburbia and the consumer lifestyle.[20]

The 1950s and 1960s witnessed a dramatic increase in consumer culture and advertising imagery. Andy Warhol's iconic artwork *Coca-Cola* references this step change in popular culture.[21]

The boom in consumption, most prominent in the United States, began to be reflected in most developed industrialised economies. In 1957, Harold Macmillan (the UK's Conservative Prime Minister between 1957 and 1963) made a speech to a group at Bedford Town football ground in which he said, 'Let us be frank about it: most of our people have never had it so good. Go around the country – go to the industrial towns, go to the farms – and you will see a state of prosperity such as we have never had in my lifetime, not indeed ever in the history of this country'.

Innovations in how consumers shopped created a sense of modernism and excitement, providing further ballast to the rise in the consumer culture. A popular innovation in the United States came with the invention of Tupperware. The emergence of Tupperware parties helped fuel the post-WWII appetite for consumer goods. The company's strategy was to discover what consumer goods the party host wanted to own and then calculate how many parties they would need to hold to make enough to acquire the desired products. The company reinforced the consumer's appetite for purchases

---

[20] Kim, W. (2022). Television and American consumerism. *Journal of Public Economics*, **208**, art. 104609.
[21] Whiteley, N. (1987). Toward a throw-away culture. Consumerism, 'style obsolescence' and cultural theory in the 1950s and 1960s. *Oxford Art Journal*, **10**(2), pp. 3–27.

with various promotions and prizes as a reward for high sales, for example kitchen appliances. This trend of outsourcing sales or work to the consumer helped to boost revenues and profit margins for consumer companies. In the United Kingdom, an important innovation in the retail sector that helped to boost company profits was the evolution of self-service shops, which allowed shoppers to select the products they wanted and take them to a cash till to pay. The system had started during the war due to the shortage of retail staff. In 1947, there were only ten self-service shops in Britain, but this had grown to 12,000 by 1962 and 24,000 by 1967. By 1952, half of Tesco's stores were self-service.[22]

This optimism about future growth and consumer brands spilled over into the equity market. Throughout the 1960s, the emergence of fast-growing global companies spurred confidence in the stock market, and in the so-called 'Nifty Fifty' stocks in the United States in particular. The idea behind investing in these stocks was that you need never worry about valuation because these companies either had strong earnings growth or high expectations of strong growth in the future, and many also had strong brands.

The boom in US consumer spending, and in public spending, had negative consequences for global imbalances. As the 1960s progressed, the US dollar, which was fixed in value against gold under the Bretton Woods system of fixed exchange rates, became overvalued.[23] A significant increase in public spending in the United States, with President Lyndon Johnson's Great Society programmes and increased military spending to fund the Vietnam War, put further stress on the system. The Gold Standard had come under significant pressure by the late 1960s and was finally dissolved by President Richard Nixon in 1971, when he announced a 'temporary' suspension of the dollar's convertibility into gold.[24] The 'Nifty Fifty'

---

[22] Eduqas (2018). *Austerity, Affluence and Discontent: Britain, 1951–1979* [GCSE History Resource].
[23] Federal Reserve Bank of Boston (1984). *The International Monetary System: Forty Years After Bretton Woods*. Boston, MA: Federal Reserve Bank of Boston.
[24] International Monetary Fund (2020). The end of the Bretton Woods System (1972–81). Available at https://www.imf.org/external/about/histend.htm.

stock bubble burst. With higher interest charges and unemployment, the high levels of consumer debt turned the virtuous cycle into a vicious one.

In most equity markets, prices had already reached a plateau around 1966 after an astonishing rise over the previous 15 years especially.[25,26] The bear market that followed was structural in nature and the US market declined in real terms by 75% between 1966 and 1982, triggered by sharply rising inflation and interest rates. This is the structural cycle that I discuss in the next chapter.

[25] Crafts, N. F. R. (1995). The golden age of economic growth in Western Europe, 1950–1973. *The Economic History Review*, 48(3), pp. 429–447.
[26] United Nations (2017). Post-war reconstruction and development in the Golden Age of Capitalism. *World Economic and Social Survey 2017*, pp. 23–48.

Chapter 5
1968–1982: Inflation and Low Returns

At some point this dam is going to break and the psychology is going to change.

—Paul Volcker

The period from the early 1970s through to the early 1980s was one of the worst decades in history for investors (Exhibit 5.1). The surge in inflation and interest rates, together with two deep recessions and otherwise sclerotic growth, weighed on both equity and fixed-income markets in an environment of what became known as stagflation. The combination drove a long-lasting 'Fat and Flat' environment of high volatility and low returns for over a decade. The key drivers were a combination of:

- High interest rates with low growth
- Social unrest and strikes
- Collapsing trade, increased protectionism and regulation
- High government debt and lower corporate profit margins

Exhibit 5.1   The period from the early 1970s through to the early 1980s was one of the worst decades in history for investors

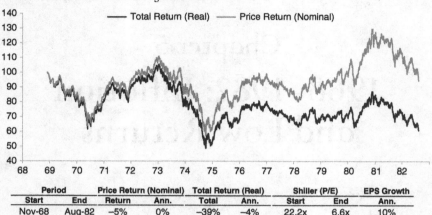

Period		Price Return (Nominal)		Total Return (Real)		Shiller (P/E)		EPS Growth
Start	End	Return	Ann.	Total	Ann.	Start	End	Ann.
Nov-68	Aug-82	–5%	0%	–39%	–4%	22.2x	6.6x	10%

NOTE: Shiller price/earnings (P/E) is a valuation measure. It is calculated by dividing the index price level by the average inflation-adjusted 10-year earnings per share (EPS).

SOURCE: Goldman Sachs Global Investment Research

After an astonishing rise over the previous 15 years, most major equity markets had reached a plateau in 1966, while in the United States the market peaked in 1968. The bear market that followed was structural in nature: the US market declined by 5% in price terms over the period and annualised no price rises in real terms between 1968 and 1982, as a consequence of sharply rising inflation and interest rates. But, as in the case of the bear markets of the 1930s and 1940s, the whole super cycle comprised at least two bear markets rolled into one.

A Lost Decade for Investors

The 1970s was a period of high volatility for investors but lower aggregate returns. In this way, it can be described as a secular 'Fat and Flat' cycle. In nominal terms, equity indices did make progress, but because inflation was so high, the aggregate returns in real terms (adjusting for inflation) were much lower. As Exhibit 5.1

shows, dividends became an important source of returns for investors in equity markets as they kept pace with inflation, providing some protection for investors against higher prices.

The combination of high inflation and high interest rates forced economies into deep recessions, resulting in a squeeze in net wealth in the household sector, together with lower profit margins in the corporate sector.

The Bubble Before the Bust

Despite the peak of most equity markets in the late 1960s, a narrow group of large companies, referred to as the 'Nifty Fifty', outperformed strongly from the late 1960s to the early 1970s. Many of these companies enjoyed remarkably high returns on capital (unlike during the technology bubble of the late 1990s, when the market was dominated by new companies with low returns on capital) and benefited from a belief that these returns could be maintained into the long-term future. For that reason, they were often referred to as 'one-decision' stocks. Investors commonly were happy to buy and hold them irrespective of the price. There was a popular shift away from 'Value' investing towards 'Growth' investing.

While no official index existed for these large-cap and multi-national companies, they prospered in an environment of growing global growth and low interest rates. They did, however, become expensive. By 1972, when the S&P 500 had a P/E of 18×, the average across the Nifty Fifty was over twice this level. Polaroid traded at a P/E of over 90×, and Walt Disney and McDonald's at over 80× forward expected earnings. Despite these lofty valuations, Professor Jeremy Siegel argued that most of these stocks did grow into their valuations and achieved strong returns.[1]

A similar narrative later drove the focus on the 'New Economy' of the late 1990s and again after the Global Financial Crisis (GFC).

---

[1] Siegel, J. J. (2014). *Stocks for the Long Run: The Definitive Guide to Financial Market Returns & Long-Term Investment Strategies.* New York: McGraw-Hill Education.

In these periods, as in the 1960s, Value (or 'Old Economy') stocks became unloved.

The speed of the decline in the valuation of financial assets as they buckled under the pressure of higher interest rates was dramatic. The maximum drawdown, or fall in value, of a typical balanced portfolio made up of 60% equities and 40% bonds was the sharpest in the post-World War II (WWII) period (Exhibit 5.2), apart from that experienced during the GFC of 2008/09 (see Chapter 7 for details).

The erosion of wealth was significant (Exhibit 5.3). In the United States, household net worth fell 25% as a proportion of gross domestic product (GDP) as inflation eroded the real value of many financial assets and equity values fell, whereas real assets and real estate rose in value.

Exhibit 5.2   Balanced portfolios have historically experienced large drawdowns: 1-year drawdowns for a 60/40 portfolio (equity/bonds). Daily returns with monthly rebalancing

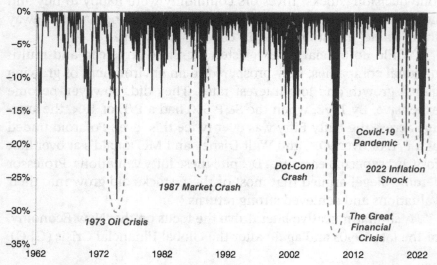

SOURCE: Goldman Sachs Global Investment Research

Exhibit 5.3 The erosion of household net worth was significant during the 1970s: household real estate, corporate equity and net worth as a percentage of GDP

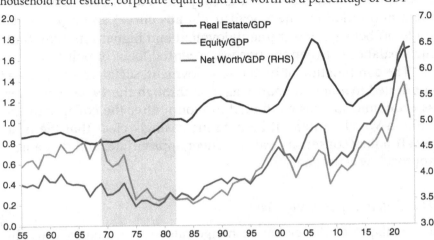

SOURCE: Federal Reserve, Financial Accounts of the United States

High Interest Rates and Low Growth

The drivers of the 'Fat and Flat' secular trend of the 1970s were macro, micro and geopolitical. On the macro side, surging inflation and interest rates triggered the two recessions and, between them, prolonged periods of weak growth. On the micro front, tougher regulation, labour market instability and lower profit margins were key factors. On the political dimension, Cold War tensions, the war in the Middle East and the resulting oil shocks were instrumental in weakening investor returns.

Economic policy also played a role. The post-WWII policy consensus was greatly influenced by the experience of the devastation wrought by the Great Depression and by Keynes's policies of stabilisation. In general, this resulted in the complementary management of demand through fiscal policy (the setting of government spending and taxation) and monetary policy (the setting of interest rates) in the pursuit of stable growth and full employment.

Throughout the 1950s and 1960s there was a widely accepted assumption that a stable relationship existed between unemployment and inflation (the so-called Phillips curve) and a presumed trade-off between lower unemployment and higher inflation; finding a balance between the two was a central focus of policy.

The combination of high unemployment, social unrest and war continued to guide the policy agenda through the 1970s. However, as economic stresses continued to mount after the collapse of the Bretton Woods system, it became increasingly clear that the post-WWII policy consensus was no longer appropriate, and that a new approach was needed.

The Collapse of Bretton Woods

The collapse of the global exchange rate system managed by the Bretton Woods Agreement and the policy mix of the 1960s contributed to the rise in inflation over this period. In the early 1960s, US President John F. Kennedy's campaign promised to 'get the economy moving again'. When elected, his administration boosted fiscal policy and introduced a series of tax cuts, tax credits for investment and faster capital depreciation.

As the 1960s progressed, the US dollar – which was fixed in value against gold under the Bretton Woods system of fixed exchange rates – became overvalued. The United States was running an increasing trade deficit with both Japan and Germany. Many US multinational companies invested in factories in Europe, given their higher productivity relative to the United States, where factories were older and where it was therefore harder to integrate innovative technologies. The emergence of the Eurodollar market provided a new source of cheap financing for these investments. The trade imbalance, together with large fiscal deficits incurred to help fund the US war in Vietnam, increased international liabilities against insufficient gold reserves.[2]

---

[2] Meltzer, A. H. (1991). US policy in the Bretton Woods era. *Federal Reserve Bank of St. Louis Review*, **73**(3), pp. 54–83.

In 1966, the Federal Reserve raised policy rates rapidly, from 1.5% at the start of the year to over 6% by September. However, in 1968 President Lyndon Johnson's plans to increase US forces in Vietnam put further pressure on the economy and on the Bretton Woods system. The United States was forced to sell 100 tons of gold on a single day in March of that year to maintain dollar to gold convertibility.[3]

To stem the tide of capital outflows, the Treasury worked with the Federal Reserve in a complementary policy approach. It focused on increasing short-term Treasury bills to attract capital, while at the same time buying long-term US government debt to hold down long-term interest rates in a policy of 'yield curve control'. The US government increased borrowing to fund tax cuts and the increased costs related to the Vietnam War. The policy of 'accommodating' the increase in government spending by keeping interest rates low boosted money supply, which contributed to rising prices (inflation), but unemployment remained high.

The Arab–Israeli War of the 1970s, together with an Organization of Petroleum Exporting Countries (OPEC) oil embargo, contributed further to rising inflation. Economists began to differentiate between 'demand-pull' inflation and 'supply-push' inflation and policymakers now faced dilemmas. Central banks could slow excess demand by raising interest rates, but this would not help to ease the supply-side problems in the oil market that were contributing to rising oil prices and higher inflation.

Prominent monetarist economists (Edmund Phelps in 1967 and Milton Friedman in 1968) pointed out that the Phillips curve relationships upon which the post-WWII economic consensus was based were no longer relevant and no longer stable. They argued that, as inflation increased, workers adjusted their demands to expect higher inflation, and the curve would shift upwards. In other words, inflation would continue to rise for any given level

---

[3] Bryan, M. (2013). The Great Inflation. Available at https://www.federalreservehistory.org/essays/great-inflation.

of employment, requiring ever higher inflation to maintain low unemployment.

Stresses in the international markets continued to grow. The United States had lower levels of interest rates relative to countries such as the United Kingdom and France, and, combined with surging gold prices, this led to widespread speculation and capital movements out of the United States. By the middle of 1971, the price of gold had increased to over $40 an ounce, and many countries around the world started to sell their dollar holdings to buy gold. The system collapsed in August 1971 when the United States suspended the convertibility of the dollar into gold and imposed a 10% temporary surcharge on dutiable imports. The Smithsonian Agreement in December 1971 attempted to resurrect the system, but it was ultimately ineffective. After the collapse of Bretton Woods, various approaches to managing currencies were tried but most currencies ended up freely floating, resulting in elevated levels of market volatility.

Economic problems, and financial market stress, were further compounded in late 1973 as tensions emerged during the Arab–Israeli War. Arab countries that were members of OPEC imposed an oil embargo against the United States following its decision to provide military supplies to Israel. The result was a surge in oil prices that had doubled the price of fuel by early 1974.

Rising oil prices inevitably increased costs of production and triggered major supply problems and, in turn, sharp rises in food prices, just as we have seen more recently in the aftermath of the Covid-19 pandemic. Global inflation rose from an average of just over 5% in 1971 to more than 10% in 1975. Some countries saw even higher price rises: US inflation went from 3.3% in 1971 to 12.3% in 1975, while Japan's inflation surged from 4.5% to over 24% over the same period.

Prior to the oil shock of 1973, annual global GDP had been growing at 5.3%, but over the rest of the decade it virtually halved to just 2.8%, and by the early 1980s it had slowed further to 1.4%.[4]

---

[4] United Nations Department of Economic and Social Affairs (2017). World Economic and Social Survey 2017: Reflecting on Seventy Years of Development Policy Analysis. New York: United Nations.

Economic difficulties in developed economies were amplified in many developing countries, which saw an even greater rise in debt levels as they increased government borrowing. This was financed, in part, by the recycling of huge volumes of petrodollars.

The deepening economic crisis of high unemployment and inflation pressures triggered a sharp reversal in the policy consensus. In October 1979, the Chair of the Federal Reserve, Paul Volker, embarked on a dramatic tightening of monetary policy to control inflation once and for all. Central banks around the world were forced to raise interest rates aggressively, and the impact was dramatic. Real interest rates surged (Exhibit 5.4) – reversing the trend that had been established in the secular bull market of 1950–1973.

The United States and many other major economies plunged into recession for a second time in a decade. For emerging economies, the burden of exploding interest costs on their debt became increasingly difficult to fund. When large international banks decided in 1981/82 that some developing countries might not be

Exhibit 5.4   Real interest rates surged in the 1970s: US 10-year real interest rate. Shaded areas show US recession (National Bureau of Economic Research)

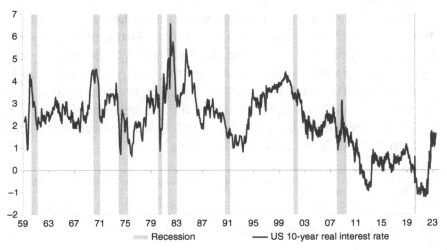

SOURCE: Goldman Sachs Global Investment Research

able to continue to service their external debts, they suddenly stopped rolling over short-term credits and forced a debt crisis globally. Starting with the Mexican debt default of August 1982, the crisis quickly spread, and a series of debt defaults occurred across the emerging economies of the world. The growth rate of international bank lending declined sharply. Within a few years, nearly 20 countries in Europe, Africa and Latin America had experienced one or more debt crises, requiring intervention by the International Monetary Fund (IMF) and other multilateral agencies.[5]

Social Unrest and Strikes

As economic stress deepened throughout the decade, companies responded by laying off workers. Unemployment surged and demand weakened further. Labour strikes had already become widespread early in the decade as unemployment increased. For example, in 1970, almost 210,000 US postal employees went on strike. The government deemed the strike illegal, so it became the largest 'wildcat' strike in US history. President Richard Nixon called out the Army and National Guard to break the strike. The number of workers involved in disputes in 1970 alone rose to the highest level since 1952; 33% higher than in 1969.[6]

Four US railroad unions also went on strike in 1970, and in 1971 two longshore strikes resulted in the closure of major ports on the East and West coasts and the Gulf. In 1975, 80,000 employees in Pennsylvania conducted the first legal strike by state workers; between 1977 and 1978 strikes spread to the coal industry. As the cost of living continued to rise, so did the number of strikes. In 1979, there was a 10-day strike by over 200,000 workers in the road and truckers' unions in the United States.[7]

---

[5] Boughton, J. M. (2002). Globalization and the silent revolution of the 1980s. *Finance & Development*, **39**(1), pp. 40–43.

[6] Hodgson, J. D. and Moore, G. H. (1972). *Analysis of Work Stoppages, 1970*. U.S. Department of Labor, Bulletin 1727.

[7] Schwenk, A. E. (2003). Compensation in the 1970s. *Compensation and Working Conditions*, **6**(3), pp. 29–32.

On the other side of the Atlantic, strikes and social unrest became widespread. In France, the May 1968 student demonstrations became a major focus of protest (Exhibit 5.5); they lasted seven weeks and 11 million people participated.

In the United Kingdom, a similar trend emerged. Over 10 million working days were lost through strike action in 1970, including those of nurses and electricity workers. A number of these strikes were unofficial and not supported by unions. By the end of the decade, the UK economy was crippled by a series of strikes (see Exhibit 5.6) that became known as the 1978–1979 'Winter of Discontent' (the

Exhibit 5.5 A student hurling rocks at the police in Paris during the May 1968 student uprising

SOURCE: Gamma-Keystone. https://www.gettyimages.co.uk/detail/news-photo/un-%C3%A9tudiant-lance-des-pav%C3%A9s-sur-le-service-dordre-au-news-photo/1264479225

Exhibit 5.6 Public sector workers' rally: public sector workers at a rally in Hyde Park during a 24-hour strike to protest against the government's 5% limit on pay rises, London, 22 January 1979. The rally was followed by a march to the House of Commons. About 1.5 million public service employees took part in the strike, including hospital and ambulance staff.

SOURCE: Photo by Steve Burton/Keystone/Hulton Archive/Getty Images. https://www.gettyimages
.com/detail/news-photo/public-sector-workers-at-a-rally-in-hyde-park-during-a-24-news-photo/
1477508105

term was taken from the opening line of William Shakespeare's *Richard III*), which led to a no-confidence vote in Prime Minister James Callaghan and an election that brought in Margaret Thatcher to lead the government 4 months later.

Political uncertainty was also running high. The Watergate scandal in the United States in 1973 and the growing geopolitical tensions around the Middle East contributed to heightening market worries. Investors' returns collapsed, pushing down equity valuations relative to risk-free government bonds and pushing up equity risk premia (the required future return in risky equities relative to safe bonds). The mood of gloom and despondency became pervasive. The collapse of businesses, particularly in the energy-intensive manufacturing industries, spilled over into social unrest.

The cultural manifestation of this in the emergence of the Punk scene in the late 1970s reflected the disillusionment of a generation of young people unable to find work and with few prospects of doing so.[8] As The Clash said in an interview with *The Times* in 1976, 'if there were jobs, we would be singing about love and kisses'.[9] The lyrics of the era reflected a sense of loss and abandonment rather than the hope and idealism of much of the music of the early 1970s. The Sex Pistols' *No Future (God Save the Queen)* and *There is No Future/In England's Dreaming* reflected the sense of anger and abandonment at that time.[10] Popular band UB40 took its name from the government's unemployment benefit form, which was also replicated on the cover of their 1980 debut album *Signing Off*. In France, too, a wave of popular songs was inspired by events, including songwriter Léo Ferré's *L'Été 68*. The images of rioting and unrest had a widespread and lasting impact. The Rolling Stones' song *Street Fighting Man* was a reference to the French riots. More recently, a Stone Roses album included a track called *Bye Bye Badman* about the events. In the world of cinema, the period also had a significant influence, and the events were depicted in many films, such as François Truffaut's *Baisers volés* (1968), set during the time of the riots. Of course, it is important not to overstate that these waves dominated the arts scene. Other mainstream music was also popular at the time, but it attracted less controversy. The fact that the Sex Pistols' *God Save the Queen* was released to coincide with the Queen's Silver Jubilee and was banned from the BBC, for example, added to its cultural significance.[11]

---

[8] Fletcher, N. (2018). "If only I could get a job somewhere": The emergence of British punk. Young Historians Conference, 19. Available at https://pdxscholar.library.pdx.edu/younghistorians/2018/oralpres/19.

[9] Church, M. (1976, November 29). Catching up with punk. *The Times*.

[10] Lydon, J., Matlock, G., Cook, P. T. and Jones, S. P. (1976). *No Future (God Save the Queen)*.

[11] 45 years after its release, on 4 June 2022, coinciding with the weekend of the Queen's Platinum Jubilee, a reissue of the song reached number 1 in the UK charts for the first time.

Collapsing Trade, Increased Protectionism and Regulation

The cocktail of high inflation and unemployment, together with low growth, led to a series of record trade imbalances in several countries, including the United States and the United Kingdom; others, such as Japan (Exhibit 5.7) and several European countries, enjoyed record surpluses. Policymakers focused on ways to reduce imports or boost major capital flows in deficit countries. The latter was difficult to achieve because of widespread capital controls.

The result was an increase in protectionism. While there were ongoing discussions about tariff reductions within the Tokyo round of General Agreement on Tariffs and Trade (GATT) trade negotiations, increased tensions flared up between the United States and Europe on one side and Japan on the other, given Japan's mounting trade surplus. In a way, these concerns

Exhibit 5.7 Japan's trade surplus surged: Japanese exports, imports and trade surplus (1960–1990)

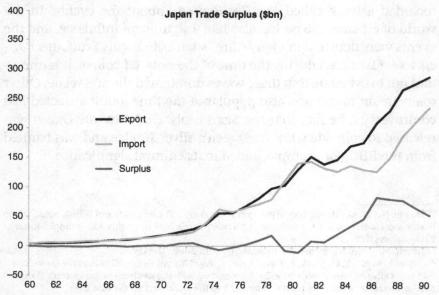

SOURCE: Ministry of Finance Japan

were not dissimilar to the fears of growing Chinese surpluses in the 2000s.

The approach used was to circumvent the GATT deal by evoking so-called 'voluntary' trade restrictions in areas not explicitly covered by GATT.[12]

The United States and Europe put pressure on Japan to restrict exports voluntarily, particularly in auto and steel manufacturing. The United States initiated an increased number of anti-dumping suits, and more protectionist measures were applied to developing countries. The Multi-Fibre Arrangement (MFA) was introduced in 1974, which imposed quotas on the amount of clothes and textiles that developing countries could export to developed countries (this lasted until 1994). As the tide turned away from free trade, costs increased and corporate margins declined.

Increased Public Spending, Lower Margins

Public spending increased dramatically in the United States and in other economies during this period. In the United States, President Lyndon Johnson's Great Society programmes and increased military spending to fund the Vietnam War contributed to rising deficits. The war, together with other tensions including the space race, also led to increased spending in the Soviet Union, which fuelled the race for military supremacy. Spending on its military and space efforts amounted to around 15% of GDP in the Soviet Union during the 1970s and 1980s, three times more than in the United States and five times more than in Europe (Maddison Database, 2010).[13]

Meanwhile, European governments increased spending to finance their welfare states and increased public ownership and

---

[12] Irwin, D. A. (1994). The new protectionism in industrial countries: Beyond the Uruguay Round. IMF Policy Discussion Paper No. 1994/005.
[13] Maddison Database (2010). https://www.rug.nl/ggdc/historicaldevelopment/maddison/releases/maddison-database-2010?lang=en.

nationalisations. In the United Kingdom, for example, large swathes of industries were brought into public control throughout the 1970s (and were already under public control in many other countries). Examples included the National Bus Company and Post Office in 1969, Rolls Royce in 1971, the local authority water supply and British Gas in 1973, British Petroleum in 1975, the National Enterprise Board (a state holding company for the full or partial ownership of industrial companies) and British Leyland (which included companies such as Jaguar and Land Rover) in 1976, British Aerospace in 1977.

The combination of increased public spending and wages led to a persistent decline in the profit share of GDP. In effect, the corporate sector was being squeezed by increased regulations, high interest rate costs and taxes, growing uncertainty and high energy and wage costs. As Exhibit 5.8 shows, the after-tax share of company profits to GDP collapsed in the United States.

Exhibit 5.8   Profit share of GDP fell in the 1970s and 1980s: shading highlights inflationary periods (1968–1982 and 2022–2023)

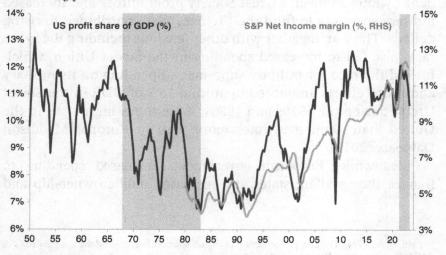

SOURCE: Goldman Sachs Global Investment Research

The End of the Downturn

By the end of the 1970s, stock markets had enjoyed some sharp rallies. In the United States, Ronald Reagan's defeat of Jimmy Carter in November 1980 and Republican control of the Senate were viewed as market-friendly. For the first time since 1976, the Dow Jones index rose back through 1,000. But the enthusiasm did not last. A further sharp round of interest rate hikes (the Fed raised its discount rate to an all-time high of 14%) forced another sharp fall in the stock market, and most economies around the world entered another recession. During 1981, inflation, high unemployment and economic stagnation sent stocks across the world down to further lows. Collapsing valuations, however, started to sow the seeds of what was to emerge as one of the most powerful and long-lived bull markets in history.

Chapter 6
1982–2000:
The Modern Cycle

Mr Gorbachev, open this gate! Mr Gorbachev, tear down this wall!
　　　　　　　　　　　　　　　　　　　　—Ronald Reagan

The secular bull market from 1982 to 2000 was, overall, a period of significant returns and low volatility in financial markets (Exhibit 6.1). That said, as with most secular bull markets, it included several cycles. Much like the 1968–1982 era, there were two recessions in most economies (the recessions of the early 1980s and 1990s were both deep and painful). However, unlike the 'Fat and Flat' trend of the 1970s period, the recessions of the 1980s were accompanied by a downward trend in inflation and interest rates that enabled markets to generate strong returns.

Over the whole super cycle, US equity generated over 1,300% total real returns, annualising at 16%, including dividends and after inflation. Dividend growth compensated for inflation (Exhibit 6.1).

Many complex factors drove the higher returns, including:

1. The Great Moderation
2. Disinflation and a lower cost of capital

Exhibit 6.1   The secular bull market from 1982 to 2000 was a period of significant returns and low volatility in financial markets

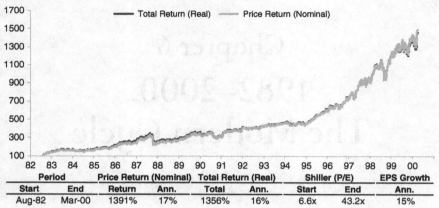

Period		Price Return (Nominal)		Total Return (Real)		Shiller (P/E)		EPS Growth
Start	End	Return	Ann.	Total	Ann.	Start	End	Ann.
Aug-82	Mar-00	1391%	17%	1356%	16%	6.6x	43.2x	15%

NOTE: Shiller price/earnings (P/E) is a valuation measure. It is calculated by dividing the index price level by the average inflation-adjusted 10-year earnings per share (EPS).

SOURCE: Goldman Sachs Global Investment Research

3. Supply-side reforms (including deregulation and privatisation)
4. The end of the Soviet Union (lower geopolitical risk)
5. Globalisation and cooperation
6. The impact of China and India
7. Bubbles and financial innovation

1. The Great Moderation

The Modern Cycle is often attributed to the 'Great Moderation' in economic variables (Exhibit 6.2). This phrase (coined by James Stock and Mark Wilson) referred to the significant reduction in the volatility of key macroeconomic variables, including inflation, interest rates, gross domestic product (GDP) and unemployment.[1] Olivier Blanchard and John Simon (2001) showed that the variability of

---

[1] Stock, J. H. and Watson, M. W. (2002). Has the business cycle changed and why? *NBER Macroeconomics Annual*, **17**, pp. 159–218.

Exhibit 6.2   Independent central banks contributed to longer and less-volatile economic cycles: GDP and inflation 10-year rolling volatility

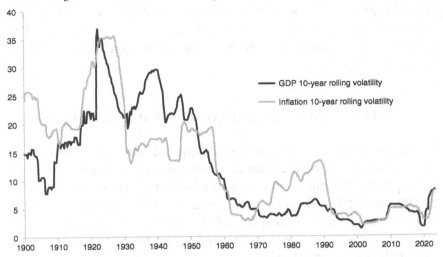

SOURCE: Goldman Sachs Global Investment Research

quarterly growth in real output (as measured by its standard deviation) had fallen by half and the variability of quarterly inflation had fallen by about two-thirds in the 20 years from the early 1980s.[2]

These improvements had many positive spinoffs for investors in financial markets. Lower volatility makes planning for the future easier and less costly for companies, and reduces the need for and cost of hedging for investors.[3] Lower output volatility also helped reduce swings in employment, which, in turn, reduced the uncertainty facing companies, households and investors. Lower uncertainty brings down the cost of capital by reducing risk premia (the higher return that investors demand to reflect the uncertainty of future outcomes). Much of the period was associated with increased household net wealth and income began to improve. Alongside this,

[2] Brookings (2001). The long and large decline in U.S. output volatility. Available at: https://www.brookings.edu/articles/the-long-and-large-decline-in-u-s-output-volatility/.
[3] Bernanke, B. (2004). The Great Moderation: Remarks before the Meetings of the Eastern Economic Association, Washington, D.C.

corporate profit margins increased, driving improved rates of return on capital. That said, although volatility remained low, it has been argued that it is a cause of greater future volatility as investors take more risk. This so-called Volatility Paradox is often attributed to increased risk in the run-up to both the technology bubble and the Global Financial Crisis.[4]

2. Disinflation and a Lower Cost of Capital

In the late 1950s and early 1960s, inflation in many economies was low and stable, hovering around 1% in the United States. It started to rise from the mid-1960s and reached more than 14% in 1980. By the latter part of the 1980s, it had fallen back to around 3.5% and, alongside this, interest rates fell materially. The general trend to lower interest rates over the period reflected a significant downward adjustment in inflation.

From August 1982 to December 1999, the compounded real return on the Dow Jones Industrial Average was 13% per year, well in excess of long-run average returns, or indeed the increase in earnings or book value over the period.[5] Much of this secular bull market therefore reflected valuation expansion – a phenomenon that pushed up both equity and fixed-income (bond) returns at the same time as the discount rate fell. However, this period was driven mostly by a powerful rise in corporate earnings per share (Exhibit 6.3) and falling interest rates and inflation (Exhibit 6.4).

European Interest Rate Convergence

One additional factor that drove interest rates lower globally was the convergence towards the European single currency that took place

[4] Danielsson, J., Valenzuela, M. and Zer, I. (2016). Learning from history: Volatility and financial crises. FEDS Working Paper No. 2016-93.
[5] Ritter, J. R. and Warr, R. S. (2002). The decline of inflation and the bull market of 1982–1999. *The Journal of Financial and Quantitative Analysis*, 37(1), pp. 29–61.

Exhibit 6.3   The Modern Cycle was characterised by a powerful rise in corporate earnings per share: S&P 500 price and EPS

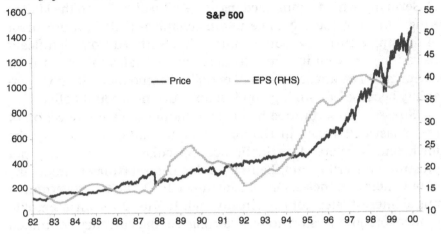

SOURCE: Goldman Sachs Global Investment Research

Exhibit 6.4   The Modern Cycle was characterised by falling inflation and interest rates: US 10y nominal bond yields (%) and US CPI y/y (%, RHS)

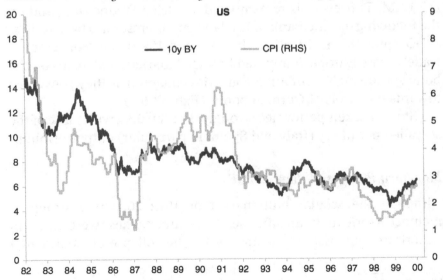

SOURCE: Goldman Sachs Global Investment Research

in the mid-1990s.[6] To be clear, this followed a period of significant stresses in Europe early in the decade, in the wake of the unification of Germany, which culminated in the ejection of Italy and the United Kingdom from the exchange rate mechanism (ERM), a precursor of the single currency. Both countries had suffered from significant recessions, making it harder to raise interest rates to defend their currencies. The impact of a weaker dollar compounded their vulnerability because of both high budget and current account deficits.

Stresses across Europe had been building since the rejection of the Maastricht Treaty in Denmark in 1992 and concerns over the forthcoming referendum in France. Speculators increasingly put pressure on sterling and the lira, forcing central banks to intervene to buy their currencies. On 16 September 1992, the UK government raised interest rates from an already high 10% to 12% in an attempt to induce foreign investors to buy sterling. As the currency continued to weaken, Chancellor Norman Lamont committed to raising interest rates to 15%, but the financial markets viewed these rate rises as unsustainable, given they would likely trigger a deep recession; by the end of the day, the government announced that it would leave the ERM. This event is remembered as 'Black Wednesday', and on the following day the Bank of England cut interest rates back to 10%.

Despite the ERM crisis, by the mid-1990s the 'convergence trade' across Europe dominated financial markets and yields on the bonds of the higher-inflation countries collapsed as they converged towards the levels of German bonds (Exhibit 6.5).

Stock markets performed strongly (Exhibit 6.6), with those of the so-called periphery (Italy and Spain, in particular) outperforming.

Monetary Policy and the 'Fed Put'

Although the secular bull market of 1982–2000 was strong, it included a series of financial crises. Chief among these were the Latin American debt crises (1982 and 1994), the collapse of Continental

---

[6] Côté, D. and Graham, C. (2004). Convergence of government bond yields in the euro zone: The role of policy harmonization. Bank of Canada Working Paper No. 2004-23.

Exhibit 6.5   10-year government bond yields converged in Europe

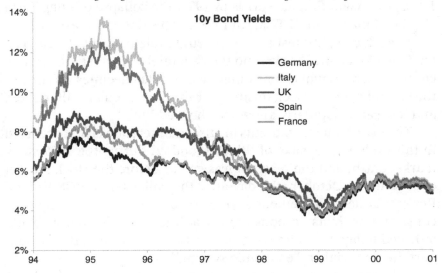

SOURCE: Goldman Sachs Global Investment Research

Exhibit 6.6   Total returns on equity indices rose sharply as bond yields fell, indexed to 100 in 1994.

SOURCE: Goldman Sachs Global Investment Research

Illinois Bank in 1984, the US Savings and Loans crisis starting in the 1980s, the Asian financial crisis in 1997, the collapse of Long-Term Capital Management (LTCM) in 1998 and the dot-com crash in 2000.

In each case, interest rates were cut to relatively low levels. The tendency for central banks, and the Federal Reserve in particular, to cut interest rates when confronted with market declines was one of the central support mechanisms over this long secular bull market, and it became popularly known as the 'Fed Put'.

The use of interest rate cuts to offset market shocks first occurred in this cycle in the wake of 'Black Monday', during the 1987 stock market crash, and the reaction was swift.[7] Before the stock market opened on 20 October (the day after the collapse), the US Federal Reserve issued a statement saying: 'The Federal Reserve System, consistent with its responsibilities as the nation's central bank, affirmed today its readiness to serve as a source of liquidity to support the financial and economic system.'[8]

Affirming the central bank's commitment to serve as a lender of last resort was intended to reverse the crisis psychology and to guarantee the safety and soundness of the banking system. The statement was accompanied by a 1% cut in the Federal Reserve's funds rate (from 7½% to 6½%) to boost liquidity and prevent the crash from spilling over into the bond market.

This aggressive intervention was utilised on several other occasions over the period of Fed Chair Alan Greenspan's tenure (he served five terms between 1987 and 2006), including during the Savings and Loans crisis (1986–1995), the Gulf War (1991), the Mexican debt crisis (1994) and the series of, mainly international, crises in 1998.

The last of these crises started in Thailand in 1997 and quickly broadened to encompass much of Asia and Latin America. By late 1998, it had spread to Russia and the ensuing turmoil led to

---

[7] Miller, M., Weller, P. and Zhang, L. (2002). Moral hazard and the US stock market: Analysing the 'Greenspan Put'. *The Economic Journal*, **112**(478), pp. C171–C186.
[8] Parry, T. R. (1997). The October '87 crash ten years later. FRBSF Economic Letter, Federal Reserve Bank of San Francisco.

the collapse of a large and highly levered hedge fund, LTCM. The Federal Reserve cut interest rates three times (each by a quarter of a percent) in the autumn of 1998, despite low unemployment of 4.5% and prevailing concerns about US inflation. The statement that accompanied the September cut focused on the risks to US growth, noting that 'action was taken to cushion the effects on prospective economic growth in the United States of increasing weakness in foreign economies and of less accommodative financial conditions'.[9]

The emphasis that central banks placed on avoiding a possible disruption to economic activity from these crises emboldened investors, who became ever more confident that the downside risks would be limited by the rapid intervention and support of the central bank.

The scale of the stimulus was such that it led to a rapid economic expansion and, in turn, contributed to the Tech, or dot.com, bubble of 1998–2000. Over this 2-year period, the S&P 500 increased by 51% (or 23% annualised). It was only after this bubble burst that the Federal Reserve switched to buying mortgage-backed securities as a form of stimulus which, in turn, contributed to the housing bubble and financial crisis of 2007/08 (see Chapter 7).[10]

3. Supply-Side Reforms (Including Deregulation and Privatisation)

The economic problems of the 1970s, coupled with labour unrest and high commodity prices, led to a growing momentum for change. During the 1980s, economic policymaking in most advanced economies moved to the right of the political spectrum, championed by

---

[9] Wessel, D. (2018). For the Fed, is it 1998 all over again? Available at https://www.brook ings.edu/articles/for-the-fed-is-it-1998-all-over-again/.

[10] Corsetti, G., Pesenti, P. and Roubini, N. (1998a). What caused the Asian currency and financial crisis? Part I: A macroeconomic overview. NBER Working Paper No. 6833. Corsetti, G., Pesenti, P. and Roubini, N. (1998b). What caused the Asian currency and financial crisis? Part II: The policy debate. NBER Working paper No. 6834.

a wave of political leaders keen to embrace a free-market approach to problems and a more libertarian approach to regulation and policy. The combination of Ronald Reagan in the US and Margaret Thatcher in the UK spearheaded an era of supply-side reforms to economic management. Helmut Kohl in Germany and Masayoshi Ohira in Japan also pursued economic reforms. The policy reforms across countries included the privatisation of public industry (particularly in the United Kingdom), deregulation aimed at increasing competition, reduced power for the trades unions, and tax reform.[11]

Central to the supply-side thesis was the Laffer Curve – a visual representation of the trade-off between taxes and growth. According to Laffer's theory, when the tax level is too high, a reduction in taxes should boost government revenues by generating more spending and, with it, higher growth.[12]

Tax Reforms

Tax reforms, and competition among countries to offer lower tax rates, became more prevalent. In the United States, for example, the tax reforms of the early 1980s were the most dramatic since the expansion of personal taxes during World War II (WWII). There were two major tax cuts: the Economic Recovery Tax Act of 1981 and the Tax Reform Act of 1986. The top marginal tax rate for individuals was reduced from 70% in 1981 to 50% initially, and eventually to 28%.[13]

Low-income families were taken out of the tax system and median-income households saw marginal rates fall by about one-third, and unemployment fell dramatically (Exhibit 6.7). However, many of the initial tax reforms initiated by the Reagan administration

---

[11] Boughton, J.M. (2002). Globalization and the silent revolution of the 1980s. *Finance & Development*, **39**(1), pp. 40–43.

[12] Feldstein, M. (1994). American economic policy in the 1980s: A personal view. In M. Feldstein (ed.), *American Economic Policy in the 1980s*. Chicago, IL: University of Chicago Press, pp. 1–80.

[13] Laffer, A. (2004). The Laffer Curve: Past, present, and future. Available at https://www.her itage.org/taxes/report/the-laffer-curve-past-present-and-future.

Exhibit 6.7   US unemployment rate started to improve

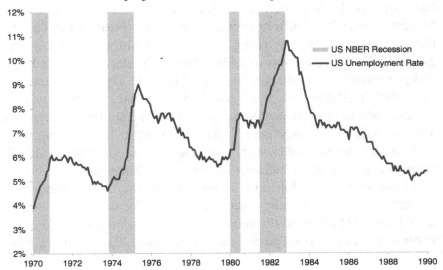

SOURCE: Goldman Sachs Global Investment Research

in the early 1980s were later reversed.[14] In the United Kingdom, the Thatcher administration reduced the top rate of income tax from 83% in 1979 to 40% in 1988, while the basic tax rate was cut from 33% to 25% over the same period. Partly, this was paid for by an increase in consumer taxes – in 1979, VAT rose from 8% to 15%.

Although governments were able to achieve lower unemployment and higher growth, their deficits increased. During the Reagan administration, the federal debt increased almost threefold to over $2 trillion, and the United States went from being the world's largest creditor to being the largest debtor nation.

The United States and the United Kingdom responded to rising deficits by cutting non-defence spending aggressively. However, the cuts to public funding were widely criticised and proved socially

---

[14] Fox, J. (2017). The mostly forgotten tax increases of 1982–1993. Available at https://www.bloomberg.com/view/articles/2017-12-15/the-mostly-forgotten-tax-increases-of-1982-1993.

divisive. In the United Kingdom, many in the establishment pushed back against the reforms. The University of Oxford refused to give Margaret Thatcher an honorary doctorate in protest at her cuts to the education budget, marking the first time since WWII that the award had not been given to a UK Prime Minister. In March 1981, 364 prominent economists wrote a joint letter to *The Times* newspaper criticising the government's fiscal and monetary policies. Indeed, it was a period of increased social unrest amid high unemployment and the collapse of manufacturing in regions previously dependent on industry. As industries were privatised and services deregulated, there was a significant increase in inequality that added to tensions and lowered social cohesion (Exhibit 6.8). In the United Kingdom, the deregulation of financial services in the 'Big Bang' of 1986 followed the 1984 strike in the coal industry, when miners walked out in protest at 20 proposed pit closures threatening 20,000 miners' jobs.

Exhibit 6.8 The top 10% share of total income increased sharply from the 1970s, particularly in the United States and the United Kingdom

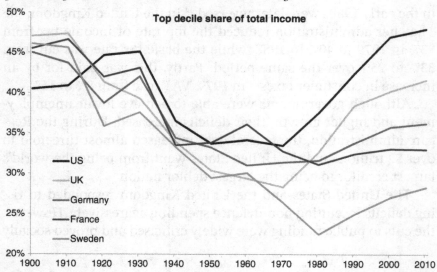

SOURCE: Piketty, T. (2014). *Capital in the Twenty-First Century*. Translated by A. Goldhammer. Cambridge, MA: The Belknap Press of Harvard University Press

The strikes turned violent with the 'Battle of Orgreave' on 18 June 1984, during which many miners were arrested. The strikes ended in defeat for the miners in March 1985.

Deregulation and Privatisation

Many governments pursued policies of deregulation and privatisation. In the United States, several industries were deregulated, including in the air transport and financial sectors. In the latter case, the partial repeal of the Glass–Steagall Act of 1933 removed barriers in the financial markets industry that had prevented institutions from combining across banking, securities and insurance businesses.

In the United Kingdom, where the state controlled many key industries, privatisation was implemented across several sectors, including utilities. The aim was to unburden companies from the inefficiencies of the state while at the same time increasing share ownership in the country, boosting what was described as a 'share-owning democracy'.

The wave of sales included companies such as British Telecom (BT), British Gas, BP and British Airways. The shares were generally sold below market price, creating a frenzy of buying. The first of these sales, that of BT in November 1984, was oversubscribed by three times. By the end of the first day of trading, the stocks had increased in value by one-third. British Airways, sold in 1987, rose 35% on the first day of trading.

The effect was far-reaching. Companies in public ownership in the United Kingdom accounted for 12% of GDP in 1979 but around just 2% by 1997.[15] By the mid-1990s the trend for privatisation had spread to the rest of Europe, even reaching Socialist-led governments such as that of Lionel Jospin in France, during 'the cohabitation' with President Jacques Chirac, which launched a $7.1 billion initial offering of France Telecom in 1997 and made a $10.4 billion secondary

---

[15] *The Economist* (2002, June 27). Coming home to roost.

offering a year later (as the fervour for telecom companies accelerated around the expanding technology bubble).

At the same time, increased globalisation and the opening up of capital markets made it possible for foreign investors to provide direct investment in these industries. From the early 1980s, reform programmes were implemented in all Organisation for Economic Co-operation and Development (OECD) countries.

Prior to the deregulation of the telecom industry, for example, most services were subsidised by long-distance traffic, which was priced five or six times higher than its marginal cost to subsidise local traffic.[16] Following deregulation, there was a significant adjustment in prices, particularly in long-distance rates.

Studies of the impact of these reforms across a variety of countries have shown a similar impact. For example, since the 1985 privatisation of Japan's Nippon Telegraph and Telephone (NTT), new entrants in the industry have created as many jobs as were lost after NTT ceased to exist. Similarly, in Finland, the liberalisation of the state PTO telecoms company resulted in more jobs being created in the sector than were lost directly (Ministry of Transport and Communications, 1995).[17]

In the United States, the liberalisation of the airline industry also resulted in lower prices. According to *The Economist*, air ticket prices had fallen by 33% and air traffic had increased by 100% by the end of the 1980s as new low-cost companies entered the market and offered a wider range of flights to smaller cities.[18] Nonetheless, this was not entirely successful. Although there was more competition in smaller cities, there was less competition in the long-haul market. *The Economist* reports that the big three US airlines doubled their market share to 60% between 1978 and the end of the 1990s because of the economies of scale needed to make these routes profitable.

---

[16] Pera, A (1989). Deregulation and privatisation in an economy-wide context. *OECD Journal: Economic Studies*, 12, pp. 159–204.

[17] Hoj, J., Kato, T. and Pilat, D. (1995). Deregulation and privatisation in the service sector. OECD Economic Studies No. 25.

[18] *The Economist* (1997, April 3). Freedom in the air.

Building regulations were also relaxed. In the United Kingdom, the Building Act of 1984 reduced the number of regulations from 306 pages to 24.[19] New compulsory competitive tendering policies required local authorities to compete with the private sector to deliver services. A range of other local authority services were privatised, including the London Bus Service and local regional bus and rail services (following the Railways Act 1993).

While these domestic reforms were in full swing, increased globalisation and the opening up of capital markets made it possible for foreign investors to provide direct investment in these newly privatised and deregulated industries.

4. The End of the Soviet Union (Lower Geopolitical Risk)

On a visit to West Berlin on 12 June 1987, Ronald Reagan called on Mikhail Gorbachev to 'tear down this wall'.[20] Little did he know that only a couple of years later, on 9 November 1989, the Berlin Wall would fall and, within a year, East and West Germany would be reunited. A wave of protest across the former Eastern Bloc in Poland, Czechoslovakia, Romania and Bulgaria, among others, paved the way for the break-up of the Soviet Union. By the summer of 1990, all the formerly Communist Eastern Bloc regimes had been replaced by democratically elected governments. Between spring 1992 and 1993, the 12 former Soviet Socialist Republics that made up the Soviet Union (together with the three Baltic States that were annexed by the Soviet Union in 1940) had joined the International Monetary Fund (IMF).[21]

Most of these governments quickly embarked on programmes of institutional change that included market liberalisation and privatisation. Optimism spilled over into financial markets and capital

---

[19] Hodkinson, S. (2019). *Safe as Houses: Private Greed, Political Negligence and Housing Policy After Grenfell*. Manchester: Manchester University Press.
[20] *Encyclopaedia Britannica* (1987). President Ronald Reagan speaking at the Berlin Wall, 1987.
[21] Boughton, J. M. (2012). *Tearing Down Walls: The International Monetary Fund, 1990–1999*. Washington, D.C.: International Monetary Fund.

flows picked up strongly in the countries that had made the most progress. Some, however, were slow to realise these benefits because of elevated levels of debt. Poland, for example, had gross debt to GDP of 80% in 1990, while places such as the Czech Republic and Hungary benefited from a perceived low risk of default.[22]

The initial economic adjustment for many countries was painful, and several experienced years of recession in the 1990s.[23] From a geopolitical perspective, the collapse of the Soviet Union was pivotal. It ended the Cold War and began an extended period of US political and economic hegemony that was unconstrained by threats from rival nations. It allowed the United States to intervene in foreign countries without the risk of retaliation but also laid the ground for the expansion of liberal democracy and capitalism.

Taken together, these events helped to reduce the equity risk premium (the required hurdle rate for investing in risky assets compared with low-risk bonds) and equity markets surged.[24] The DAX, the main German stock market index, rose sharply by 22% between October 1989 and July 1990.

5. Globalisation and Cooperation

Following the collapse of the Bretton Woods system, several attempts were made to find new agreements that would encourage a greater sense of cooperation to help moderate currency volatility.

---

[22] Lankes, H., Stern, N., Blumenthal, M. and Weigl, J. (1999). Capital flows to Eastern Europe. In M. Feldstein (ed.), *International Capital Flows*. Chicago, IL: University of Chicago Press, pp. 57–110.

[23] Dabrowski, M. (2022). Thirty years of economic transition in the former Soviet Union: Macroeconomic dimension. *Russian Journal of Economics*, **8**(2), pp. 95–121.

[24] The decline in geopolitical risk premia was largely a function of a perception of the lower risk of large-scale wars. However, it should be noted that, between 1989 and 2000, the IMF reports that more than 4 million people are estimated to have died in conflicts. International terrorist attacks also increased from about 342 a year between 1995 and 1999 to 387 between 2000 and 2001. While US military hegemony reduced the risks of major confrontations among developed economies, lower- and middle-income countries experienced almost 70% of major conflicts and more than 20% of terrorist attacks between 1996 and 2000.

Debt crises had become a recurrent risk in the early 1980s, as had currency fluctuations. Solutions were needed to find ways to check wild swings in currency markets that were no longer anchored to gold. The focus on currency volatility increased in the mid-1980s across Asia, Europe and the United States, with the introduction of the so-called Plaza Accords (a series of exchange rate management policies agreed at a meeting in the New York Plaza Hotel in 1985), under which the value of the US dollar was reduced by about 50% through a coordinated agreement among the central banks of France, Germany, Japan and the United Kingdom to sell dollars. This was followed 2 years later by the signing of the Louvre Accord with the aim of stabilising the dollar.

These accords helped to stabilise currencies, while other attempts were made to stabilise debt. One such attempt was the Baker Plan, proposed by US Treasury Secretary James Baker in 1985.[25] It envisioned helping highly indebted emerging economies by exploiting part of the Chinese trade surplus. The plan centred around cooperation between the United States and other international institutions, such as the World Bank and the IMF, and commercial bank creditors to restructure the debt of developing countries that entered programmes to pursue structural adjustments. While it was only partially successful, initially because the plan focused on rescheduling debt payments rather than cancelling them, by 1989 Baker proposed the cancellation of some troubled debt. In the same year, the Managing Director of the IMF, Michel Camdessus, described the transformation of many countries that were implementing reform programmes to strengthen their economic growth as a 'silent revolution'. Many of these changes were seen in emerging economies in Africa, and programmes in China, Korea, Mexico and Poland encouraged private entrepreneurship not tied to the state. Across the industrial world,

---

[25] International Monetary Fund. Money Matters: An IMF Exhibit – The Importance of Global Cooperation. Debt and Transition (1981–1989), Part 4 of 7. Available at https://www.imf.org/external/np/exr/center/mm/eng/dt_sub_3.htm.

a focus on longer-term macroeconomic management emerged to reduce inflation and deregulate the private sector.[26]

Global companies, particularly those based in the United States, expanded rapidly to take advantage of the new markets that were opening up. As international relations warmed, and trade restrictions were eased, consumers in emerging economies were able to access Western goods for the first time. Western products gained traction as cigarettes, jeans and fast food became symbols of Western lifestyles and American culture.

In a highly symbolic event, the first McDonald's was opened in the Soviet Union on 31 January 1990 (Exhibit 6.9), serving over 30,000 people on its first day (three times the previous first-day record in Budapest), with lines several kilometres long on Pushkinskaya Square in the centre of Moscow.

The opening up of new markets boosted the value of the multinational companies that were best placed to take advantage of the new opportunities and had the global brands to which many aspired. By 2000, 62 of the 100 most valuable brands in the world were American (according to Interbrand methodology), even though the United States accounted for just 28% of world GDP.

In 1994, the interim committee on the International Monetary System issued the 'Madrid Declaration', which called on all countries to adopt sound domestic policies and embrace international cooperation and integration; the Declaration was endorsed by the world's finance ministers. The IMF was then charged with adopting new standards on data dissemination and fiscal transparency. It also implemented the Basel Committee's Core Principles for Effective Banking Supervision, which became the cornerstone of international banking supervision.

In the mid-1990s, Russian President Boris Yeltsin and US President George H. W. Bush signed trade agreements designed to make it easier for US citizens to conduct business in Russia. In 1997, for the first time, Russia participated in economic discussions at the G7 Summit in

---

[26] Boughton, J. M. (2002). Globalization and the silent revolution of the 1980s. *Finance & Development*, **39**(1), pp. 40–43.

Exhibit 6.9   McDonald's opening in the USSR: customers stand in line outside the just-opened first McDonald's in the Soviet Union on 31 January 1990 at Moscow's Pushkin Square

SOURCE: Photo by VITALY ARMAND/AFP via Getty Images. https://www.gettyimages.com/detail/news-photo/soviet-customers-stand-in-line-outside-the-just-opened-news-photo/1239070707

Denver, Colorado, and in 1998 Russia was integrated as a full member, making the G7 the G8. By the early 2000s, Russian President Vladimir Putin was working to create a free-trade zone in Russia, and the country eventually joined the World Trade Organization in 2012.

Suddenly, there was a new drive towards integration and globalisation. World merchandise exports as a share of GDP increased from 12.7% in 1990 to 18.8% in 2000, and the total value of global trade almost trebled between 1980 and 2000. There was also an explosion of foreign direct investment (FDI). In developing countries, in particular, FDI increased from $2.2 billion in 1970 to $154 billion in 1997.[27]

---

[27] Williamson, J. (1998). Globalization: The concept, causes, and consequences. Keynote address to the Congress of the Sri Lankan Association for the Advancement of Science, Colombo, Sri Lanka, 15th December.

World capital flows also accelerated sharply. The proportion of assets owned by foreign residents as a share of GDP ballooned from 25% in 1980 to nearly 49% in 1990, and then to 92% by 2000, five times greater than the peak level of the early twentieth century.[28]

Technology and the Labour Market

By the end of the 1980s, the former Soviet Bloc countries had scrapped restrictions on the rights of their citizens to leave the country, and those who stayed were effectively absorbed into the global capitalist trading system. At the same time, the European Union abandoned limits on the movement of people within the Union, and the United States and Canada began to liberalise their own immigration policies.

The drivers of this impressive integration were policy and technology. From around 1990, personal computers had a significant impact on the trend of globalisation. Workers in developed economies had to compete with low-wage workers in emerging economies, now part of the global trading system, who had access to new technology supplied by companies in the developed world.

As a result of these changes, the effective supply of labour increased massively. Today, the total labour pool from China, India and the former Soviet Bloc that is economically active stands at around 1.3 billion (40% of the world's total). Many of these workers became economically active as they were integrated into the global economy from the 1990s.

6. The Impact of China and India

China's impact on the rest of the world began with the setting up of 'special economic zones' along its eastern coast in 1980. These gave local governments discretionary powers over taxation and the building of modern infrastructure, while business rules were

---

[28] Crafts, F. R. N. (2004). The world economy in the 1990s: A long run perspective. Department of Economic History, London School of Economics, Working Paper No. 87/04.

relaxed. The zones attracted large-scale investment from foreign investors, which eventually spilled over to other regions.

Growth was further stimulated by the state-owned enterprise reforms of the mid-1990s, relieving corporations of social responsibilities and freeing them to invest in new technologies. China adopted a model akin to those of Japan and Korea, to develop export-orientated markets by connecting its cheap and excess labour supply to the global market.

China's share of global manufacturing output increased from 2.7% in 1990 to 7% in 2000, while its share of manufactured exports more than doubled to 4.7% in 2000.

The reforms in India began in 1991. The advantage of existing property rights meant that its reforms were directed initially at lifting restrictions on manufacturing and trade. Prior to 1991, foreign competition was highly restricted by a series of licensing requirements and government involvement in industry restricted innovation and investment. Reforms lifted these requirements and tariffs fell, opening India's financial markets to the global economy. India benefited from several advantages that helped boost capital flows, including its large population and an English-speaking corporate sector. Initially, foreign investment took advantage of these conditions by outsourcing customer services, aided by new and lower-cost telecommunications and computing. However, this soon broadened out into software, financial, legal and medical services, as well as pharmaceuticals, supported by a highly educated workforce in engineering and technology. India joined the World Trade Organization in 1995 and China followed at the end of 2001.[29]

7. Bubbles and Financial Innovation

Such an extended period of economic growth and stability, coupled with lower interest rates and confidence in the 'Fed Put', not surprisingly resulted in growing financial speculation. As with many

---

[29] Syed, M. and Walsh, J.P. (2012). The tiger and the dragon. *Finance & Development*, **49**(3), pp. 36–39.

other bubbles in history, this was facilitated by financial innovation, particularly in derivatives.

The derivatives markets took off in the 1970s as demand increased for solutions to deal with the uncertainty and volatility unleashed by the collapse of Bretton Woods and the oil crisis of 1973/74. A key proponent of financial innovation was Professor Milton Friedman, who wrote an influential paper for the Chicago Mercantile Exchange (CME) calling for the development of futures markets in foreign currencies. The US Treasury gave permission to establish the International Money Market on this exchange, and it opened in 1972. High inflation and interest rates led to the development of markets for several other contracts, including gold futures and Government National Mortgage Association (Ginnie Mae) futures in 1975, Treasury bond futures in 1976 and oil futures in 1978.

This innovation meant that, for the first time, buyers and sellers of commodities did not need to deliver physical commodities at the end of a contract. A further important innovation came in 1976 with the introduction of the Eurodollar interest rate futures contract at the CME. Later, regulators agreed that it was no longer necessary to deliver the actual contract and that cash delivery would be acceptable instead. This provided support for an explosion of index futures on equities, such as the S&P 500 index future, which opened on the CME in 1982. Additional financial instruments started to evolve, and the process of 'securitisation' – for example, splitting parts of a financial instrument between income and capital – became popular.

The Japan Bubble and the Tech Bubble

The secular bull market of 1982–2000 became famous for two spectacular financial bubbles.

Japan's legendary bubble of the 1980s resulted in increases in stock and land prices that were extraordinary by any measure. Fuelled by falling interest rates (the Bank of Japan had cut rates from 5% to 2.5% by early 1987) and the 1985 Plaza Accord (which triggered a depreciation of the dollar against the yen aimed at reducing the US current account deficit by making exports cheaper), asset prices enjoyed a long and steady rise. Japanese companies used their appreciating currency to go on an overseas buying spree that included the purchase of the Rockefeller Center in New York and golf courses in Hawaii and California.

This exuberance was particularly rampant in the property market. The Imperial Palace in Tokyo was reported to be worth more than the entire value of France or California. The value of land in Japan in 1988 was theoretically more than four times that of land in the United States, even though the latter was 25 times the size.[30] It was argued that a ¥10,000 note dropped in Tokyo's Ginza district was worth less than the size of the ground that it covered.[31] The bubble became so big that the combined capital gains on stocks and land amounted to 452% of nominal GDP for the 1986–1989 period, while the subsequent losses were 159% of nominal GDP for the 1990–1993 period.[32] The surge in stock prices meant that Japanese companies had become some of the largest in the world. Mitsui & Co., Sumitomo Corp., Mitsubishi Corp. and C. Itoh all had higher sales than the largest company in the United States, General Motors.[33]

A more recent expression of confidence and, eventually, overvaluation came prior to the collapse of the technology bubble in the late 1990s. Before this bubble burst, shares in new companies were rising exponentially. I will turn to this period in the next chapter.

---

[30] Cutts, R. L. (1990). Power from the ground up: Japan's land bubble. *Harvard Business Review*, **May/Jun**. https://hbr.org/1990/05/power-from-the-ground-up-japans-land-bubble.

[31] Johnston, E. (2009, January 6). Lessons from when the bubble burst. *The Japan Times*.

[32] Okina, K., Shirakawa, M. and Shiratsuka, S. (2001). The asset price bubble and monetary policy: Experience of Japan's economy in the late 1980s and its lessons. *Monetary and Economic Studies*, **19**(S1), pp. 395–450.

[33] Turner, G. (2003). *Solutions to a Liquidity Trap: Japan's Bear Market and What it Means for the West*. London: GFC Economics.

Chapter 7

2000–2009: Bubbles and Troubles

September and October of 2008 was the worst financial crisis in global history, including the Great Depression.

—Ben Bernanke

The cycle between 2000 and 2009, like the 1970s cycle, can be described as 'Fat and Flat' – the low returns were punctuated by periods of sharp falls and powerful rallies. In total return terms, and adjusting for inflation, the swings were even larger. Overall, however, it was a decade of bubbles and significant market busts, underpinned by growing geopolitical uncertainty. The major market-moving events included the collapse of the technology bubble between 2000 and 2002, the 9/11 terrorist attacks in the United States in 2001, the Iraq war of 2003 and the Global Financial Crisis (GFC) of 2007–2009. Of these, the technology collapse and financial crisis were the most significant.

Total returns over the super cycle were −58% after inflation and dividends, with annualised declines of 9% (Exhibit 7.1).

Exhibit 7.1   Total returns over the cycle between 2000 and 2009 were –58% after inflation and dividends, with annualised declines of 9%

Period		Price Return (Nominal)		Total Return (Real)		Shiller (P/E)		EPS Growth
Start	End	Return	Ann.	Total	Ann.	Start	End	Ann.
Mar-00	Mar-09	–56%	–9%	–58%	–9%	43.2x	20.3x	0%

NOTE: Shiller price/earnings (P/E) is a valuation measure. It is calculated by dividing the index price level by the average inflation-adjusted 10-year earnings per share (EPS).

SOURCE: Goldman Sachs Global Investment Research

As Exhibit 7.1 shows, the bursting of the technology bubble lowered broad equity indices – such as the S&P 500 – by just under 50% between March 2000 and March 2002. The equity market then recovered sharply, rising by just under 100% between its trough in 2002 and the peak in October 2007 (generating an average annualised return of around 15%). That said, overall the market generated very little return, just 2.5%, between the peak in 2000 and the peak in 2007. Over the whole period, the market fell 55%, declining 9% at an annualised rate and 9% after adjusting for dividends and inflation.

The GFC generated the second major bear market of the decade, resulting in a 57% fall in the S&P 500 between 2007 and March 2009 (an annualised fall of 44%). The S&P 500 index closed the day at 676 on 3 September 2009.

The combination of these bubbles and crises meant that:

1. Growth expectations declined
2. The equity risk premium increased – as uncertainty rose
3. Equity/bond correlations turned negative – falling interest rates were generally negative for equities as they reflected fears of deflation.

The Bursting of the Technology Bubble

The scale of the bubble in technology stocks that emerged at the end of the last century was staggering, pushing valuation to record levels (Exhibit 7.2). Stock prices rose sharply, fuelled by a combination of cheap money (partly because of interest rate cuts that followed the Asian financial crisis of 1998) and a powerful narrative.

Flows into new emerging technology companies grew strongly as investors looked to gain access to these high-growth companies. By 1999, 39% of all venture capital investments went to internet companies. According to Paul Gompers and Josh Lerner, venture capital funds rose to around 1% of US GDP at the peak of the boom, with around 85–90% of this going into the technology sector.[1] The technology sector grew sharply in the public market, reaching a peak of 35% in 2000, and the internet sector alone reached a market capitalisation share of around 10% in the United States, with similar sharp rises in emerging growth indices in many other countries.

Exhibit 7.2 The S&P 500 cyclically adjusted P/E ratio peaked at c. 45× in the dotcom bubble: Real price divided by the 10y rolling average real earnings.

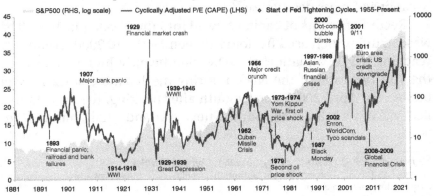

SOURCE: Robert Shiller, Goldman Sachs Global Investment Research

---

[1] Gompers, P. A. and Lerner, J. (2004). *The Venture Capital Cycle*, 2nd ed. Cambridge, MA: MIT Press.

As with many financial bubbles throughout history (see Peter Oppenheimer, 2020), a strong narrative developed: tech innovations such as the internet would change the world.[2] As we now know, such predictions were not without foundation.

In 1999, 295 of the 457 initial public offerings (IPOs) that year were related to internet companies, and these were followed by 91 in the first quarter of 2000 alone.[3] When the internet-based company Yahoo! made its IPO in April 1996, the price of its stock rose from $13 to $33 (having peaked at over $40) within a single day, nearly trebling the worth of the company. This became a familiar pattern in the period that followed. In 1999, for example, Qualcomm shares rose in value by 2,619%. This scale of price appreciation became commonplace. Thirteen major large-cap stocks all increased in value by over 1,000%, and another seven large-cap stocks each rose by over 900%.[4]

Financial innovation – which played a central role in the bubble that preceded the financial crisis of 2008 – was another significant factor, and the growth of derivative markets was an important driver. Between 1994 and 2000, the notional amounts of derivatives in interest rates and currency grew 457%, equivalent to the 452% increase between 2001 and 2007.[5] Warren Buffett called derivatives 'weapons of mass destruction'.[6]

Record amounts of capital flowed into the Nasdaq in 1997. The Nasdaq index increased fivefold between 1995 and 2000, eventually reaching a P/E valuation of 200×, significantly higher than even the 70× P/E ratio of the Nikkei during the Japanese stock market bubble. By April 2000, just 1 month after peaking, the Nasdaq had lost 34% of its value, and over the next year and a half, hundreds of

[2] Oppenheimer, P. C. (2020). *The Long Good Buy*. Chichester: Wiley.
[3] Hayes, A. (2023). Dotcom bubble definition. Available at https://www.investopedia.com/terms/d/dotcom-bubble.asp.
[4] Norris, F. (2000, January 3). The year in the markets; 1999: Extraordinary winners and more losers. *New York Times*.
[5] Perez, C. (2009). The double bubble at the turn of the century: Technological roots and structural implications. *Cambridge Journal of Economics*, **33**(4), pp. 779–805.
[6] Berkshire Hathaway (2022). Annual Report.

companies saw the value of their stock drop by 80% or more. Price-line, for example, fell 94%. Eventually, by the time it troughed in October 2009, the Nasdaq itself had fallen nearly 80%. The scale of the valuation excess also bore all the hallmarks of a classic speculative bubble.[7]

By the end of the stock market downturn of 2002, stocks had lost $5 trillion in market capitalisation since the local peak. At its trough on 9 October 2002, the Nasdaq-100, the technology-heavy index that had been a major outperformer over the previous couple of years, had dropped to 1,114, down 78% from its peak.

The collapse of the stock market bubble that ended the structural bull market of the 1982–2000 disinflationary era triggered a major reset in financial markets, pushing down interest rates. It was not long, however, before a major event rocked markets and shocked the world: the 9/11 attack on the World Trade Center in New York triggered global political uncertainty and the subsequent war in Iraq.

Confidence was already fragile given the stock market collapse, and the economic data that dominated in the summer of 2001 remained weak. Poor profit results continued and a profit warning from Sun Microsystems (one of the market leaders before the tech bubble burst) triggered a renewed sell-off: the Dow Jones index fell below 10,000 for the first time since April of that year. Labour market data in the United States deteriorated through the summer and investors became more pessimistic about growth prospects across Europe following a collapse in industrial production in July. The fears about another global economic downturn resulted in further stock market declines across the world. Between late May and 10 September 2001, the S&P had fallen by 17%, while more cyclical markets, such as Germany and Japan, had dropped by around a quarter, with most falling back to their lowest levels since the 1998 Asian crisis.[8]

---

[7] McCullough, B. (2018). A revealing look at the dot-com bubble of 2000 — and how it shapes our lives today. Available at https://ideas.ted.com/an-eye-opening-look-at-the-dot-com-bubble-of-2000-and-how-it-shapes-our-lives-today/.

[8] Cohen, B. H. and Remolona, E. M. (2001). Overview: Financial markets prove resilient. *BIS Quarterly Review*, **Dec**, pp. 1–12.

When the World Trade Center attacks occurred on 11 September, the impact was dramatic. The US stock market closed and remained closed for four days (the only other occasions on which it had been closed for a prolonged period were in World War I and during the Great Depression). Trading in US bonds ceased – the leading government bond broker, Cantor Fitzgerald, was housed in the World Trade Center – and on the commodities futures exchange (the New York Mercantile Exchange).[9] Initially, other markets remained open and suffered big losses. The MSCI World equity index fell by 12% between 10 and 26 September, losing roughly $3 trillion in value.

The policy intervention, however, was swift. The US Federal Reserve cut interest rates by 50bp on 17 September and many other central banks followed suit.

Despite the severity of the technology bubble collapse, the sector recovered and began to outperform again. The combination of low economic growth and interest rates stimulated further interest in faster-growing companies. The first iPhone was introduced in 2007 (Exhibit 7.3), spawning a new generation of companies and applications.

The Financial Crisis of 2007–2009

The collapse in interest rates that followed the Asian crisis in 1998 led, at least indirectly, to the loose credit conditions that facilitated the scale of the technology bubble at the end of the 1990s. In a similar way, the rapid interest rate cuts that followed the 11 September attacks created a fertile environment for a new wave of speculation as investors, on the lookout for returns, combined increased risk appetite with financial innovation to form the basis of the US housing boom in the mid-2000s. Both crises were a function of low interest rates that were put in place as a result of shocks. Carlota Perez expresses this

---

[9] Makinen, G. (2002). *The Economic Effects of 9/11: A Retrospective Assessment.* Congressional Research Service Report RL31617.

Exhibit 7.3   The long-awaited Apple iPhone goes on sale across the United States: people line up to be the first to buy an iPhone at Apple's flagship store on Fifth Avenue on 29 June 2007 in New York City.

SOURCE: Photo by Michael Nagle/Getty Images. https://www.gettyimages.com/detail/news-photo/people-line-up-to-be-the-first-to-buy-an-iphone-at-apples-news-photo/74959434

neatly in an academic article for the *Journal of Economics* (2009): 'the two boom and bust episodes of the turn of the century – the internet mania and crash of the 1990s and the easy liquidity boom and bust of the 2000s – are two distinct components of a single structural phenomenon. They are essentially the equivalent of 1929 developed in two stages, one centred on technological innovation, the other on financial innovation'.[10]

But she argues that, while the initial bubble in technology was more about the narrative and attraction of the story (rather than particularly low interest rates), 'that of the 2004–07 boom was driven

---

[10] Perez, C. (2009). The double bubble at the turn of the century: Technological roots and structural implications. *Cambridge Journal of Economics*, **33**(4), pp. 779–805.

by both low interest rates and abundant liquidity'. Low interest rates found their way into higher house prices; average home prices in the United States more than doubled between 1998 and 2006, experiencing their sharpest rise in history, while home ownership rose from 64% in 1994 to 69% in 2005 in the United States.[11] The sharp rise in house prices and low funding costs boosted home construction, and residential investment grew from about 4.5% of US gross domestic product to about 6.5% over the same period. The Federal Reserve reported that roughly 40% of net private sector job creation between 2001 and 2005 was accounted for by employment in housing-related sectors. Boosted by low interest rates and higher prices, household mortgage debt in the United States rose from 61% of GDP in 1998 to 97% in 2006.

Leverage and Financial Innovation

This is where the boom in mortgage-backed securities came in. Low interest rates and financial innovation combined to encourage banks to securitise significant volumes of new business in the form of mortgage-backed securities. This resulted in a rapid expansion of access to housing credit which, in turn, fuelled more demand that put further upward pressure on house prices. However, as low interest rates and rising housing markets resulted in higher loan-to-value mortgages (and banks taking on more risk), the high-risk loans became difficult to sell. Consequently, banks began to package loans together with high- and low-risk mortgages collated in what were called collateralised debt obligations (CDOs).[12] The idea is that the assets serve as collateral if the

---

[11] Weinberg, J. (2013). The Great Recession and its aftermath. Available at https://www.federalreservehistory.org/essays/great-recession-and-its-aftermath.

[12] A collateralised debt obligation (CDO) is a structured financial product that pools together assets that generate cash, such as mortgages, and then packages this asset pool into different tranches that can be sold to investors. Each varies significantly in risk profile.

loan defaults. Different tranches of a CDO were sold with different risk levels that reflected the risk of the underlying assets.[13]

The originators argued that if the lower-risk BBB-rated loans were pooled together, this would create diversification benefits that would reduce their risk, and the rating agencies generally agreed. If only one of the underlying loans went bad, it was argued, this would be offset by many others and the investors in the pooled instruments would be paid.

As Perez put it, 'the term "masters of the universe", often quoted to refer to the financial geniuses that were supposed to have engineered the unending prosperity of the mid-2000s, expresses the way in which they were seen as powerful innovators, spreading risk and somehow magically evaporating it in the vast complexity of the financial galaxy'.[14]

Derivatives exposure in the currency and interest rate markets ballooned (Exhibit 7.4). According to Bank for International Settlements (BIS) estimates, there was $432 trillion of derivatives exposure in 2007, equivalent to approximately eight times the annual size of global GDP (which stood at $54 trillion in 2007). Credit default swaps and equity swaps accounted for another $68 trillion, according to the same source.[15]

In the Financial Crisis Inquiry Commission report, the authors explain that not only were the underlying mortgages backed by debt – increasingly with a high loan-to-asset value at the time – but mortgage-backed securities and CDOs created further leverage because they were financed with debt. And the CDOs were often purchased as collateral by those creating other CDOs with yet another round of debt. Synthetic CDOs consisting of credit default swaps amplified the leverage; even the investor who bought the

[13] The Financial Crisis Inquiry Commission (2011). The CDO machine. *Financial Crisis Inquiry Commission Report*, Chapter 8. Stanford, CA: Financial Crisis Enquiry Commission at Stanford Law.

[14] The term 'Masters of the Universe' in relation to finance was popularised by Tom Wolfe in his book *The Bonfire of the Vanities*, published in 1987.

[15] Perez, C. (2009). The double bubble at the turn of the century: Technological roots and structural implications. *Cambridge Journal of Economics*, 33(4), pp. 779–805.

Exhibit 7.4 Derivatives exposure in the currency and interest rate markets ballooned: over-the-counter interest rate derivatives, notional amount outstanding ($ trillion)

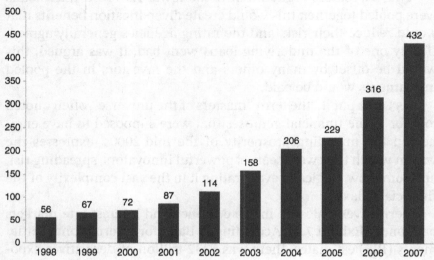

SOURCE: Bank of International Settlements

CDOs could use leverage. Structured investment vehicles (SIVs) – a type of commercial paper programme that invested mostly in triple-A-rated securities – were leveraged at an average of just under 14:1. In other words, these SIVs would hold $14 in assets for every dollar of capital. The assets would be financed with debt. It did not stop there: many of the investors in these products, particularly hedge funds, were also highly leveraged.[16] The problem was compounded because these vehicles were less regulated than other investment structures and were typically held off-balance-sheet by large financial institutions, reducing the impact of the assets and liabilities of the issuing bank.

---

[16] The Financial Crisis Inquiry Commission (2011). The CDO machine. *Financial Crisis Inquiry Commission Report*, Chapter 8. Stanford, CA: Financial Crisis Enquiry Commission at Stanford Law.

A huge amount of leverage therefore depended on the continued success of ever-higher real estate prices (just as had been the
case in Japan in the late 1980s before its bubble burst). The seem-
ingly virtuous cycle pushed up levels of debt across the private sector, with the banks, non-bank financial institutions (such as hedge
funds), corporates and households all experiencing significant
increases in leverage. The only offset to this were governments,
which had relatively (by the standards of today) low and stable debt
levels. When the party was eventually over – just like after the Japanese bubble of the late 1980s – the systemic fallout wreaked havoc
in financial markets and economies. As the private sector, saddled
with huge amounts of debt, was forced to de-lever and increase savings, governments stepped in. This time, cutting interest rates was
not enough to stimulate demand and governments had to increase
spending. This resulted in a transfer of debt from the private to
the public sector (as Exhibit 7.5 shows), a topic that I will cover in
Chapter 10.

In August 2007, pressures in financial markets began to mount
and asset-backed commercial paper markets came under stress as
investors tried to reduce exposure to the banks with the riskiest
mortgages. Bear Stearns was one of the most exposed and highly
leveraged banks.

In 2007, Bear Stearns had derivative contracts with a 'notional'
(or face value) worth of $13.4 trillion. It had net equity of $11.1
billion and supporting assets of $395 billion, resulting in a lever-
age ratio of nearly 36:1. The balance sheet comprised many illiquid
assets, and many of questionable value.[17]

Bear Stearns had to bail out one of its funds that was largely
invested in CDOs but, shortly afterwards, two of its hedge funds –
heavily exposed to subprime mortgages – had lost nearly all their
value. As panic spread, the Federal Reserve Bank of New York
stepped in. Initially it provided a $25 billion loan to Bear Stearns,

---

[17] Weinberg, J. (2013). The Great Recession and its aftermath. Available at https://www
.federalreservehistory.org/essays/great-recession-and-its-aftermath.

Exhibit 7.5 Imbalances shifted away from the private sector to the public sector and central banks

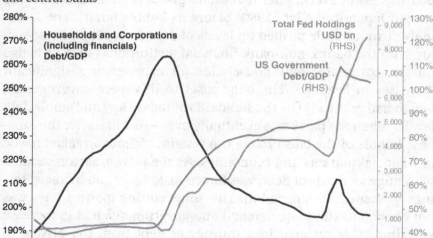

SOURCE: Goldman Sachs Global Investment Research

but it soon changed the deal by creating a new company to buy $30 billion of Bear Stearns' assets; the company itself was bought by JPMorgan Chase in a distressed sale for less than 7% of its market value just two days earlier.[18]

Fears continued to grow through the summer and the focus turned to Lehman Brothers. For a while, the credit default spreads (CDSs – financial derivatives that allow an investor to swap their credit risk with that of another investor) were relatively stable. Investors seemed to take the view that if the regulators had stepped in to bail out Bear Stearns 6 months earlier, it would likely do the same in the case of Lehman, which was a far bigger bank.[19]

---

[18] Torres, C., Ivry, B. and Lanman, S. (2010). Fed reveals Bear Stearns assets it swallowed in firm's rescue. Available at https://www.bloomberg.com/news/articles/2010-04-01/fed-reveals-bear-stearns-assets-swallowed-to-get-jpmorgan-to-rescue-firm.

[19] Skeel, D. (2018). History credits Lehman Brothers' collapse for the 2008 financial crisis. Here's why that narrative is wrong. Available at https://www.brookings.edu/articles/history-credits-lehman-brothers-collapse-for-the-2008-financial-crisis-heres-why-that-narrative-is-wrong/.

But, in a surprise to investors, the regulators decided not to extend a federal guarantee to Lehman or bail it out. Instead, other attempts were made to save the bank. Bank of America, one of the parties involved in the discussions, decided not to acquire it. Another attempt was made at a rescue that involved the splitting of Lehman's 'good' assets (the brokerage arm and other assets) in a sale to Barclays Bank, leaving the troubled real estate 'bad assets' to be funded by a consortium of other systemically important banks.

This solution also failed as the UK securities regulator (the Financial Services Administration) refused to allow Barclays to guarantee Lehman's operations during the period of the sale. As the options available to save Lehman evaporated, the bank filed for bankruptcy on 15 September 2008. The systemic fallout continued, and a major money market fund called the Reserve Primary Fund, which had a large exposure to Lehman's commercial paper, announced that it would 'break the buck' – a term used to describe the inability of the fund to pay its investors a dollar for each dollar that they had invested, causing further panic as more investors tried to pull their funds.

On the day of the Lehman collapse, the S&P 500 fell by close to 5% and the money and commercial paper markets became more stressed, prompting regulators to intervene with a bailout of insurer AIG the day after the Lehman collapse. Soon after, the US Congress intervened with the passing of the $700 billion Troubled Asset Relief Program (TARP), aimed at stabilising the financial system.

The problem was that a vicious cycle developed when the housing market began to fall, just as had occurred in Japan two decades earlier. Banks collapsed and the credit risk that had spread to institutions around the world resulted in systemic weakness in asset markets. Many of the CDOs were valued on a 'mark to market' basis, which, as prices fell, caused a collapse of credit markets with its spillover effects. Banks were forced to make dramatic write-downs.[20]

---

[20] Pezzuto, I. (2012). Miraculous financial engineering or toxic finance? The genesis of the U.S. subprime mortgage loans crisis and its consequences on the global financial markets and real economy. *Journal of Governance and Regulation*, 1(3), pp. 113–124.

The financial crisis of 2007–2009 and its aftermath were highly traumatic, in terms of both the collapse in the value of risk assets and the global economic fallout. US home prices fell by more than 20% between the first quarter of 2007 and the second quarter of 2011. As a result of these declines, and the leverage that was exposed to them, financial strains had begun to appear by the summer of 2007. Demand for asset-backed commercial paper collapsed as investors and money market funds tried to reduce exposure to subprime mortgages.

The impact of the financial crisis on the global economy has been estimated at over $10 trillion, equivalent to more than one-sixth of the global economy in 2010 alone. Over $2 trillion of assets in financial institutions were written down. The decline in overall economic activity was modest at first, but it steepened sharply in the fall of 2008 as stresses in financial markets reached their climax. From peak to trough, US GDP fell by 4.3%, making this the deepest recession since World War II. It was also the longest, lasting 18 months. The unemployment rate more than doubled, from less than 5% to 10%.[21]

Some analysts suggest that the impact may have been even greater; one such study estimates that the financial crisis persistently lowered US output by roughly 7 percentage points, representing a lifetime income loss in present-discounted value terms of about $70,000 for every US citizen.[22] Then Governor of the Bank of England Sir Mervyn King said at the time: 'This is the most serious financial crisis at least since the 1930s, if not ever.'[23]

Unsurprisingly, given the economic impact, the collapse in equity markets was also substantial: US equity markets fell 57% and the world stock market (MSCI World) fell 59%, placing this period firmly in the group of rare 'structural' bear markets, based on the

[21] Weinberg, J. (2013). The Great Recession and its aftermath. Available at https://www.federalreservehistory.org/essays/great-recession-and-its-aftermath.

[22] Romer, C. and Romer, D. (2017). New evidence on the aftermath of financial crises in advanced countries. *American Economic Review*, **107**(10), pp. 3072–3118.

[23] Mason, P. (2011, October 7). Thinking outside the 1930s box. BBC News.

definitions in Chapter 2. The downturn was so sharp that the public sector stepped in, and debt was effectively transferred from the private sector to the public sector (Exhibit 7.5), eventually moderating the risks of further de-leveraging, but leaving governments saddled with large debts and questions about the sustainability of government balance sheets, particularly in Southern Europe.

In terms of market moves going into the crisis and at the start of the bear market, the pattern initially followed a 'typical' path after the initial collapse and Hope phase in the rebound. However, the recovery that followed the trough broke the patterns of the past: the typical phases of the cycle were knocked off course by a series of shock waves as the second-round effects of the crisis made their way across the world. While the epicentre had been the US housing market, with the collapse of subprime mortgages and associated credit and banking problems, the stresses extended into European banks (which were highly levered at the time and heavily exposed to real estate in Southern Europe, which also suffered large losses). Consequently, this emerged as the European sovereign debt crisis (2010–2012). A third wave was felt mainly in Asia when, in August 2015, China devalued its currency against the US dollar following a period of weak growth. Commodity prices also collapsed, with Brent oil prices more than halving in value from nearly $100 per barrel in the summer of 2014 to $46 in January 2016.

I turn to the post-financial-crisis super cycle in the next chapter.

The Decline in Long-Term Growth Expectations

The consequence of these financial crises, the de-leveraging of private sector balances that they triggered and the decline in inflation all contributed to a fall in consensus on long-term real economic growth assumptions. Given that equity markets make a claim on future growth, the concerns regarding slower economic activity spilled over into profit growth expectations and equity returns (Exhibit 7.6).

Exhibit 7.6   Long-term real GDP expectations declined in the United States as well as Europe: US and Europe GDP consensus growth expectations for the next 6 to 10 years

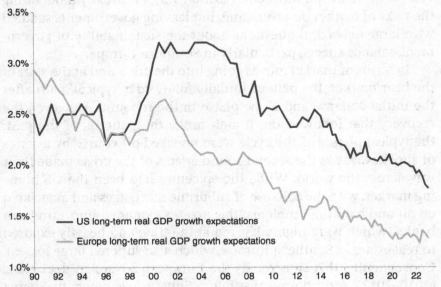

SOURCE: Goldman Sachs Global Investment Research

The Rise in the Equity Risk Premium

Alongside the collapse in growth expectations, there was a significant increase in uncertainty. This reflected growing doubts about future economic growth and a loss of confidence in the narrative that the technological innovations that had led to the technology bubble of the late 1990s would realise their potential. The rise in interest in technology during the late 1990s had sparked a new generation of private investors. This was the case even in Europe, which had hitherto had much less exposure to equity investment.

When Deutsche Telekom was privatised in 1996, for example, one of the motivations was to increase the equity culture. While the offering was global, two-thirds of the shares were allocated to German investors, of which roughly 40% went to retail investors.

More than three million German retail investors signed up for interest in the deal and the offering was several times oversubscribed.[24] The problem was that when the bubble burst, the losses were spectacular. At its peak, the stock traded at close to €100, but it had fallen to a low of €8 by 2002. The collapse was highly damaging to confidence more broadly. In 2014, Germany's Supreme Court (BHG) said that Deutsche Telekom had failed to adequately inform investors of the risks when buying shares in its 2000 IPO. This is just one of the many examples of how the impact of the technology collapse increased investor uncertainty and the prospective return investors would require for investing.

This was reflected in a higher equity risk premium (ERP, the excess return investors require to invest in a risky asset, such as equities, over and above the risk-free rate – such as a government bond, which compensates investors for taking on the higher risk of buying equity; Exhibit 7.7).[25] The ERP rose significantly again in the aftermath of the financial crisis as the risk of deflation mounted, and concerns around sovereign debt payments emerged in Europe.

While the required rate of return rose in equities – as greater risks meant that investors demanded a higher prospective return to invest – the actual return achieved in equities deteriorated relative to government bonds. This measure, known as the ex-post risk premium, exhibited relatively poor returns in aggregate over this period (Exhibit 7.8), particularly relative to the returns achieved in the previous cycle. The lower the returns, the more investors worried about investing in risky assets such as equities.

---

[24] Gordon, J. N. (1999). Deutsche Telekom, German corporate governance, and the transition costs of capitalism. Columbia Law School, Center for Law and Economic Studies, Working Paper No. 140.

[25] A one-stage DDM allows us to estimate a forward-looking (ex-ante) ERP using the following formula: ERP = dividend yield + expected nominal dividend growth – risk-free rate. Commonly, the dividend yield is the observable current trailing one, dividends are assumed to grow in line with trend real GDP growth, expected inflation is equal to the trailing 5-year average of inflation and we can use 10-year bond yield for the risk-free rate.

Exhibit 7.7 The rise in uncertainty was reflected in a higher equity risk premium: US multi-stage equity risk premium with long-term growth assumptions from Consensus Economics at the time

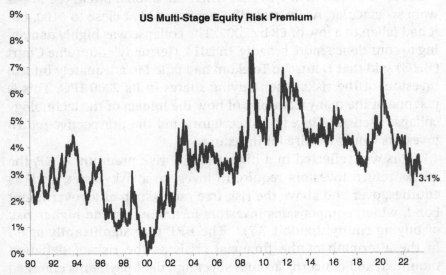

NOTE: Goldman Sachs Multistage Equity Risk Premium.
SOURCE: Goldman Sachs Global Investment Research

The Negative Correlation Between Bonds and Equities

The changing relationship between bonds and equities over different super cycles can also be seen in the way the correlation between equity prices and bond yields (or interest rates) has evolved through these cycles. Normally, equity and bond prices are positively correlated – this means that falling interest rates (which push up bond prices) are also a positive for equity markets.

Negative equity/bond correlations (that is, when yields fall – or bond prices rise – equity prices fall) became a familiar pattern at the end of the technology bubble in 2000 (Exhibit 7.9). Prior to this, only during the 1920s and the 1950/60s were equity/bond

Exhibit 7.8   Ex-post risk premium exhibited poor returns in aggregate over this period: annualised excess return of European equities over German 10-year bonds based on 10-year holding periods and total returns

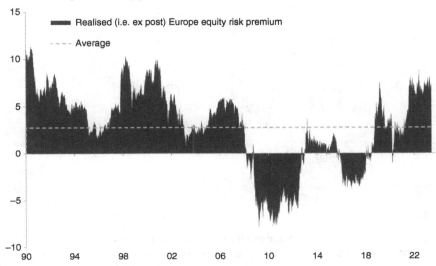

SOURCE: Goldman Sachs Global Investment Research

correlations negative, as inflation was generally very low. In these periods, ultra-low interest rates (which pushed up bond prices) often signified recessionary risks and, as a result, weaker equity prices. This was particularly true in the decade after the GFC when very low inflation and growth increased the risk of stagnation or even deflation. This is a bad outcome for equities (which make a claim on future growth). Over this period, understandably, the equity risk premium went up: dividend yields on equities had to be higher relative to the yield on bonds to compensate for the risk of deflation.

Only since the lifting of restrictions from the Covid-19 crisis have 12-month rolling correlations turned positive again, as stronger economic growth and higher inflation have been broadly more positive for equity markets than for bonds.

Exhibit 7.9   Negative bond/equity correlations have become a familiar pattern since the end of the technology bubble in 2000: S&P 500 vs US 10-year bond correlation (daily returns where available, otherwise monthly returns)

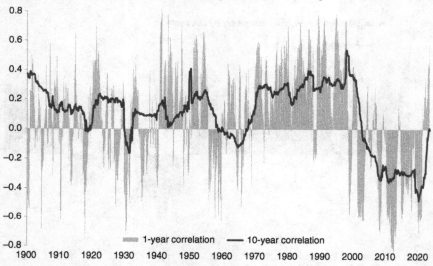

SOURCE: Goldman Sachs Global Investment Research

Chapter 8

2009–2020:
The Post-Financial-
Crisis Cycle and Zero
Interest Rates

We cannot solve problems by using the same kind of thinking we used when we created them.

—Albert Einstein

The period between 2009 and 2020 represented the third great secular bull market since World War II.

Total returns after inflation and including dividends were 417% over this period (Exhibit 8.1), annualising at 16%. Falling interest rates resulted in sharp rises in valuations: the Shiller P/E (the price divided by 10-year trailing earnings) rose from an already high 20× in 2009 to over 31× in 2020 which, coupled with strong profit growth (earnings annualising at over 10%), drove remarkable returns.

Exhibit 8.1 Total returns after inflation and including dividends were 417% over the cycle between 2009 and 2020, annualising at 16%

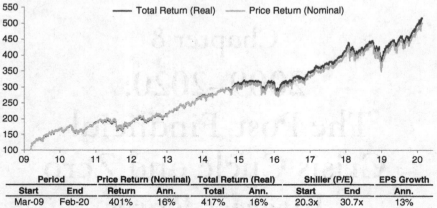

Period		Price Return (Nominal)		Total Return (Real)		Shiller (P/E)		EPS Growth
Start	End	Return	Ann.	Total	Ann.	Start	End	Ann.
Mar-09	Feb-20	401%	16%	417%	16%	20.3x	30.7x	13%

NOTE: Shiller price/earnings (P/E) is a valuation measure. It is calculated by dividing the index price level by the average inflation-adjusted 10-year earnings per share (EPS).

SOURCE: Goldman Sachs Global Investment Research

The main characteristics were:

1. Weak growth but high equity returns
2. The era of free money
3. Low volatility
4. Rising equity valuations
5. Technology and the outperformance of Growth versus Value
6. The outperformance of the United States versus the rest of the world

1. Weak Growth but High Equity Returns

Unlike the secular bull markets of the previous 70 years, the period after the financial crisis was unusual in that the economic recovery was relatively weak.

As Exhibit 8.2 shows, the pace of US real GDP, for example, was much weaker than the average recovery from other recessions since the 1950s.

Exhibit 8.2 Weak economic recovery: US real GDP from trough 10 years onward: indexed to 100

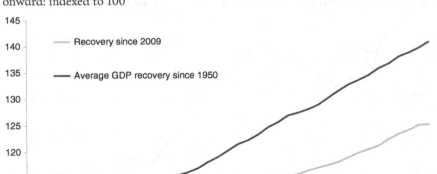

SOURCE: Goldman Sachs Global Investment Research

The underwhelming economic recovery post-financial crisis was reflected in declining expectations for future growth in the economy and in corporate profits. Exhibit 8.3 shows a 10-year rolling average (to smooth out the data) of corporate sales growth in the stock markets of Europe, Japan, the United States and the world aggregate. Lower inflation and a slow recovery in economic activity resulted in generally weaker sales for companies. The 10-year annualised growth rate in revenues across the developed world has converged towards the levels that Japan has experienced since the collapse of its asset bubble in the late 1980s.

Despite the weaker economic and profits growth, the equity market recovery was much stronger than the 'average' over the period since the 1960s, as Exhibit 8.4 shows.

The explanation for the gap between the economic recovery and the equity market owed much to the impact of zero interest rate policies and the implementation of quantitative easing (QE).

Exhibit 8.3 Top-line sales growth fell along with declining nominal GDP: year-over-year sales growth (10-year rolling average). Market excluding financials

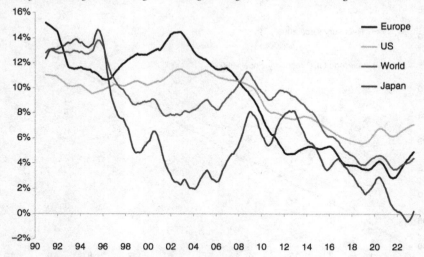

SOURCE: Goldman Sachs Global Investment Research

Exhibit 8.4 An unusually strong financial recovery: S&P 500 indexed to 100 on 9 March 2009

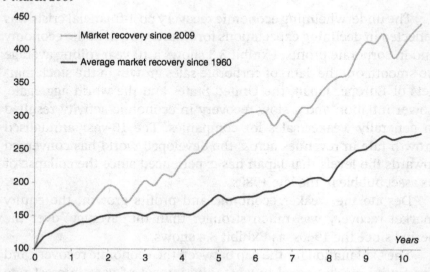

SOURCE: Goldman Sachs Global Investment Research

The Aftershock of the Financial Crisis

While the financial crisis bear market reversed in 2010 on the back of huge policy support, the post-financial-crisis cycle was distorted by the aftershock of the initial crisis, which resulted in Europe and, with a lag, emerging markets decoupling from the United States. The aftershock came in waves that can be characterised by the causes of stress evident as they erupted in the different regions.

Wave 1 in the United States started with the housing market collapse and spread into a broader credit crunch when Lehman Brothers filed for bankruptcy. It ended with the Troubled Asset Relief Program (TARP)[1] and QE.[2]

Wave 2 in Europe began with the exposure of banks to leveraged losses in the United States and spread to a sovereign debt crisis given the lack of a debt-sharing mechanism across the Euro area. It peaked with the Greek debt crisis and pressure for private investors to be 'bailed in' when it came to losses. It ended with the introduction of Outright Monetary Transactions (OMT), the European Central Bank (ECB)'s commitment to do 'whatever it takes' and, finally, the introduction of QE.[3]

Wave 3 in emerging markets (EMs) coincided with the collapse in commodity prices and activity that hit EM equities hard, particularly between 2013 and the start of 2016.

So, while all major equity markets troughed in 2009 and recovered sharply together, the secular bull market from then on was unusual because the different regions performed very differently as

---

[1] The Troubled Asset Relief Program (TARP) was a US government programme that helped to stabilise the financial system through a series of measures that included the 'TARP bailout program', which authorised the use of $700 billion to bail out banks, AIG and auto companies. It also provided relief to credit markets and homeowners.

[2] Quantitative easing (QE) – for large-scale asset purchases – refers to monetary policy that entails a central bank creating money that is used to buy predetermined amounts of government bonds or other financial assets in order to inject liquidity into the economy.

[3] Outright Monetary Transactions (OMT) is a programme of the European Central Bank under which the Bank makes purchases ('outright transactions') in secondary, sovereign bond markets, under certain conditions, of bonds issued by Euro area member states.

the shocks spread geographically from the initial wave. In the context of this rolling crisis, 2016 marked an important turning point as global equity markets rose on the back of strong synchronised growth and receding political and systemic risks (Exhibit 8.5). The improvement in growth and profits meant that, for the first time in the cycle, a large share of the return in equity markets came from profit growth as opposed to valuation expansion.

The impact of the three waves on US, European and EM equity markets is highlighted in Exhibit 8.5. The US wave quickly became a global shock as credit markets and banks' balance sheets around the world became impaired. All the main equity markets fell together and EMs (which have a higher beta and are most vulnerable to a collapse in world trade growth) suffered the largest declines. The rebound, triggered by zero interest rate policies and the start of US QE, also had a global impact, and EM equities (which had initially suffered the most) rebounded strongly.

Exhibit 8.5   Global equity markets rose as the EM wave ended in 2016: price performance in USD

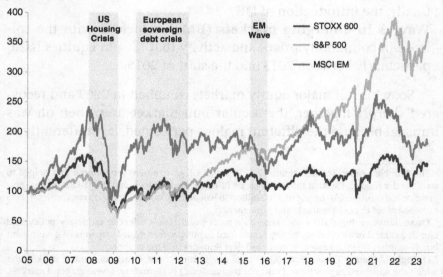

SOURCE: Goldman Sachs Global Investment Research

But the recovery was interrupted as the crisis extended to Europe. Here, the combination of levered banks and the institutional weaknesses of the Euro area fiscal framework led to a sovereign debt crisis and another severe drawdown. For much of this period, however, the US economy and stock market managed to decouple from the rest of the world and continued to make rapid progress.

For Greece, the impact was severe: bond yield spreads rose sharply, and the government was forced to implement 12 rounds of tax increases and spending cuts between 2010 and 2016. Additionally, there were a series of bailouts in 2010, 2012 and 2015 from the International Monetary Fund (IMF), Eurogroup and ECB, as well as a negotiated 50% 'haircut' on debt owed to private banks in 2011 (amounting to a €100 billion debt relief programme). In July 2012, the Euro area financial sector was in acute crisis. Greece had already experienced a surge in government bond yields to 50% as markets feared a possible exit from the euro. Spanish 10-year sovereign yields had reached levels above 7.5% and the 2-year rate was approaching 7%. A flattening of the Spanish government yield curve at levels inconsistent with fiscal and macroeconomic sustainability threatened to cause the sovereign market to seize up. And, given the central role played by the government bond market in the wider functioning of the Spanish financial system (and the deep connectivity between banks and the sovereign), the Spanish banking sector came under threat. Contagion to other Southern European countries became acute as Italian sovereign yields were also climbing towards 7%, and existential risks to the euro and to the Euro area were widely considered to be high.

Finally, equity markets globally rebounded in mid-2012 as risk premia moderated following aggressive policy intervention by the ECB and verbal assurances that the ECB would do 'whatever it takes' to preserve the euro, demonstrating, once again, the power of central banks to change market expectations. Following his comments, ECB President Mario Draghi announced the ECB's OMT programme in a September 2012 press meeting. For Euro area countries that had accepted the conditionality implicit in a European

Stability Mechanism (ESM) and simultaneously retained market access, the ECB stood ready to purchase shorter-dated government debt in potentially unlimited amounts.

But just as things appeared to be calming down, significant weakness in commodity markets and EM equities triggered a third wave of the downturn, with China at the epicentre. Europe was hit once again, given its large exposure to EM markets, while the US equity market experienced a milder and shorter correction and was once again seen as a relative haven.

Since the middle of 2016, equity and fixed-income (bond and credit) markets have moved higher together, although with significant differences in relative returns. Aggressive monetary easing and quantitative easing had a powerful effect in pushing up valuations in financial markets. Various academic papers have examined the impact of QE on bond prices, particularly following the announcement of QE programmes. Others have shown that it had a meaningful impact on equity markets as well, with some estimates that, in the case of the UK FTSE All-Share index and the US S&P 500, 'unconventional policy measures adopted caused increases in equity prices of at least 30%'.[4]

2. The Era of Free Money

However, the main reason for this extraordinary and unusual pattern of returns largely boils down to the move in inflation and interest rates that followed the financial crisis, helping to bring down the cost of capital and boost valuations.

The decline in interest rates (both nominal and real) was an almost constant feature of the cycles after 1982. From the 2000s,

[4] Balatti, M., Brooks, C., Clements, M. P. and Kappou, K. (2016). Did quantitative easing only inflate stock prices? Macroeconomic evidence from the US and UK. Available at SSRN: https://ssrn.com/abstract=2838128 or http://dx.doi.org/10.2139/ssrn.2838128. They argue in this paper that median estimates indicate a peak impact on equities, at the end of the 24-month horizon, of around 30% for the FTSE All-Share and around 50% for the S&P 500.

more effective forward guidance by central banks and the impact of new technologies and globalisation all contributed to lower and more stable inflation, alongside a flatter Phillips curve (the relationship between unemployment and inflation), resulting in much more stable inflation expectations.[5]

Other factors played a role in lowering interest rates. One explanation is that an excess of global savings over investment had driven equilibrium real interest rates down even before the start of the financial crisis. Lawrence Summers (2015), for example, in his 'secular stagnation hypothesis', suggests that chronically weak aggregate demand, together with ultra-low policy rates, kept desired saving above investment and pushed the natural rate below market rates.[6] The global savings glut (Bernanke, 2005) and the shortage of safe assets (Caballero and Farhi, 2017) drove excess savings in emerging market economies, reflected in their current account surpluses, into advanced economies, depressing real rates there.[7] But others point out that slower economic growth and lower inflation (partly reflecting the impact of demographics and partly the impact of rapid technological disruption) were also responsible.

Whatever the reasons, there was another notable shift lower in interest rates after the financial crisis and, alongside this, market measures of inflation fell dramatically relative to other cycles. To some degree, the impact of QE was also responsible.[8]

---

[5] Cunliffe, J. (2017). The Phillips curve: Lower, flatter or in hiding? Speech given at the Oxford Economics Society. Available at https://www.bankofengland.co.uk/speech/2017/jon-cunliffe-speech-at-oxford-economics-society.

[6] Summers, L. H. (2015). Demand side secular stagnation. *American Economic Review*, **105**(5), pp. 60–65.

[7] Bernanke, B. S. (2005). The global saving glut and the U.S. current account deficit. Speech at the Sandridge Lecture, Virginia Association of Economics, Richmond, VA, March 10. Caballero, R. J. and Farhi, E. (2017). The safety trap. *The Review of Economic Studies*, **85**(1), pp. 223–274.

[8] Borio, C., Piti, D. and Rungcharoenkitkul, P. (2019). What anchors for the natural rate of interest? BIS Working Paper No. 777. They argue that 'to the extent that monetary policy, which sets the price of leverage, can influence the financial cycle, it too may have a persistent impact on the economy's long-run path, and hence also on real interest rates. If the definition of equilibrium also precludes the occurrence of boom–bust cycles, as one would reasonably expect, then it may not be possible to define a natural rate independently of the monetary regime'.

According to long-term data (from the Bank of England), the level of interest rates globally fell sharply after the financial crisis and moved rapidly towards the lowest levels in history (before rising sharply in 2021 – a topic I cover in Part III).

The Collapse in Government Bond Yields

What was notable about this period was that, not only did nominal interest rates and inflation fall, but there was also a significant shift downwards in real long-term rates (nominal rates minus inflation; Exhibit 8.6).

The falls in bond yields became so dramatic in some cases that roughly 30% of government debt globally had a negative yield by 2020. This meant that investors were effectively paying the government to take their money. Even a quarter of investment-grade corporate bonds (that is, those of companies with a robust balance sheet) had a negative yield (Exhibit 8.7).

Exhibit 8.6 The German real yield turned negative: 10-year nominal yield minus current inflation

SOURCE: Goldman Sachs Global Investment Research

Exhibit 8.7   Proportion of negative-yielding global government bonds

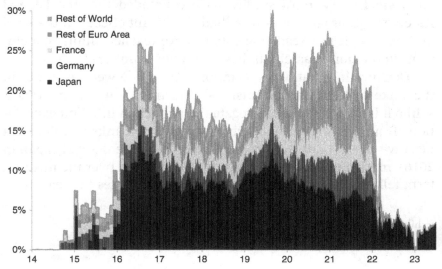

SOURCE: Goldman Sachs Global Investment Research

This may seem an odd concept, but it became a reality in the era following the financial crisis as central banks pushed the level of interest rates down rapidly to soften the blow to economies and avoid the mistakes made with much slower action following previous financial collapses (Japan in the late 1980s and the United States in the 1930s, in particular). The 'anchoring' of interest rates by central banks was then further cemented in longer-term interest rates and bond yields through the QE programmes.

QE, in theory, has an impact on yields by pushing down investor expectations about future interest rates through a 'signalling effect', as the purchase of government debt by the central bank signals that the target level of interest rates will stay lower than might otherwise have been the case. Another argument is that central bank purchases of government securities encourage investors to increase their demand for riskier assets as they seek to achieve an acceptable return, thereby pushing down yields on other debt securities, such as corporate bonds, more risky bond markets or longer-duration bond markets.[9] Although estimates of the direct impact of QE on bond yields vary, most studies have concluded that the Federal Reserve's QE programmes have had significant effects on the level of Treasury yields. Academic studies have reached similar conclusions in relation to asset purchases in other countries.[10]

Declines in inflation expectations, alongside weaker output in the wake of the financial crisis, also justified lower bond yields. While it is difficult to disaggregate the impact on inflation expectations from QE and growth, when the central banks introduced a negative interest rate policy (the ECB in 2014, the Bank of Japan in 2016), market expectations about future inflation over the medium term fell as well (Exhibit 8.8).[11] Inflation swap rates (a measure of

Exhibit 8.8   Market expectations about future inflation fell

SOURCE: Goldman Sachs Global Investment Research

[9] Christensen, J. and Krogstrup, S. (2019). How quantitative easing affects bond yields: Evidence from Switzerland. Available at https://res.org.uk/mediabriefing/how-quantitative-easing-affects-bond-yields-evidence-from-switzerland/.

[10] Gilchrist, S. and Zakrajsek, E. (2013). The impact of the Federal Reserve's large-scale asset purchase programs on corporate credit risk. NBER Working Paper No. 19337.

[11] Christensen, J. H. E. and Spiegel, M. M. (2019). Negative interest rates and inflation expectations in Japan. *FEBSF Economic Letter*, 22.

future inflation expectations) also dropped meaningfully in the United States and Europe following the start of QE.

In the case of Europe, ECB QE and negative German Bund yields had a meaningful impact on sovereign spreads. During the epicentre of the European sovereign debt crisis in 2011, Greek bond yields spiked above 40% in March 2012, and again briefly to around 20% in 2015 (Exhibit 8.9). The country was forced into a series of austerity programmes and debt relief that helped to stabilise concerns. Since then, as fears of a breakup of the Euro area faded and QE strengthened, the spillover effect of negative German yields to other European bond markets has been dramatic, resulting in Greek 10-year yields converging with those of the United States by the time of the pandemic; they are now similar to the levels in the United States and the United Kingdom.

Falling bond yields also reflected a collapse in the so-called term premium. Theory tells us that the yield on a default-free government bond is the sum of expected policy rates over the life of the

Exhibit 8.9 Greek bond yields surged amid uncertainty: Greece and US 10-year bond yield

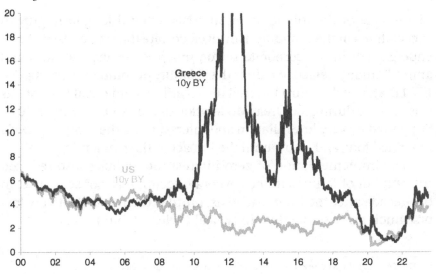

SOURCE: Goldman Sachs Global Investment Research

bond plus a term premium. When bond yields change, therefore, it is either because expectations of short-term rates are revised or market prices (and/or the quantity) of the risks associated with lending money far out into the future ('duration') change.

This term premium exists because investors need to be compensated for bearing economic risks (just as with equities and the equity risk premium). For bondholders, two risks are particularly relevant. One is inflation, as unexpected inflation erodes the real value of fixed nominal payments, reducing real returns on nominal bonds. This means that bond investors will require a higher term premium when they expect inflation to be high and/or they are more uncertain about its medium-term trajectory. The second is the risk of recession. This is, of course, the primary risk for equity investors. Because recessions imply lower expected wealth and consumption growth, they also result in higher risk aversion, thereby causing investors to demand higher compensation for holding risky assets, and a lower premium for fixed-income assets that are safer.

3. Low Volatility

The impact of the rolling financial crisis reduced long-term growth expectations in the economy. However, despite the slower pace of revenue growth in the corporate sector, much lower interest rates and ample liquidity helped to reduce the volatility of company earnings (or EBITDA), which in turn lowered the volatility in financial markets, as was the case during the Great Moderation of the 1990s (Exhibit 8.10).[12] Supported by very low inflation and interest rates, the economic cycle remained long and stable until the impact of the pandemic.

The implementation of zero interest rate policies also reduced the number of failures in the corporate sector. As a consequence, in the decade after the financial crisis, profit growth was relatively low but much more stable than in typical cycles (Exhibit 8.11).

---

[12] EBIDTA = earnings before interest, tax, depreciation and amortisation.

Exhibit 8.10   Median S&P 500 company trailing 10-year EBITDA growth variability

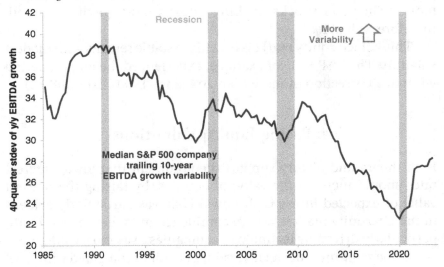

SOURCE: Goldman Sachs Global Investment Research

Exhibit 8.11   EPS rarely falls outside of recessions: MSCI AC World annual realised earnings growth. Grey shading indicates recessions (United States, Europe, Japan or EM)

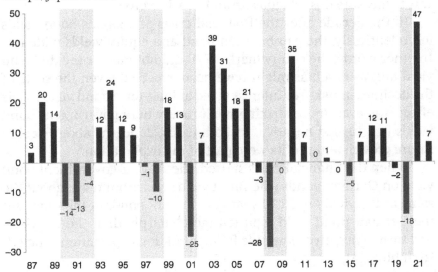

SOURCE: Goldman Sachs Global Investment Research

The de-leveraging of private sector balance sheets (of banks, corporates and households) meant that the private sector appeared more resilient to shocks, making returns more predictable and, therefore, valuable.

This helped equity markets to achieve stable returns with modest volatility. The S&P 500, for example, experienced the longest period without a correction of more than 20% since 1900 (Exhibit 8.12).

4. Rising Equity Valuations

Both theory and history support the argument that lower interest rates should increase the value of equities, by raising the present value of expected future cash flows. This was particularly evident in the US equity market, where confidence in longer-term growth, particularly driven by technology companies, was most evident.

At the same time, the relative value of equities compared with 'safe' government bonds fell. The uncertainty about the future meant that the yield on equities rose relative to the yield on government bonds. The so-called yield gap – the difference between the S&P 500 earnings yield (the inverse of the P/E) and the 10-year US Treasury yield – is one way to measure this relationship and how it evolves.

In the decade after the financial crisis of 2008, as bond yields fell relentlessly, the gap between bond and equity yields widened. In other words, the equity market P/E did not rise (or the dividend yield fall) as much as might have been expected given the scale of the declines in risk-free interest rates, or long-term bond yields. This effect was even more striking in Europe where government bond yields had turned negative. In both cases, concerns about weaker future growth and profits were part of the explanation.

When the financial crisis started, the 10-year government bond yield on German bonds (the Bund yield) was around 4%, about the same as the yield on US 10-year government bonds at the time. But the German Bund yield then fell more sharply than the US yield, and turned negative alongside falling inflation expectations and QE (Exhibit 8.13).

Exhibit 8.12 2009–2020 was the longest bull market in equities without a 20% drawdown: S&P 500

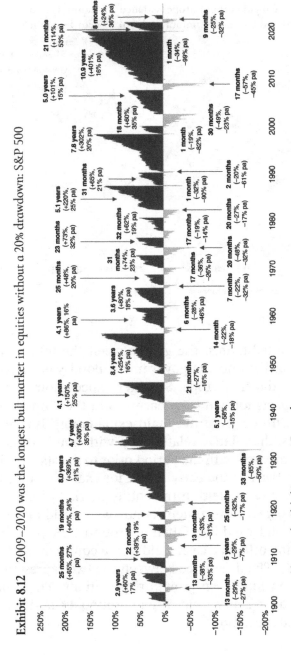

SOURCE: Goldman Sachs Global Investment Research

Exhibit 8.13   The yield gap in Europe widened: 12-month forward dividend yield for STOXX 600 and German nominal and real 10-year bond yield

SOURCE: Goldman Sachs Global Investment Research

In the United States, the gap between the total cash yield in the equity market and the government bond yield never became as wide as it did in Europe. Stronger expectations for long-term growth prospects for company earnings in the United States compared with Europe were the main explanation. But, even in the United States, the relative relationship with bond yields changed a great deal compared with the period prior to the start of the twenty-first century. Back in the early 1990s, for example, an investor was being offered a cash yield in the equity market of around 4% at a time when 10-year government bonds were yielding 8%. By 2020, the 10-year bond yield had fallen to around 1.5% but equity investors were being offered a cash yield in the equity market of over 5% (Exhibit 8.14). The difference between the two represents a significant decline in long-term growth expectations. Then, in 2022/23, the US 10-year treasury yield rose to around 4% and was twice the S&P 500 dividend yield.

Exhibit 8.14 In 2022, the US 10-year treasury yield rose to around 4% and was twice the S&P 500 dividend yield: 12-month forward dividend yield for S&P 500 and US nominal and real 10-year bond yield

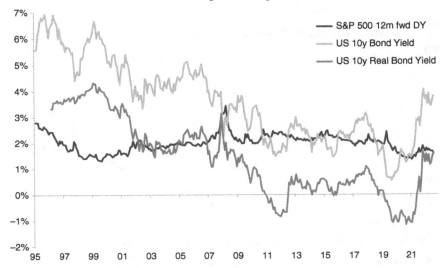

SOURCE: Goldman Sachs Global Investment Research

5. Technology and the Outperformance of Growth versus Value

Another important influence on the evolution of the equity cycle since the financial crisis was the impact of technology on financial returns. The dramatic growth of some technology companies (or companies that utilise new technologies to disrupt traditional industries, including retail, restaurants, taxis, hotels and banking) meant that the distribution of profits has diminished compared with past cycles. As Exhibit 8.15 shows, the technology sector has experienced a spectacular rise in profits since the crisis. While the world stock market (excluding technology) saw a strong improvement in earnings as the global economy recovered in 2016, it had only just returned to the levels prevailing before the financial crisis by the time the Covid-19 pandemic hit in 2020. The technology sector,

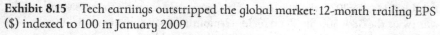

Exhibit 8.15 Tech earnings outstripped the global market: 12-month trailing EPS ($) indexed to 100 in January 2009

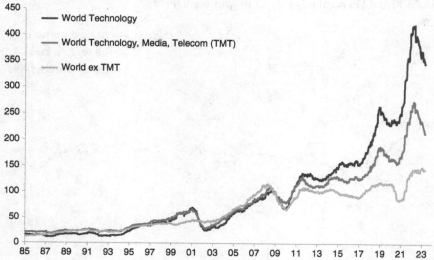

SOURCE: Goldman Sachs Global Investment Research

meanwhile, enjoyed a surge in earnings per share over the same period (albeit in part driven by the boom in share buybacks).[13]

This dramatic trend resulted in a much wider dispersion of returns between relative winners and losers in terms of stock market performance.

The Extraordinary Gap between Growth and Value

The post-financial-crisis cycle also resulted in a persistent and sustained divergence of returns within and across equity markets that was very unusual relative to other cycles. In particular, as shown in Exhibit 8.16, the Value segment of stock markets (low valuation companies, generally in older, mature industries) had significantly

---

[13] Lazonick, W. (2014). Profits without prosperity. *Harvard Business Review*, **Sept**. https://hbr.org/2014/09/profits-without-prosperity.

Exhibit 8.16   MSCI World Value significantly underperformed versus Growth: price performance

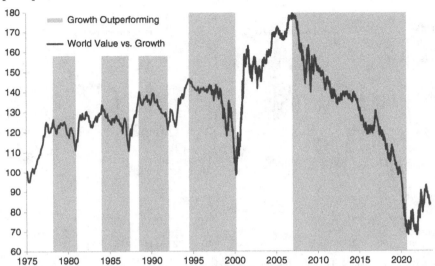

SOURCE: Goldman Sachs Global Investment Research

underperformed so-called Growth companies (those with higher expected future growth, typically in 'new economy' industries dominated by technology).

There are several reasons for this, related to the unique nature of the post-financial-crisis cycle.

First, growth was scarce and, therefore, generally highly valued. We have already seen that revenue growth trended downwards after the financial crisis, but in general the proportion of companies with high growth also fell in most equity markets. Exhibit 8.17, for example, shows the share of high-growing versus low-growing companies globally over time. Growth companies are defined here as those expected to grow revenues above 8% annually over the next 3 years, and low-growth companies as those expected to grow at a rate below 4%.

Second, lower bond yields enhanced the value of Growth versus Value as a result of the longer 'duration' of growth stocks, that is, the sensitivity of their valuations to lower interest rates (Exhibit 8.18).

Exhibit 8.17   Few companies have high projected sales growth: MSCI AC World

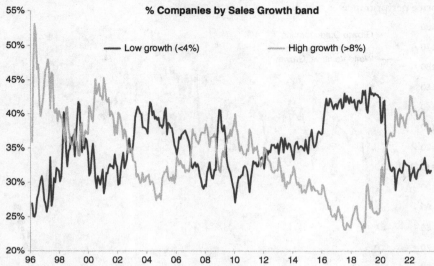

SOURCE: Goldman Sachs Global Investment Research

Exhibit 8.18   Lower bond yields tend to weigh on value stocks

SOURCE: Goldman Sachs Global Investment Research

Companies with expected growth in profits far into the future are more sensitive to changes in interest rates because the net present value of their future profits becomes more valuable with lower interest rates (the rate at which these are discounted), and less valuable when they rise.

Third, as seen in Exhibit 8.19, lower yields boosted Defensive companies (companies in business sectors that are less impacted by the economic cycle, such as healthcare or consumer staples) relative to Cyclicals (those that are more sensitive to changes in growth in the broader economy). This is a similar theme to Growth versus Value. Many of the Cyclical sectors are those with a low P/E, while most of the Defensives are seen to offer better growth or, more importantly, predictable growth, particularly in an uncertain economic environment.

Fourth, lower bond yields increased the value of companies with low volatility and strong balance sheets (Exhibit 8.20), as well

Exhibit 8.19   Cyclicals versus Defensives have also moved with the US 10-year bond yield

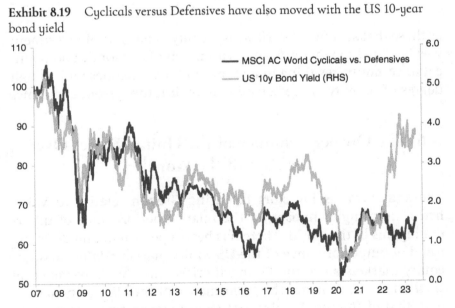

SOURCE: Goldman Sachs Global Investment Research

Exhibit 8.20   Low-volatility stocks have underperformed as yields and inflation expectations have risen

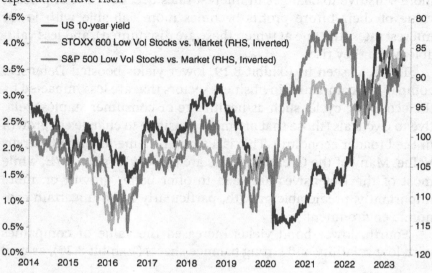

SOURCE: Goldman Sachs Global Investment Research

as those that are often described as 'quality'. This style of investment was favoured in what was an environment of economic and political uncertainty, resulting in a premium for companies with a high degree of stability or predictability in their future revenue streams.

6. The Outperformance of the United States Over the Rest of the World

The shift towards investors favouring Growth relative to Value had a meaningful impact on the relative performance of different regions of the world. There has been a persistent and dramatic trend of outperformance of the US equity market relative to other equity markets since the financial crisis, and this is particularly clear when we compare the performance of the US equity market with that of Europe. Exhibit 8.21 shows the relative performance

Exhibit 8.21   The relative performance of Europe over the United States has mirrored the relative performance of Value over Growth

SOURCE: Goldman Sachs Global Investment Research

of the S&P 500 and the Euro STOXX 50 index (the main benchmark of equities in the Euro area) over time. Between 1990 and 2007 there was no clear trend; the relative performance between these markets was cyclical – sometimes the United States outperformed and sometimes Europe outperformed. The period since the financial crisis has seen a persistent trend of outperformance of the US equity market.

What is interesting here is that this trend of relative performance correlates well with the relative performance of the Value versus Growth indices. The United States is considered a Growth market given its high concentration of companies that enjoy fast growth (such as technology companies). By contrast, the European market has a high proportion of low-growth, 'cheaper' companies in relatively mature industries (industrials, autos, commodities, financials and the like), and a smaller proportion of the market is made up of high-growth companies.

The significant differences in regional equity performance that have emerged since the financial crisis also reflect the difference between the growth of earnings per share across major equity markets. For example, as illustrated in Exhibit 8.22, from the last peak in the levels of earnings per share (EPS) just before the financial crisis began up until the start of the pandemic in 2020, the level of US EPS increased by nearly 80%. A good deal of this had been generated by the technology sector but, even excluding this sector, the level of EPS had increased by a healthy 75%.

In Japan, the equivalent increase was 20%, while across Europe (shown here as the STOXX 600, that is, the 600 largest public companies in Europe), the aggregate rise in EPS was a meagre 7%. Just as with the United States, the weighting of industries within these

Exhibit 8.22   The gap between US and European EPS roughly halves when adjusting for sector composition: EPS peaked in 2006 in the US (S&P 500) and Japan (TOPIX), and peaked in 2007 in Europe (SXXP) and Asia ex Japan (MXAPJ).

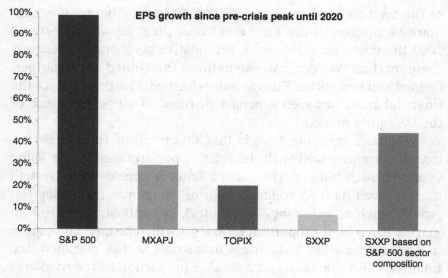

SOURCE: Goldman Sachs Global Investment Research

stock markets matters. In the United States, the heavy weight of technology companies boosted earnings, while Europe had a heavy weight in banks (where earnings have largely fallen). When an adjustment is applied to the European numbers to calculate what EPS growth might have been if Europe had the same sector weightings as the United States (more tech and fewer banks, for example), the progression of earnings would have been much stronger, close to 45%.

Zero Rates and the Demand for Risk Assets

Another interesting aspect of zero, or negative, interest rates post-financial crisis is their impact on the preference for risk assets among long-term investing institutions, such as pension funds and insurance companies.

For these institutions, one of the main effects is that, as interest rates fall, the net present value of the future liabilities (the discounted value of future cash flows) of a pension plan or an insurance company would increase. For a typical defined-benefit pension plan, a 100bp drop in long-term bond yields could mean, all else equal, an immediate increase in liabilities on the order of 20%.[14]

As the Organisation for Economic Co-operation and Development (OECD) put it: 'the main concern for the outlook is the extent to which pension funds and insurance companies have been, or might become, involved in an excessive 'search for yield' in an attempt to match the level of returns promised to beneficiaries or policyholders when financial markets were delivering higher returns, which might heighten insolvency risks'.[15]

---

[14] Antolin, P., Schich, S. and Yermi, J. (2011). The economic impact of protracted low interest rates on pension funds and insurance companies. *OECD Journal: Financial Market Trends*, **2011**(1), pp. 237–256.
[15] For a good discussion on the asset/liability mix and the risks of 'searching for yield', see *OECD Business and Finance Outlook* 2015, Chapter 4: Can pension funds and life insurance companies keep their promises?

There has been some evidence of this effect in the United States where, on balance, institutions took on more risk as risk-free rates and funding rates have fallen.[16] Others have shown that searching for yield is not confined to institutions but applies to investors as well.[17]

There were also widespread implications for pension funds and companies that have large future pension liabilities, as falling interest rates increased the net present value of the deficits.[18] For insurance companies, the fall in rates can threaten guaranteed yields of life assurance contracts and make them less resilient in a downturn, or locked into structurally lower returns if they increase their weighting in government bonds.[19]

In some regions, and in Europe in particular, the high-risk weighting applied to equities for pension and insurance companies for regulatory purposes makes it much harder to increase weightings in risky assets, thereby increasing the demand for bonds. Consequently, the increased demand for bonds, through the need to hedge interest rate and liability risks, put further downward pressure on bond yields. Indeed, as Exhibit 8.23 shows, European pension and insurance companies in aggregate have continued to focus on debt investments such as government bonds in recent years, even as bond yields fell below zero. The problem, as we see later, is that when interest rates eventually started to rise again with the emergence of inflation post-Covid-19, the risks of asset liability mismatches had increased.

---

[16] Gagnon, J., Raskin, M., Remache, J. and Sack, B. (2011). The financial market effects of the Federal Reserve's large-scale asset purchases. *International Journal of Central Banking*, 7(1), pp. 3–43. These authors also found that US State and Municipal sponsors with weak balance sheets have increased their risk exposure as bond yields have fallen. They estimate that up to a third of funds' total risk was related to underfunding and low interest rates between 2002 and 2016.

[17] Lian, C., Ma, Y. and Wang, C. (2018). Low interest rates and risk taking: Evidence from individual investment decisions. *The Review of Financial Studies*, **32**(6), pp. 2107–2148.

[18] Antolin, P., Schich, S. and Yermi, J. (2011). The economic impact of protracted low interest rates on pension funds and insurance companies. *OECD Journal: Financial Market Trends*, 2011(1), pp. 237–256.

[19] Belke, A. H. (2013). Impact of a low interest rate environment – global liquidity spillovers and the search-for-yield. Ruhr Economic Paper No. 429.

Exhibit 8.23   Pension and insurance funds continue to focus on debt investments (and largely ignore equity): quarterly flows into equity and long-term debt by Euro area pension and insurance funds (€ billions)

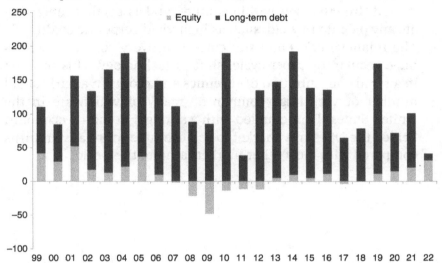

SOURCE: Goldman Sachs Global Investment Research

In summary:

The 2009–2020 super cycle was characterised by several factors:

1. A relatively weak economic cycle in terms of nominal and real GDP growth, resulting in an unusually aggressive period of monetary easing and the advent of QE.
2. Despite the cuts in interest rates, long-term growth expectations moderated and average revenue growth across the corporate sector in Western economies slowed.
3. Notwithstanding the weaker than average economic and profits growth, financial markets were unusually strong, both in fixed-income markets (as policy rates and inflation moderated) and in equity and credit markets (as lower interest rates pushed up valuations).
4. Inflation expectations collapsed, and bond yields fell to record low levels, both globally and in many individual economies.

5. The impact of slow growth and record low interest rates meant that both income and growth were relatively scarce, driving a secular shift in relative performance towards low-volatility Quality and Growth assets within equities, and assets that can generate any pick-up in yield, such as high-yield corporate credit.

6. The financial crisis and subsequent recovery coincided with a huge secular, or super-cycle, shift in technology. This resulted in a rapid concentration of revenues and profits in a fairly small number of very large companies, many of which are in the United States. This, coupled with a stronger domestic economy, helped the US equity market to achieve superior relative returns compared with most other markets around the world.

Chapter 9
The Pandemic and the Return of 'Fat and Flat'

The magnitude and speed of collapse in activity . . . is unlike anything experienced in our lifetimes.

—Gita Gopinath

T he economic shock of the pandemic generated a period of falling returns for equity investors (Exhibit 9.1). Markets recovered with the support of governments and the introduction of Covid vaccines.

Pandemic Pandemonium

The onset of the Covid-19 pandemic ushered in the end of an era defined by disinflation, quantitative easing (QE) and record low interest rates, which caught policymakers and investors largely by surprise.

Exhibit 9.1   Pandemic heralds the return of 'Fat and Flat'

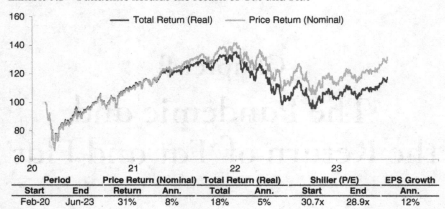

Period		Price Return (Nominal)		Total Return (Real)		Shiller (P/E)		EPS Growth
Start	End	Return	Ann.	Total	Ann.	Start	End	Ann.
Feb-20	Jun-23	31%	8%	18%	5%	30.7x	28.9x	12%

NOTE: Shiller price/earnings (P/E) is a valuation measure. It is calculated by dividing the index price level by the average inflation-adjusted 10-year earnings per share (EPS).

SOURCE: Goldman Sachs Global Investment Research

The Pandemic Shock

The outbreak of Covid-19 and the ensuing pandemic resulted in an abrupt halt to global economic activity and, with it, global equities entered a bear market in one of the fastest collapses in stock prices since World War II. The US equity market opened down 7% on 8 March 2020, triggering a circuit-breaker for the first time since the financial crisis of 2007/08. Other equity markets followed suit, and the STOXX 600 index of the largest companies in Europe fell more than 20% below its level earlier in the year. As fears of recessions deepened, the yield on government debt collapsed, and US 10- and 30-year Treasury yields fell below 1% for the first time in history.[1]

As one government after another implemented shutdowns, large parts of the global economy shuddered to a halt. By the first week of April 2020, 3.9 billion people, more than half of the world's

---

[1] Franck, T. and Li, Y. (2020, March 8). 10-year Treasury yield hits new all-time low of 0.318% amid historic flight to bonds. CNBC.

Exhibit 9.2   Empty shelves in a central London supermarket on the eve of the first Covid-19 lockdown in March 2020

SOURCE: Photo by Peter C. Oppenheimer

population, were in lockdown, causing uncertainty and panic buying (Exhibit 9.2).[2]

Almost all economies experienced a significant decline in economic output, and in the first 3 months of 2020 the G20 economies together fell 3.4% year-on-year.[3]

In the United Kingdom (a particularly vulnerable economy due to its high exposure to service industries), GDP declined by 11% in 2020. This was the steepest fall since consistent records began in 1948 (Exhibit 9.3), and the largest drop since the Great Frost of 1709.

During the first lockdown, UK GDP was 25% lower in April 2020 than it had been only 2 months earlier.[4] The wider effects on society and on employment were quickly becoming obvious. During the

[2] Sandford, A. (2020, April 2). Coronavirus: Half of humanity on lockdown in 90 countries. Euronews.
[3] Organisation for Economic Co-operation and Development (2020). G20 GDP Growth – First quarter of 2020.
[4] Harari, D., Keep, M. and Brien, P. (2021). Coronavirus: Effect on the economy and public finances. House of Commons Briefing Paper No. 8866.

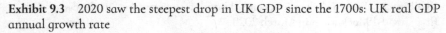

Exhibit 9.3   2020 saw the steepest drop in UK GDP since the 1700s: UK real GDP annual growth rate

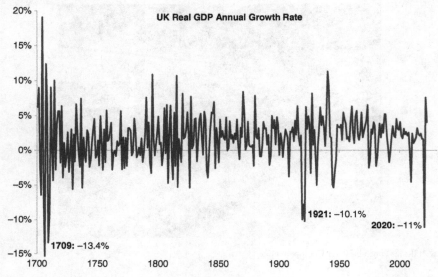

SOURCE: Goldman Sachs Global Investment Research

pandemic, the closure of schools and universities around the world affected more than 1.5 billion students, with the most vulnerable learners hit the hardest.[5]

By March 2020, 6.6 million workers had filed for unemployment in the United States, and the British Chamber of Commerce reported that, by early April 2020, 32% of businesses would have laid off staff. The income earned by workers globally fell 10% in the first 9 months of 2020, equivalent to a loss of over $3.5 trillion.[6]

Fears of mass unemployment were growing: St Louis Fed President James B. Bullard argued that US unemployment could rise to

---

[5] UNESCO (2020). Education: from school closure to recovery. Available at https://www.unesco.org/en/covid-19/education-response.
[6] Strauss, D. (2020, September 23). Pandemic knocks a tenth off incomes of workers worldwide. *Financial Times*.

30% unless urgent action were taken.[7] Something had to be done, and quickly. Governments around the world stepped up borrowing and implemented a wide range of support programmes. By as early as May 2020, the group of 20 largest economies (the G20) had implemented fiscal support measures worth around $9 trillion, equivalent to around 4.5% of GDP on average, making the support programmes bigger than those during the financial crisis, where moral hazard issues had made intervention more complex.[8]

The disruption to economic activity even resulted in a move into negative oil prices. Oil buyers were paid around $30 a barrel of WTI (West Texas Intermediate) in April 2020 to take delivery of physical oil as futures contracts expired, given that the severe lack of storage capacity had led to huge excess supplies.[9]

The economic crisis and the increase in fiscal support resulted in a huge rise in government debt levels.

Meanwhile, central banks continued to pump vast amounts of money into the global economy. Between 2007 (the financial crisis) and 2021, the European Central Bank (ECB)'s balance sheet increased more than fourfold, the Bank of Japan (BoJ)'s around sixfold and the US Federal Reserve's eightfold (Exhibits 9.4 and 9.5). As a result, the ECB's balance sheet exceeded €7 trillion at the beginning of 2021, more than 60% of Euro area GDP, and the BoJ's rose to 130% of Japan's GDP.[10]

As a result, interest rates fell even further (Exhibit 9.6), this time to the lowest levels in history.

---

[7] Matthews, S. (2020). U.S. jobless rate may soar to 30%, Fed's Bullard says. Available at https://www.bloomberg.com/news/articles/2020-03-22/fed-s-bullard-says-u-s-jobless-rate-may-soar-to-30-in-2q.

[8] The support programmes were taken up with significant effect. In the United States, for example, financial assistance from the US Paycheck Protection Program (PPP) was requested by 61.7% of companies with employees and received by 58.3% during the Covid-19 pandemic in 2020. United States Census Bureau (2022). Impacts of the COVID-19 pandemic on business operations. Available at https://www.census.gov/library/publications/2022/econ/2020-aces-covid-impact.html.

[9] Reed, S. and Krauss, C. (2020, April 20). Too much oil: How a barrel came to be worth less than nothing. *The New York Times.*

[10] Cerclé, E., Bihan, H. and Monot, M. (2021). Understanding the expansion of central banks' balance sheets. Banque de France Eco Notepad, Post No. 209.

Exhibit 9.4   Central banks' balance sheets increased massively from 2007: central bank balance sheets as a percentage of GDP

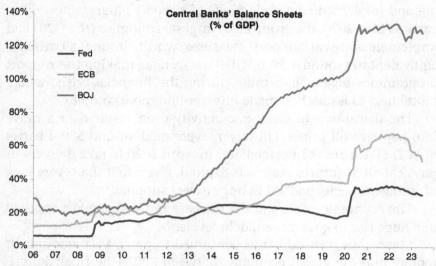

SOURCE: Goldman Sachs Global Investment Research

Exhibit 9.5   The Fed significantly expanded its balance sheet from 2007: US government and agency securities held outright by all Federal Reserve banks ($ trillion)

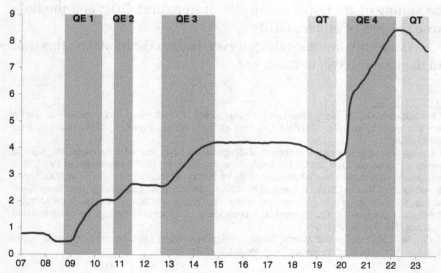

SOURCE: Goldman Sachs Global Investment Research

Exhibit 9.6   In 2020, interest rates collapsed to the lowest levels in modern history: effective fed funds rate

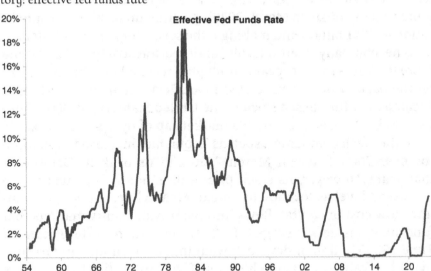

SOURCE: Goldman Sachs Global Investment Research

Another Tech Bubble

As the scale of lockdowns and restrictions spread, technology companies were among the major beneficiaries, which meant that the equity rebound was, once again, highly concentrated. Consumer demand for hardware and technology services surged as consumers were forced to stay at home. A survey by Twilio suggested that the pandemic had accelerated the digital transformation by 6 years; it reported that 97% of executives had accelerated their digital transformation because of Covid-19, and 79% had increased budgets for digital transformation.[11]

---

[11] Koetsier, J. (2020). 97% of executives say Covid-19 sped up digital transformation. Available at https://www.forbes.com/sites/johnkoetsier/2020/09/10/97-of-executives-say-covid-19-sped-up-digital-transformation/.

Chipmaker Nvidia was the best performing of the mega cap technology stocks in 2021, with a 127% increase in value (a rise of more than 350% since March 2020), pushing up its market capitalisation to $741 billion and making it the seventh-biggest tech stock.[12]

The company then sharply underperformed in 2022, falling more than 50% from its peak, although it reached new highs in 2023 on the back of optimism related to artificial intelligence (AI), and became the fifth-biggest stock in the United States (up c. 300% from its lows in October 2022, with a market cap of over $1 trillion).

Other tech companies, such as Zoom, had increased even more (by over 700% between March 2020 and its peak in October of that year). However, its stock price subsequently returned to the pre-Covid level as lockdowns ended. Meanwhile, supported by an ultra-low cost of capital, flows into the private equity markets that fund new businesses surged. In 2021, according to the *Financial Times*, $330 billion of new cash went into US technology start-ups, twice the value in 2020, which itself was twice the level 3 years earlier.[13]

Venture capital investment (early-stage investment) also ballooned. FactSet estimates that over $600 billion in venture capital was invested globally in 2021, more than double the total in 2020.[14] Low interest rates supported ever higher valuations. Over 500 venture-capital-backed companies became 'unicorns' in 2021 (companies with a valuation of over $1 billion), nearly three times the number that had achieved that valuation in 2020 (FactSet). Some start-ups increased in value in the private markets to over $10 billion – this group included the cryptocurrency exchange FTX Trading, which reached a valuation of $25 billion (it later collapsed on 11 November 2022).

---

[12] Levy, A. (2021, December 24). Here are the top-performing technology stocks of 2021. CNBC.
[13] Waters, R. (2022, August 1). Venture capital's silent crash: When the tech boom met reality. *Financial Times*.
[14] Haley, B. (2022). Venture capital 2021 recap—a record breaking year. Available at https://insight.factset.com/venture-capital-2021-recap-a-record-breaking-year.

According to McKinsey, fundraising in the private equity space increased by 20% in 2021, or $1.2 trillion; assets under management surged to an all-time high of nearly $10 trillion.[15]

Ultra-low interest rates and government furlough schemes had buoyed confidence in retail demand for stocks. Retail investors lacked alternative assets to generate decent returns, the so-called TINA effect: there is no alternative.[16] In January 2021 alone, roughly six million Americans downloaded a retail stock brokerage app, adding to the 10 million who had already done so in 2020.[17]

One of the most emblematic symbols of this bubble was the emergence of so-called MEME stocks (companies that gained an almost cult-like following among retail investors through social media on investor platforms such as Reddit). Perhaps one of the most infamous of these was the video game company GameStop Corp. Its stock became the target of short selling by hedge funds and roughly 140% of its public float stock had been sold short (hedge funds pay a fee to 'borrow' the stock and sell it, hoping to gain from a fall in the stock and then buy it back at a lower price). Its stock rose from $5 in the summer of 2020 to over $300 in January of 2021, and then reached a high of $483, causing huge losses for some hedge funds.[18]

Buoyed by furlough cheques sent out in the United States, private investors started to take on more leverage. According to *Forbes*, margin debt balances (money borrowed to buy shares) hit an all-time high of $778 billion in early 2021, nearly 37 times the value held in March 2000 at the peak of the technology bubble, while the ratio of margin debt to cash (debt used to fund equity investments

[15] Averstad, P., Beltrán, A., Brinkman, M., Maia, P., Pinshaw, G., Quigley, D., *et al.* (2023). McKinsey Global Private Markets Review: Private markets turn down the volume. Available at https://www.mckinsey.com/industries/private-equity-and-principal-investors/our-insights/mckinseys-private-markets-annual-review.

[16] The term 'There is No Alternative' was coined during the Thatcher years when it was used as a political slogan.

[17] Deloitte Center for Financial Services (2021). The rise of newly empowered retail investors. Availableathttps://www2.deloitte.com/content/dam/Deloitte/us/Documents/financial-services/us-the-rise-of-newly-empowered-retail-investors-2021.pdf?ref=zoya-blog.

[18] Kaissar (2021). GameStop Furor Inflicts Lasting Pain on Hedge Funds. Bloomberg.

relative to the cash balance of investors) reached 72% versus 79% at the peak of the technology bubble.[19]

The fervour for anything 'tech' that could benefit from this ultra-low cost of capital flowed into public markets as well. On 19 November, the tech-heavy Nasdaq stock index in the United States reached an all-time high of 16,057, an astonishing 133% higher than the trough it had reached in March of that year. By the end of 2021, on most measures, the US equity market was trading at record valuations.

Within markets, the leadership in performance of the technology sector, which had been dominant since the financial crisis, accelerated. This sector had generally experienced better earnings growth, but the surge in spending online and on technology platforms during the pandemic appeared to boost the relative competitive advantage of tech companies. The valuation of the future cash flows of these 'Growth' companies accelerated dramatically as interest rates fell (see Exhibit 9.7).

The biggest stocks got bigger and more concentrated in the main indices. The largest US technology companies (Facebook, Apple, Amazon, Microsoft and Google parent Alphabet) continued to outperform the broader market. By July 2020, these five companies had risen by around 30% since the start of the year, while the rest of the market was virtually flat. These Big Tech companies had grown to 22% of the S&P 500 market capitalisation, the highest concentration of the index since the early 1980s.[20]

Adding to bubble concerns was the other exceptional feature of the recent initial public offering (IPO) surge – the preponderance of Special Purpose Acquisition Companies (SPACs) – or 'blank cheque' companies, which are publicly held investment vehicles created to be merged with a company, thereby bringing it public.

---

[19] Ponciano, J. (2021). Is the stock market about to crash?
[20] Scheid, B. (2020). Top 5 tech stocks' S&P 500 dominance raises fears of bursting bubble. The previous highest yearly average concentration was in 1982 when AT&T, IBM, Exxon, GE and GM reached a combined market capitalisation worth 17% of the broader market – although these stocks spanned a number of different industries.

Exhibit 9.7   The premium of Growth relative to Value has increased sharply since 2018: 12-month forward P/E premium

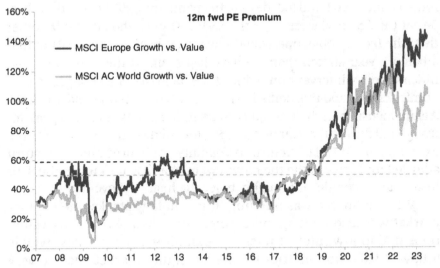

SOURCE: Goldman Sachs Global Investment Research

SPAC IPOs comprised over 50% of US IPOs in 2020 – reaching by far the highest number on record. And in the first three weeks of 2021 alone, 56 US SPACs were brought to market.[21]

The Medicine Worked

The combination of extreme policy support and success with Covid vaccines broadened out the market rally. The scale of the financial market rebound in 2021 should not be understated.

The combination of huge fiscal expansions, zero interest rate policies, QE and the success of vaccinations boosted optimism as quickly

---

[21] A SPAC begins with a sponsor forming a corporation and working with underwriters to list the SPAC on a public exchange. In the IPO, a SPAC sells units consisting of a share and a fractional warrant. The proceeds of a SPAC's IPO are placed in a trust and invested in Treasury notes. The SPAC typically has 2 years to identify a merger target and complete the merger, otherwise the SPAC liquidates and distributes the funds in the trust back to the public shareholders.

as it had previously collapsed. In 2021, the S&P 500 rose by 27% (or 29% including dividends), ranking in the 85th percentile of all annual returns since 1962. Indeed, despite the pandemic, 2021 capped the best 3-year (and 5-year) stretch for the S&P 500 since the late 1990s; other than the tech bubble, one would have to go back to the 1930s to find a better 3-year stretch than we have just seen. At the same time, significant policy intervention reduced the 'tail risk' of a collapse in economic activity, and this helped to reduce volatility in financial markets. Again, focusing on the US equity market, the largest S&P 500 peak-to-trough fall during the year was just 5%, the mildest in 25 years (with the exception of 2017). The 'return-to-volatility' (or Sharpe ratio, the return adjusted for how volatile the moves were) was 2.2, ranking in the 83rd historical percentile and roughly twice the historical average.

While a bubble was building in technology stocks, the broader market was also looking increasingly stretched, with rising valuations due to low interest rates. As Exhibit 9.8 shows, most widely followed valuation metrics for the US equity market became very

Exhibit 9.8 S&P 500 absolute and relative valuation as of 31 December 2021: data for percentiles since 1972

Valuation metric	Aggregate index		Median stock	
	Dec-21	Historical %ile	Dec-21	Historical %ile
US Market Cap / GDP	221%	100%	NA	NA
EV / Sales	3.5x	100%	4.0x	99%
Cash Flow Yield (CFO)	5.3%	98%	5.3%	100%
EV / EBITDA	16.5x	97%	15.1x	98%
Price / Book	5.0x	96%	4.5x	100%
Cyclically Adjusted P/E (CAPE)	34.7x	95%	NA	NA
Forward P/E	22.0x	3%	20.4x	97%
Free Cash Flow Yield	3.5%	63%	3.7%	73%
Median absolute metric		97%		99%
Yield gap vs real 10-year UST	582bp	63%	634bp	29%
Yield gap vs IG	243bp	46%	295bp	33%
Yield gap vs 10-year UST	326bp	42%	378bp	28%
Median relative metric		46%		29%

SOURCE: Goldman Sachs Global Investment Research

stretched relative to their longer-term history. This was true for the majority of equity markets at the index level, but also became true for the median stock, particularly in the United States.

Another way to look at this is to consider the ratio of the value of market capitalisation (the market value of companies) to GDP. Of course, these two measures are quite different: GDP is the value of output in a single year, and the value of companies reflects the expected return long into the future. Nonetheless, this ratio had surpassed even the high values experienced during the technology bubble in 2000. It only started to reverse as interest rates began to rise coming out of the pandemic (Exhibit 9.9).

The pandemic bear market also marked the beginning of a new cycle, and one in which concerns around deflation (the main risk that investors had faced since the collapse of the tech bubble at the turn of the century) were starting to fade. As investors became less fearful of deep recessions, bond yields began to rise after years of declines. The US 10-year Treasury (government bonds with a maturity of 10 years) returned −4%, ranking in just the 8th percentile.

Exhibit 9.9   On longer-term comparisons, the US equity market continues to look stretched: market cap to GDP (%)

SOURCE: Goldman Sachs Global Investment Research

The 33 percentage point spread between the S&P 500 and the US 10-year Treasury return ranked in the 95th percentile.

The Pandemic and Inflation

The optimism that dominated markets in 2021 was, however, about to be dealt yet another blow, this time with the emergence of inflation – something that investors and policymakers had ignored as a risk given that it had remained dormant for so long. According to the World Bank, at the end of 2021, 12-month inflation was running above 5% in over half of the 34 countries they define as 'advanced economies' and in over 70% of the 109 emerging economies, about twice as high as it had been at the end of 2020.

Initially, many of the inflationary problems appeared to be related to supply-chain issues caused by the pandemic, excess savings (Exhibit 9.10) and pent-up demand.

Exhibit 9.10   US savings rate spiked above 30% during the pandemic: US personal savings rate

SOURCE: Goldman Sachs Global Investment Research

Exhibit 9.11 Market pricing implies a 30% probability that US headline CPI will exceed 3% over the next 5 years

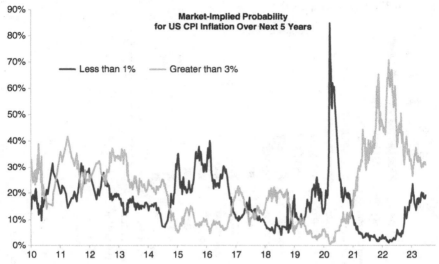

SOURCE: Federal Reserve

By January 2022, oil prices had surged 77% from their level in December 2020. A strong dollar did not help the emerging economies, as many suffered from currency weakness that exacerbated the problem. Food prices also started to rise, with 79% of emerging economies experiencing food price inflation of above 5% during 2021 (World Bank).

For the first time since before the financial crisis, inflation expectations in many countries started to rise (Exhibit 9.11).

From Disinflation to Reflation

The backdrop of the Global Financial Crisis was disinflationary in the real economy because the collapse in asset prices and private sector de-leveraging increased savings. But, as it was also associated with significant falls in interest rates and credit creation (via QE and related policies), it ultimately led to rising asset prices.

Exhibit 9.12   Wide dispersion between asset price inflation and real economy inflation: total return performance in local currency, January 2009–February 2020

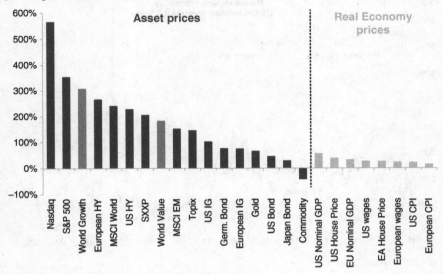

SOURCE: Goldman Sachs Global Investment Research

As Exhibit 9.12 shows, since 2009, most prices in the real economy (on the right-hand side of the chart) had been very subdued, while across asset markets there had been significant inflation. Furthermore, the highest inflation was in the longest-duration Growth assets (the Nasdaq and 'Global Growth' factor), while the weakest was seen in the markets more levered to Value (Europe and Japan) and in shorter-duration 'Global Value' stocks.

By contrast, in the post-pandemic recovery phase, the shift towards a combination of monetary support and fiscal expansion, coupled with a strong synchronised economic rebound (from a record deep recession), resulted in a more reflationary cycle. Supply-side constraints also became a significant problem at a time when accumulated savings boosted pent-up demand as lockdowns came to an end.

As Exhibit 9.13 shows, on average, equities have the highest valuations when inflation is low, at between 1% and 2% – any lower

Exhibit 9.13   Since the 1970s, the highest valuations have been reached when inflation is below 3%: average 12-month forward P/E within US CPI bands

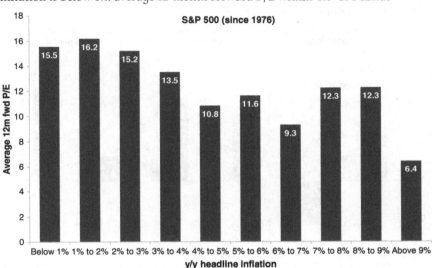

SOURCE: Goldman Sachs Global Investment Research

and the valuation starts to soften as fears of recession emerge. High inflation is nearly always associated with lower valuations.

An additional perspective can be taken from both levels of, and changes in, inflation. The combination that tends to be most supportive for equity markets is either when inflation is rising from very low levels (and the risks of deflation are falling), or when high levels of inflation are moderating.

For equities and bonds, the worst combination is high inflation (above 3%) that is rising (Exhibit 9.14). By contrast, the impact on markets tends to be more benign when inflation is above 3% but moderating. For equities in particular, the highest returns tend to be available when inflation is below 1% but rising; this is often associated with a recovery from a recession and the diminishing risk of deflation (and therefore is not particularly supportive for bond markets).[22]

[22] Mueller-Glissmann, C., Rizzi, A., Wright, I. and Oppenheimer, P. (2021). The Balanced Bear – Part 1: Low(er) returns and latent drawdown risk. GOAL – Global Strategy Paper No. 27. Available at:https://publishing.gs.com/content/research/en/reports/2017/11/28/d41623eb-3dd2-4e45-a455-3d19d310e998.html.

Exhibit 9.14   Steady returns with range-bound inflation – a reversal from extremes tends to be bullish: annualised average monthly real total returns (data since September 1929)

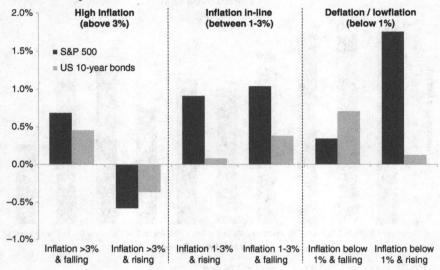

SOURCE: Goldman Sachs Global Investment Research

Getting Real – The Shift Higher in the Real Cost of Capital

As inflation picked up, central banks rapidly started to raise interest rates. Gradual moves in inflation expectations, and therefore in bond yields, tend to be more benign for equity markets than fast moves. Equity markets do not tend to perform well in periods of sharp and sudden changes in bond yields. S&P 500 returns, for example, have typically been negative in months when bond yields have risen by more than two standard deviations.

When interest rates began to rise, they did so at an extraordinary pace, albeit from an extremely low starting point. In 2022, the rise in global interest rates ranks among the 11 fastest changes, over any given year, since the fourteenth century, and the fastest since 1900 (Exhibits 9.15 and 9.16).

Exhibit 9.15   The 2022/23 rise in global interest rates is among the fastest changes since the fourteenth century: 5-year change in world nominal interest rates (2020/23 change for latest value)

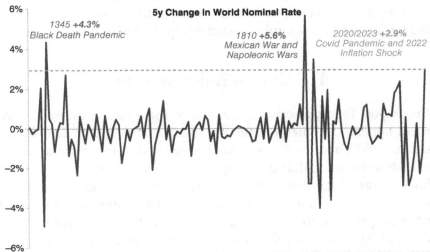

SOURCE: Bank of England Millennium Dataset

Exhibit 9.16   World nominal interest rates reached historically low levels in 2020

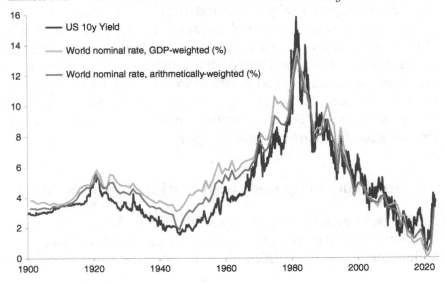

SOURCE: Bank of England Millennium Dataset

A shift in the cost of capital of this speed was likely to cause rapid changes in financial markets and it did so in various ways. Valuation and diversification began to matter again, sector leadership started to reverse, with Value areas of the market outperforming Growth, and geographical leadership started to broaden out.

The Golden Rules Resurface

In the post-financial-crisis cycle, two of the golden rules of investment appeared to turn on their heads. The first is that diversification should enhance risk-adjusted returns, and the second is that valuation matters, that is, things that are expensive should offer a lower return than things that are cheap. But these golden rules no longer seemed to apply. Diversification across asset markets would not have greatly enhanced returns: a simple split between 60% equities and 40% bonds would have generated some of the highest risk-adjusted returns for a century without the need to invest in other asset classes. In the equity world, diversification would not have helped. A portfolio made up solely of US stocks – and for that matter US technology – would have significantly outperformed anything more geographically mixed and diversified by industry.

In 2022, however, diversification began to help investors. A mix of real and nominal assets would have boosted returns, for example. In the equity world, the United States no longer outperformed: a more geographically spread portfolio would have achieved higher returns. Valuation also started to become relevant again as the cost of capital increased. For the first time since before the financial crisis, valuation had started to matter again.

Sector Leadership and the Rotation Towards Value

As discussed earlier, the post-financial-crisis cycle was dominated by Growth companies (long-duration stocks and beneficiaries of falling interest rates) significantly outperforming Value companies (cheaper companies typically in mature and heavily disrupted industries that were most negatively impacted by lower inflation and interest rates).

With stronger economic growth and higher inflation expectations, the leadership of equity markets shifted for the first time since before the financial crisis of 2008/09. Rising bond yields and increasing nominal GDP (real GDP plus inflation) were most positive for Cyclical and Value sectors, such as banks, autos, basic resources and construction, which are also among the sectors with the highest operational leverage (the highest beta of earnings to changes in global nominal GDP).

The impact of inflation and bond yields on sector returns started to be reflected at the regional level as some markets are much more exposed to Growth sectors (for example, the United States and China), while others are more exposed to Value sectors (such as Japan and Europe). Value sectors, such as commodities and banks, had been the biggest laggards of the post-financial-crisis era because they are the most positively correlated to higher yields and inflation. With the rise in interest rates and inflation, they started to outperform. The pattern of relative returns started to resemble that of the secular 'Fat and Flat' era of the 1970s. Exhibit 9.17 shows that this was a period of low returns in financial assets that generally failed to keep up with inflation in the real economy (on the right-hand side of the chart). Real assets such as gold, real estate and commodities were the best-performing assets, while long-duration equities such as the US equity market and Nasdaq had been among the worst (the latter also suffered after the 'Nifty Fifty' bubble that had preceded it burst). This pattern was the opposite of the one in the period between 2009 and 2020, shown in Exhibit 9.12.

As Exhibit 9.18 shows, the pattern of returns in markets from 2022 was reversed relative to the 2009–2020 era (Exhibit 9.12 shown earlier) and was much more akin to the pattern between 1973 and 1983 (Exhibit 9.17).

This time, rising inflation in the real economy (on the right-hand side of the chart) meant that most financial assets (on the left)

Exhibit 9.17   Asset price inflation and 'real economy' inflation during 1973–1983: total return performance in local currency

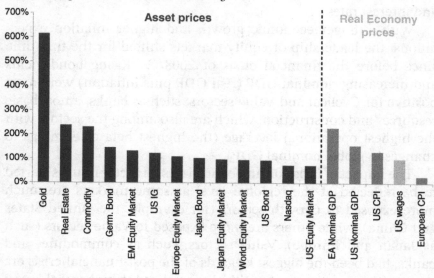

SOURCE: Goldman Sachs Global Investment Research

Exhibit 9.18   The pattern of returns since 2022 shows a reversal of the cycle post-financial crisis: total return performance in local currency since January 2022

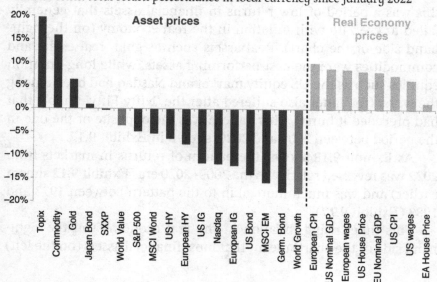

SOURCE: Goldman Sachs Global Investment Research

de-rated and generated a negative return. Leadership rotated away from high-growth strategies (the major beneficiaries of low interest rates) and the US equity markets, both the Nasdaq and a group of global high growth companies, were among the poorest performers. This leadership rotation benefited some of the more traditional industries, which are the bigger beneficiaries of higher inflation. For example, the commodity sector can pass on higher costs (commodities) to their consumers, while banks generally benefit from higher interest rates as they can achieve a wider spread between deposits and lending rates. Commodities and 'real' assets were in the driving seat, just as they had been in the inflationary era of the 1970s.

The shift towards higher inflation and interest rates also reversed the pattern of leadership geographically. The United States, with a higher exposure to technology and other growth industries, benefited disproportionately from low interest rates in the post-financial-crisis cycle of 2009–2020 (Exhibit 9.19). The net present value of

Exhibit 9.19   Europe's outperformance versus the United States has reversed despite the improvement in earnings: price return performance and 12-month forward EPS, STOXX 600 versus S&P 500 (in local currency)

SOURCE: Goldman Sachs Global Investment Research

expected long-term future growth (how equities are valued) rose as a consequence of the lower discount rate.

At the same time, the historically low level of interest rates granted easy access to a cheap and plentiful source of funding for Growth companies. With sharply higher interest rates, these benefits weakened. By contrast, the more traditional industries that have a higher weight in the stock markets of Europe and Japan – such as banks, utilities, industrials, auto makers and commodity producers – experienced stronger demand coming out of the pandemic and were generally able to pass on many of their higher costs to consumers.

Part III

The Post-Modern Cycle

Chapter 10
The Post-Modern Cycle

We live in the postmodern world, where everything is possible and almost nothing is certain.

—Vaclev Havel

I describe the super cycle from 1982 to 2020 as the Modern Cycle because it differed from most of the more traditional cycles that preceded it, in that it was unusually long and characterised by low macro volatility (economic activity and inflation) and a falling cost of capital.

There were crises over this period, of course, but mainly financial markets rebounded strongly from these as they responded to policy interventions, largely in the form of interest rate cuts. Investors became increasingly conditioned to expect policy support when faced with growth weakness or other exogenous shocks. At the time, investment returns across nearly all financial assets were heavily influenced by the trend to lower interest rates.

In the post-financial-crisis era of quantitative easing (QE), equity markets staged a powerful recovery, but selectivity mattered. Returns became increasingly bifurcated by 'factors' – the macro sensitivities of companies to the key drivers. In this case, what mattered was the impact of zero interest rates in an environment of low growth. So-called Growth (or long-duration) companies, with prospects of high growth into the longer-term future, prospered, whereas companies in mature industries, often experiencing excess supply, generally underperformed.

Leadership and return profiles in equity markets shifted once again with the end of pandemic restrictions and the era of ultra-low interest rates in 2021. A new inflationary dynamic unfolded, forcing interest rates to rise from the historically low emergency levels that were put in place after the Global Financial Crisis. The shift in the level of interest rates has driven a new discipline in the economic system and in valuations of financial assets as we enter what I describe as the Post-Modern Cycle.

Investors naturally focus on the shorter-term inflection points in markets – assessing when interest rates will move down or economic growth improve, for example – but less focus is placed on the longer-term trends. Examining the structural factors that are shifting relative to those of the Modern Cycle can help investors to be better positioned to deal with the risks and opportunities of the Post-Modern Cycle.

Structural Shifts and Opportunities

A new paradigm for investors is gradually unfolding, reflecting the way macroeconomic and political dynamics are evolving. Several key drivers of markets that have been dominant over the past generation are reaching inflection points.

It is likely that the Post-Modern Cycle will reflect elements of classical cycles (such as those before the 1980s, when there tended to be higher inflation and higher government spending), as well as some characteristics of the Modern Cycle (with lower levels of interest rates and economic growth). But entirely new developments around issues such as decarbonisation, greater regionalisation and the impact of artificial intelligence (AI) are likely to generate new risks and opportunities, creating different sets of winners and losers, and, as new economic and geopolitical realities emerge, different styles of investment and opportunities will follow.

Generally, over the Modern Cycle, when economic problems arose, they tended to be driven by weakening demand; the source of the shock may have varied but the impact was generally via weaker consumption and, therefore, weaker economic activity. This was particularly true in the post-financial-crisis era, which was driven by a negative demand shock as the private sector de-levered (or needed to increase savings in the face of higher unemployment and lower house prices). The period became dominated by a backdrop of low interest rates and low inflation, accompanying very low economic growth.

Since many of these fundamentals had remained stable for such a long period of time, largely throughout the Modern Cycle and the post-financial-crisis cycles, investors increasingly priced a continuation of these trends into the future.

In contrast, the cycle that is emerging is being driven as much by a series of negative supply shocks emanating from the pandemic itself and the Russian war in Ukraine as it is by weaker demand. For the first time in decades, the reliance on complex integrated supply chains and 'just in time' inventories has come into question. Many companies have switched their attention away from efficiency and more towards the resilience of supplies. Geopolitical tensions between the United States and China have led companies to focus on the need to diversify supply chains and, as a result, a more regionally based economic model is starting to emerge. In addition, however, underinvestment has led to increasingly tight commodity markets at a time of historically low unemployment.

Differences from the Modern Cycle

In summary, the Post-Modern Cycle is likely to be driven by the following dynamics:

1. **A rise in the cost of capital.** Since the early 1980s interest rates and inflation have trended lower; they are now trending higher (albeit from record low levels) as we transition from QE to quantitative tightening (QT). This cycle is likely to experience higher yields, both nominal and real (adjusted for inflation).
2. **A slowdown in trend growth.** Lower population growth is reducing the long-term trend rate of growth, although the prospects for AI to boost productivity could provide an offset.
3. **A shift from globalisation to regionalisation.** Since the late 1980s we have been in an era of increasing globalisation triggered by technology (cheaper and more effective communication) and geopolitics (with the collapse of the Berlin Wall in 1989, India's accession to the World Trade Organization, WTO, in 1995 and China's in 2001). We are now entering an era of greater regionalisation driven by technology. Cheaper and less labour-intensive production is making on-shoring or near-shoring more viable. Decarbonisation is also shifting the emphasis to more locally sourced production, while increased geopolitical tensions and protectionist trade policies are creating a different set of commercial incentives.
4. **A rise in the cost of labour and commodities.** While the last 20 years were characterised by cheap and plentiful energy and labour, we are emerging from the pandemic with an environment of tighter labour and commodity markets.
5. **An increase in government spending and debt.** From the early 1980s we saw a combination of deregulation, smaller government, lower taxes, falling interest expenses for companies, rising profit shares of GDP and higher corporate profit margins; we are now entering a period of more regulation, bigger government (higher government shares of GDP), higher taxes,

rising interest expenses for companies and potentially lower profit shares of GDP.

6. **A rise in capital and infrastructure spending.** Since the start of this century, the share of capex spending to sales (investment in traditional capital such as plant and machinery) has trended down amid lower nominal GDP. Supported by a very low cost of capital, significant investment flowed into building new technology platforms and software, but this largely happened at the expense of spending on physical capital expenditure and infrastructure. Over the next decade, demands to simplify supply chains from a security and environmental, social and corporate governance (ESG) perspective, coupled with increased spending on defence and decarbonisation, are likely to push capex spending higher.

7. **Changing demographics.** An ageing of populations in many developed economies, with rising dependency ratios and increased cost burdens for governments, driving higher government borrowing and a higher tax burden.

8. **An increase in geopolitical tensions and the multipolar world.** In the aftermath of the collapse of the Soviet Union, a unipolar world generated an environment of greater perceived geopolitical stability. A move towards a more multipolar world order may increase uncertainty and, with it, risk premia and the cost of capital.

1. A Rise in the Cost of Capital

The modern era of disinflation started in the early 1980s. When Paul Volcker became Fed Chair in the summer of 1979, US inflation stood at over 11% and 10-year US Treasury yields had reached nearly 16%. Restrictive monetary policy designed to reduce inflation by constraining demand heralded a prolonged period of low inflation and strong growth, supported by positive supply-side reforms (Exhibit 10.1).

Exhibit 10.1 US financial conditions tightened significantly in 2022. Shaded areas: US NBER recessions

SOURCE: Goldman Sachs Global Investment Research

The downward trend in inflation, aided by the move towards independent central banks and inflation targets in the 1990s, accelerated following the collapse of the technology bubble in 2000 and China's accession to the WTO in 2001.

Inflation took another leg down following the financial crisis in 2008, which, with the de-leveraging of the private sector, prompted another major negative demand shock.[1] As we have seen, equities performed strongly from the 1980s through to the end of the century and the collapse of the technology bubble. Financial conditions indices – which measure the broad impact of monetary policy – trended ever lower.[2]

---

[1] The impact of the financial crisis was a sharp fall in demand, estimated to be around one-sixth of GDP in 2010 alone, and over $2 trillion worth of assets in financial institutions were written down. Oxenford, M. (2018). The lasting effects of the financial crisis have yet to be felt. Chatham House Expert Comment.

[2] Financial conditions are broad indexes that estimate the overall impact of financial variables on economic activity and typically include policy rates, credit spreads, equity prices and exchange rates.

Over this period, equity returns were high: for example, 10-year real returns in US equities bought between 1982 and 1992 annualised at around 15%. At the same time, corporate earnings growth was strong, although valuation expansion (for example, rising price/earnings ratios) accounted for a large share of the returns as interest rates fell.

Even after the trauma of the financial crisis, equities continued the secular bull market supported by ever lower interest rates; the total return of the S&P 500 was positive in 17 of the 19 years leading up to 2021. The collapse in inflation and interest rates benefited bond returns as well.

The Re-emergence of Inflation

During the pandemic, financial markets were pricing very little probability of inflation or interest rates rising in the future (Exhibit 10.2). For example, at the end of 2020, the markets (based on options pricing) were pricing around a 90% probability that inflation would be below 2% in the Euro area. Put another way, markets were pricing a probability close to 100% that inflation would not be above 3%. This, as we know, turned out to be entirely incorrect: Euro area-wide inflation peaked in October 2022 at 10.7%.

The speed of the changes largely came as a shock to both investors and policymakers.

As inflation expectations collapsed, so too did government bond yields. This was also supported by years of central bank buying of debt through QE.

The negative demand shock unleashed by the pandemic proved to be more temporary than had been assumed. Demand had been delayed rather than reduced. Household balance sheets were strong as a function of forced savings and furlough schemes. As a result, the negative supply shock turned out to be more significant and persistent than the weakness in demand. The war in Ukraine added to these supply problems, ultimately making these shocks more inflationary.

Exhibit 10.2   During the pandemic, financial markets were pricing very little probability of inflation: option-implied distribution of inflation based on 5-year inflation caps/floors

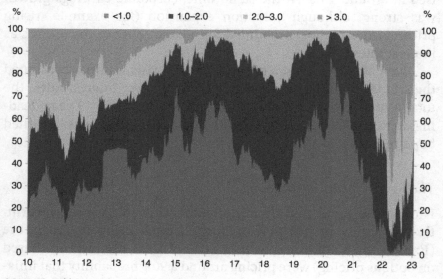

SOURCE: Goldman Sachs Global Investment Research

As pandemic restrictions began to unwind and demand recovered, central banks were caught off guard by the persistence of higher inflation. Chair Jerome H. Powell of the Federal Reserve had argued that the inflationary impact of supply-side disruptions from the pandemic was 'transitory'. It was not until late November 2021, in answer to a question during a testimony to the Senate Banking Committee, that he said 'it's probably a good time to retire that word'. Having guided the markets to assume very modest rate rises in 2021, the Federal Reserve then increased its rate by 25bp in March 2022, the first increase in 3 years, but followed with a 50bp hike in May and then a series of 75bp hikes in June, July, September and November.

Consequently, the pricing of everything – from interest rates to equity markets – ultimately needed to adjust to this dramatic shift.

For stocks, however, there is some protection. Equities are shares in businesses and, in aggregate, these businesses make a claim on future growth. But, as the revenues of companies are nominal – that is, they grow in line with nominal GDP – their profits and dividends typically grow if inflation picks up. If companies can raise their prices as much as their costs rise, then they will protect investors to some extent from higher inflation.

Of course, this is not true for government bonds or cash. These may be safe, in so far as the governments that back them can honour their debt (and avoid a default), and they also provide a coupon or guaranteed income. However, this income is not linked to inflation and, therefore, becomes less valuable in an environment where prices are rising and the fixed income that you receive in the future is worth much less when you consider inflation.

As Exhibit 10.3 shows, the gap between dividend yields and nominal or real yields had reached extremely high levels as investors increased exposure to low-risk government bonds given

Exhibit 10.3 The gap between dividend yields and nominal or real yields reached extremely high levels after the financial crisis: S&P 500 24-month-forward dividend yield vs US 10-year rates

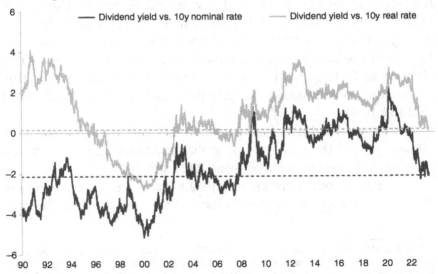

SOURCE: Goldman Sachs Global Investment Research

concerns about recession and deflation after the financial crisis and the impact of QE, and as regulation forced purchases by insurance companies and pension funds. While equities may not have much upside in absolute terms, the risk balance has shifted, thereby raising the relative attractiveness in portfolio allocation towards real assets and equities.

Nevertheless, across financial assets, a higher cost of capital and inflation should leave much less room for valuations to expand, leading to lower returns overall. The value of companies that can compound returns over longer periods of time should also prosper; these would include companies that are reinvesting at a higher rate to generate longer-term growth, as well as those that are paying out regular and predictable dividends.

2. A Slowdown in Trend Growth

While a rising cost of capital should reduce the current value of equities, weaker longer-term economic growth (which companies are making a claim on) will have a similar impact. Global real (adjusted for inflation) GDP growth had already slowed from an average of 3.6% per year in the decade before the financial crisis to 3.2% in the decade before the pandemic. The main driver of this slowing in GDP growth was a combination of lower population growth and weaker productivity, in part related to less globalisation (Exhibit 10.4).

However, Goldman Sachs economists estimate that we have already passed the peak rate of global economic growth and that the pace will average 2.8% between 2024 and 2029.[3]

Population will play an important role in the global growth deceleration. Population growth has halved over the past 50 years,

---

[3] Daly, K. and Gedminas, T. (2022). The path to 2075 — slower global growth, but convergence remains intact. Goldman Sachs Global Investment Research, Global Economics Paper. Available at https://publishing.gs.com/content/research/en/reports/2022/12/06/af8feefc-a65c-4d5e-bcb6-51175d816ff1.html.

Exhibit 10.4 Global potential growth on a gradually declining path. Global GDP growth: solid line – 5-year centred average; dotted line – annual growth

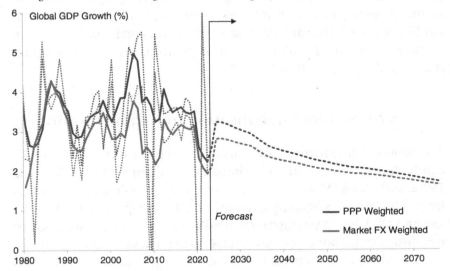

SOURCE: Goldman Sachs Global Investment Research

from around 2% annually to around 1% currently and, according to the United Nations, will slow to zero by 2075.[4]

Other factors may also play a role. The Congressional Budget Office (CBO) in the United States, for example, has projected that climate change will lower real GDP in 2051 by 1% relative to what it would have been if climate conditions between 2021 and 2051 were the same as at the end of the twentieth century.[5]

Slowing economic growth implies lower aggregate growth in company revenues and earnings. This, coupled with higher interest rates and cost of capital, implies lower longer-term index returns for investors. There are, however, likely to be some offsets to these trends. Perhaps one of the most important potential

---

[4] United Nations (2022). *World Population Prospects* 2022: *Summary of Results*. New York: United Nations Department of Economic and Social Affairs.

[5] Congressional Budget Office (2021). Budgetary effects of climate change and of potential legislative responses to it. CBO Publication No. 57019.

drivers of higher growth in the future could come from improved productivity. While productivity gains have generally been elusive in recent years, new technologies in the areas of robotics and AI could enhance future growth relative to trend, particularly based on population trends. I look at this, and the impact of technology on markets, in the next chapter.

3. A Shift from Globalisation to Regionalisation

The geopolitical environment is also evolving in a way that is significantly different to the one that shaped the secular bull market of the 1990s and 2000s 'Modern' era. The economic problems of the 1970s helped to bring in sweeping economic reforms in the 1980s. The Reagan and Thatcher 'revolutions' resulted in waves of deregulation, lower unionisation, privatisation, lower taxes and the end of credit controls.

The pivotal Uruguay Round of General Agreement on Tariffs and Trade (GATT) negotiations that took place in 1986 included services and capital, as well as textiles and agriculture, and was the first time that developing countries played an active role. This marked the start of a new era of globalisation that was to expand rapidly following the collapse of the Berlin Wall in 1989, the signing of the North American Free Trade Agreement (NAFTA) in 1994, India joining the WTO in 1995 and, finally, China joining in 2001, around the time of the Doha Development Round, whose objective was to lower trade barriers around the world, and thus facilitate increased global trade.

Between 1995 and 2010, the pace of world trade growth was twice that of global GDP (Exhibit 10.5), although it peaked after the financial crisis.[6]

As Exhibit 10.6 shows, China experienced a sharp rise in its share of global trade as it increasingly took on the mantle of factory of the world (just as the United Kingdom had done during the Industrial Revolution).

---

[6] Cigna, S., Gunnella, V. and Quaglietti, L. (2022). Global value chains: Measurement, trends and drivers. ECB Occasional Paper No. 2022/289.

Exhibit 10.5   Global goods trade peaked as a share of GDP in 2008: world
merchandise imports plus exports (% of GDP)

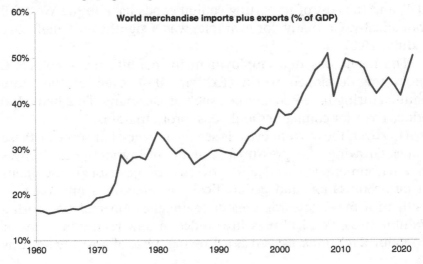

SOURCE: Goldman Sachs Global Investment Research

Exhibit 10.6   China's share of global trade and manufacturing increased sharply
after its entry to the WTO

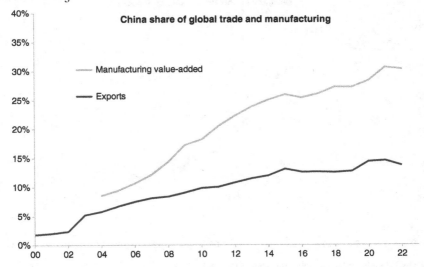

SOURCE: Goldman Sachs Global Investment Research

The outsourcing of manufacturing to China and other lower-cost regions of the world boosted global trade and profit shares of GDP, and the cost of importing capital goods back to the West fell dramatically. Germany, for example, was a significant beneficiary (Exhibit 10.7).

The result was that employment in manufacturing collapsed across the developed world (Exhibit 10.8), even in the more manufacturing-based economies such as Germany. This helped to reduce costs for companies and boost profit margins.

However, the current cycle is seeing a reversal of some of these trends. Growing ESG pressures (a model of investing that focuses on environmental, social and governance priorities), the focus on decarbonisation and geopolitical considerations are likely to result in a move towards greater regionalisation and on-shoring (Exhibit 10.9). Political pressures reflect a new reality in terms of geopolitical tensions, as well as a growing sense of hostility towards

Exhibit 10.7 German import prices decreased after China joined the WTO

SOURCE: Goldman Sachs Global Investment Research

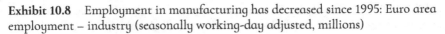

Exhibit 10.8   Employment in manufacturing has decreased since 1995: Euro area employment – industry (seasonally working-day adjusted, millions)

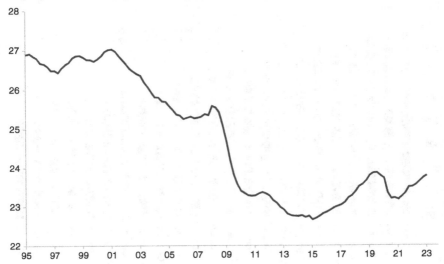

SOURCE: Goldman Sachs Global Investment Research

the implications of globalisation among the voting public in Western democracies (Exhibit 10.10).

The increased role of protectionism reflects these political realities and the way in which social attitudes have changed: virtually all countries now have a worse perception of globalisation. This has been reflected in the rise in populist political parties and leaders, as well as in increased nationalism in many countries.

While there may be many reasons for the change in public opinion towards globalisation, including the loss of manufacturing jobs in the West, anxiety has increased due to rising inequalities, as reflected in both incomes and wealth.[7]

An Ipsos survey conducted with the World Economic Forum shows a cooling of support for globalisation. Only 48% of those

---

[7] Organisation for Economic Co-operation and Development (2017). Towards a better globalisation: How Germany can respond to the critics. Better Policies Series.

Exhibit 10.9   Western democracies are less in favour of globalisation: percentage of respondents who agree with the statement 'overall, globalisation is a good thing for my country'

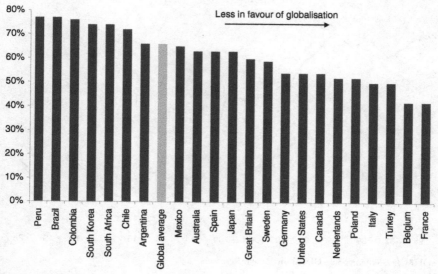

SOURCE: Ipsos

surveyed across 25 countries believe that globalisation is a good thing for their country, 10 percentage points below the number in 2019, with support as low as 42% in the United States, 40% in Italy and 27% in France. Furthermore, 37% across the 25 countries agreed that there should be more trade barriers to limit imports of foreign goods and services in their country, compared with 27% who disagreed.

Geopolitical shifts are also shaping attitudes in the world's two biggest economies. A 2021 survey by the Pew Research Center showed that 89% of US adults now see China as a competitor or enemy, and 67% have 'cold' feelings towards China, up from 46% in 2018.[8]

A further driver of the shift towards more localisation and regionalisation has come from the impact of the pandemic on

---

[8] Myers, J. (2021). This is what people think about trade and globalization. World Economic Forum.

Exhibit 10.10   Periods of increasing globalisation saw a rise in inequality: United States, income and wealth ratio of top 1% to bottom 50%

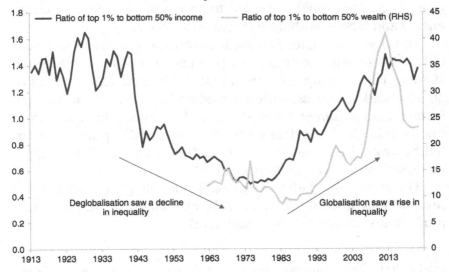

SOURCE: World Inequality Database, Goldman Sachs Global Investment Research

supply chains. The fragility and over-reliance on 'just in time' inventory systems and supply chains that have arisen since the pandemic, coupled with growing trade tensions, have prompted many companies actively to diversify to improve supply-chain resilience.

Less world trade and a replication of supply chains should result in higher costs for companies and lower profit margins. Investors are likely to continue to reward companies that can sustain high and stable margins.

4. A Rise in the Cost of Labour and Commodities

Significant investment in the 1990s and 2000s meant that there was excess capacity in commodity exploration in the post-financial-crisis era. Meanwhile, globalisation pushed labour costs down in real terms, particularly for unskilled labour, as it facilitated significant outsourcing of lower-skilled manufacturing jobs from Western economies. The combination led to an era of plentiful and cheap energy and labour, with little incentive to invest.

The Organisation for Economic Co-operation and Development (OECD) calculates, for example, that between 1990 and 2009 the share of labour compensation in national income fell in 26 out of 30 advanced countries, with the median labour share of national income falling from 66.1% to 61.7%. In the United Kingdom, Office for National Statistics data shows that the relative price of labour fell by around 20% between 2009 and 2015 as the labour supply increased by almost 4 million, or 12.5%.

The expansion of effective global labour supply (Exhibit 10.11) resulted in a downward trend in labour shares of output, while profit shares moved to record high levels.

Exhibit 10.11   The expansion of effective global labour supply resulted in a downward trend in labour shares of output: US nonfarm business sector labour share (portion of output remitted to labour in the form of compensation)

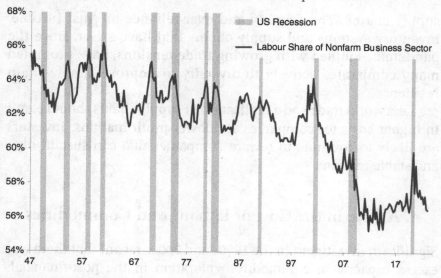

SOURCE: Goldman Sachs Global Investment Research

Exhibit 10.12   The corporate sector has experienced a significant rise in its share of GDP: United States

SOURCE: Goldman Sachs Global Investment Research

The relentless rise in corporate profit margins since the financial crisis certainly helped to offset what has been a weakening backdrop of sales growth (Exhibit 10.12). There are potentially many reasons why corporate margins increased dramatically over this period. The lack of pricing power in the labour market (reflecting the growing power of technology) and the rapid rise in margins in the faster-growing technology companies were both partly responsible. In addition, the growing trend of globalisation has been important. German wage inflation had, until the pandemic, been low and stable for many years, partly because if unions and workers pushed for higher wages, there would have been a greater likelihood of these higher-paid jobs shifting to Central Europe and other countries where the labour market is closely integrated into the German economy.

As labour supply increased, so too did the supply of commodities (albeit for different reasons). Following the collapse of the

Exhibit 10.13   Capex in real terms (adjusted for inflation) for both energy and metals has fallen over the past few years: 2002 $bn

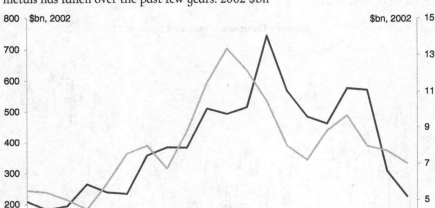

SOURCE: Goldman Sachs Global Investment Research

technology bubble and the financial crisis, there were excess energy supplies (Exhibit 10.13).

The shale gas revolution resulted in record low natural gas prices in the United States and had a profound impact on the energy industry globally.[9]

Oil prices increased from around $10 per barrel in the late 1990s to over $140 by mid-2008, before falling back into the mid-$30s later in 2008 as demand fell during the financial crisis. However, prices then accelerated back to around $100 by mid-2014, encouraging US exploration in shale gas and a sharp upward trend in production. The low-growth environment resulted in weaker demand, excess supply and little incentive to invest. Later, this resulted in a lack of energy as global demand recovered after the pandemic.

[9] Medlock, K.B. (2016). The shale revolution and its implications for the world energy market. *IEEJ Energy Journal*, **Special Issue**, pp. 89–95.

Post-Pandemic Reversal

The move towards more localisation since the pandemic has supported a shift towards tighter labour market conditions. Unemployment has reached record lows (Exhibit 10.14), and in many countries wages are rising. Data from the U.S. Bureau of Labor Statistics (BLS) shows that the number of workers involved in major work stoppages (strikes and similar activities) was about three times as high in 2021 as in 2020. In a sign of the times, Amazon workers in a New York warehouse voted to join a union for the first time in the United States, and labour disputes have become more commonplace across developed economies.

The tightness of the labour market continues to be a double-edged sword, supporting consumption on the one hand but contributing to a higher-for-longer risk of inflation on the other. This is true even in Germany, where an agreement reached in the summer

Exhibit 10.14   After the pandemic, unemployment rates reached a record low: US unemployment rate

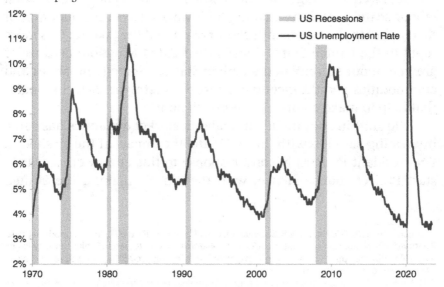

SOURCE: Goldman Sachs Global Investment Research

of 2023 on a public sector pay rise worth nearly 12% over 2 years (that is, about 6% per year) for around 2½ million employees at the federal and local level set a strong benchmark.

Energy markets have also become tight, following years of under-investment in an environment of excess supply after the financial crisis. The growth of ESG-based mandates in the investment community has starved many of these traditional carbon operators of capital.[10]

The Consequences and Investment Implications

This shift in the tightness of labour and energy markets will create winners and losers. Just as we saw in the 1970s, high labour and commodity costs are likely to generate more investment by companies in efforts to become more efficient. These will likely be technology companies creating logistics solutions, as well as technological implementations to build production using labour-saving techniques, including robotisation.

Research starting with Sir John Habakkuk has argued that labour scarcity, and the ensuing high wages, led to the adoption of machinery in the nineteenth century and that the take-up was more rapid in the United States than in the United Kingdom because of greater labour scarcity in the United States.[11] Scarcity of labour and commodities should incentivise more investment in technologies that help to make companies more efficient.

The shift in commodity and labour market dynamics has some interesting parallels with the 1970s and the impact of the oil shocks. US President Richard Nixon's response to this energy crisis was to start Project Independence, with the aim of making the United

[10] Oppenheimer, P., Jaisson, G., Bell, S., Peytavin, L. and Graziani, F. (2022). The Postmodern Cycle: Positioning for secular change. Goldman Sachs Global Investment Research, Global Strategy Paper. Available at https://publishing.gs.com/content/research/en/reports/2022/05/09/521c316d-2d20-4784-b955-57641712e9d0.html.
[11] Habakkuk, H. J. (1962). *American and British Technology in the Nineteenth Century: The Search for Labour-Saving Inventions.* Cambridge: Cambridge University Press.

States self-sufficient in meeting its own energy demands, a move that is echoed across Western governments today. The programme called on US citizens to make sacrifices, including lowering thermostats in homes (similar programmes were pursued in Europe following Russia's invasion of Ukraine).

High energy costs generated significant investment and innovation in energy efficiency. In the United States, several laws were adopted to increase fuel efficiency in the auto sector, such as the Energy Policy and Conservation Act (1975). By 1985, passenger cars were required to achieve fuel efficiency of 27.5 miles per gallon (mpg), and manufacturers would be required to pay a penalty of $5 per vehicle for each 0.1 mpg more than the standard (Exhibit 10.15).

Whereas US car manufacturers were slow to move away from large and fuel-inefficient cars, the Japanese were faster at developing smaller and more efficient cars, and so gained market share.

Exhibit 10.15   Fuel efficiency has increased by roughly 50% since 1950, with the biggest gains in the late 1970s and 1980s: miles per gallon – light-duty vehicles, short wheelbase

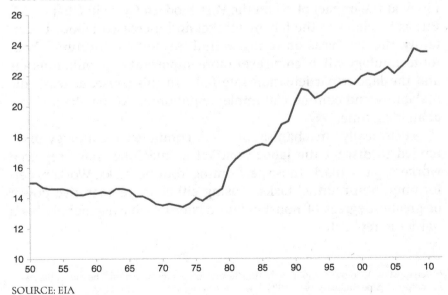

SOURCE: EIA

Furthermore, the rise in fuel costs triggered investment in new technologies, including the ethanol revolution in Brazil and the use of turbocharging, front-wheel-drive trains, lighter-weight materials and eight-speed automatic gearboxes. In other industries that were heavily energy consumptive, other savings were made. Tougher regulation, for example, helped the Swedish pulp and paper industry reduce fossil fuel use by 80% between 1973 and 1990.[12]

Consequently, while higher input costs are an overall risk for corporate margins and, therefore, equity returns, investors should focus on 'innovators': companies that can save money for businesses, particularly in areas related to greater efficiency in energy and labour substitution. In relation to energy efficiency, this includes carbon storage, modular nuclear plans and battery storage. The trend towards innovation should also raise investment in labour substitution, for example in machine learning, robotics and AI.

AI and the Labour Market

I look at the impact of AI on the Post-Modern Cycle in Chapter 11. But as it relates to the labour market and increased labour uncertainty, the emphasis on trying to find ways of substituting labour for technology will become ever more important as populations age and the labour participation rate falls. In this sense, at least, the scalability and commercial implementation of AI may be arriving at an ideal time.

Historically, mechanisation and computer technology have tended to disrupt the labour market as machines have replaced workers, particularly those performing 'routine' tasks. Workers performing 'non-routine' tasks – using either more cognitive power or greater degrees of nonstandard dexterity – have generally been harder to replicate.

---

[12] Bergquist, A.-K. and Söderholm, K. (2016). Sustainable energy transition: The case of the Swedish pulp and paper industry 1973–1990. *Energy Efficiency*, **9**(5), pp. 1179–1192.

This evolution tended to increase 'job polarisation' between the 1980s and 2010. As technology reduced the demand for routine middle-wage jobs, it increased demand for non-routine, low- and high-wage jobs. For example, hairdressers and lawyers have been difficult to replace with machines. In contrast, manufacturing and routine service process jobs, such as factory lines and typing pools, have been easily disrupted. A study by Acemoglu and Autor (2011) shows that this occurred from 1993 to 2010 in the 16 Western European countries that they examined, and similar evidence exists for the United States.[13]

AI has the potential to disrupt the labour market in different ways by making higher-paid jobs that require a high level of cognitive ability more vulnerable, given that these technologies can perform 'non-routine' tasks. Collectively, this could mean the replacement of large swathes of the labour market, alleviating labour scarcity driven by ageing populations and potentially reducing income inequality.[14]

Nevertheless, the overall impact of AI on the workforce and on wages is complex. Although AI is likely to displace jobs, it will also likely create new ones. This process is, of course, not new. By boosting productivity, technology tends to increase growth and incomes, thereby generating more demand (the so-called X effect).[15]

Autor (2022) estimates that, in the United States, more than 60% of employment in 2018 was found in job titles that did not exist in 1940. It is therefore quite likely that new jobs will be created as a result of AI, while other jobs will be displaced, helping to push against the trend towards labour tightness.

---

[13] Acemoglu, D. and Autor, D. (2011). Chapter 12 – Skills, tasks and technologies: Implications for employment and earnings. *Handbook of Labor Economics*, **4**(Part B), pp. 1043–1171.

[14] The White House (2022). The Impact of Artificial Intelligence on the Future of Workforces in the European Union and the United States of America. Available at https://www.whitehouse.gov/wp-content/uploads/2022/12/TTC-EC-CEA-AI-Report-12052022-1.pdf.

[15] Autor, D. (2022). The labor market impacts of technological change: From unbridled enthusiasm to qualified optimism to vast uncertainty. NBER Working Paper No. w30074. Available at SSRN: https://ssrn.com/abstract=4122803 or http://dx.doi.org/10.2139/ssrn.4122803.

According to a report by PwC commissioned by the UK Department for Business, Energy and Industrial Strategy, many of the new jobs created will be 'in providing relatively hard-to-automate services (e.g., health and personal care) that are in greater demand due to the additional real incomes and spending arising from higher productivity generated by AI'.[16]

5. An Increase in Government Spending and Debt

The supply-side reforms of the 1980s triggered a trend of smaller governments and less government spending. In his inaugural address in 1981, US President Reagan famously said: 'Government is not the solution to our problem, government is the problem.' The opportunities to reduce the size of government spending increased after the fall of the Berlin Wall; in November 1989, President George H. W. Bush and UK Prime Minister Margaret Thatcher talked about a 'peace dividend'.

Following the collapse of the Soviet Union, in a speech to the nation in 1991, President Bush announced plans to scrap US tactical nuclear weapons in Europe and Asia, and called off long-range nuclear bombers from 24-hour flights. The United Kingdom announced its 'options for change' policy of restructuring the armed forces in the summer of 1990. US spending on defence fell between 1985 and 1993, and then remained flat between 1993 and 1999.

The declines in government spending relative to GDP meant that by 1997, under President Bill Clinton, the United States recorded a budget surplus for the first time since 1969. In December 2000, he announced that the United States was on track to eliminate its public debt within the following decade.[17]

---

[16] PwC (2021). *The Potential Impact of Artificial Intelligence on UK Employment and the Demand for Skills*. A Report by PwC for the Department for Business, Energy and Industrial Strategy.
[17] President Clinton (2000). The United States on track to pay off the debt by end of the decade. Available at https://clintonwhitehouse5.archives.gov/WH/new/html/Fri_Dec_29_151111_2000 .html.

When the financial crisis hit in 2008, things could not have been more different. The scale of the collapse forced massive fiscal support in many economies and a material shift towards higher public sector debt and lower private sector debt.

However, concerns about unsustainable deficits in European countries led to a new set of austerity measures on the continent, spurred by the sovereign debt crisis. The pandemic shifted the policy priorities. The issues of moral hazard that weakened the case for fiscal support after the financial crisis were no longer relevant (Exhibit 10.16).

Therefore, there has been an historic increase in government spending financed by borrowing since the start of the pandemic. Covid-19 and the impact of the war in Ukraine have both resulted in sharply rising deficits. According to the International Monetary Fund (IMF), 2020 saw the largest 1-year surge in debt since World

Exhibit 10.16 There has been a historic increase in government spending since the start of the pandemic: world debt as a percentage of GDP

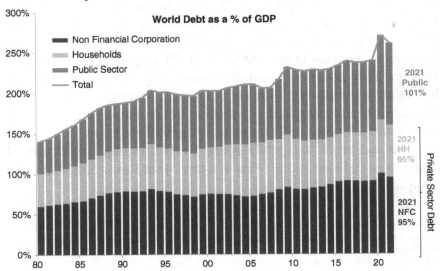

SOURCE: IMF Global Debt Database, World Economic Outlook, Goldman Sachs Global Investment Research

War II, with global debt rising to $226 trillion and global debt as a share of GDP increasing 28% to 256% of GDP.[18]

A recent report by the Office for Budget Responsibility (OBR) in the United Kingdom, for example, shows that three-quarters of the roughly 70% increase in public debt since the start of this century occurred in the 6 years hit hardest by the financial, pandemic and energy crises.

Climate change poses an additional 'contingent liability' that could result in meaningful increases in government spending. As climate-related problems become less of a tail risk and more frequent, insurance companies may increasingly restrict coverage, forcing governments to step in. The Coalition of Finance Ministers for Climate Action argues that 'the additional fiscal costs could lower the fiscal space for MoFs, potentially requiring budget cuts in critical sectors (e.g. healthcare, education), necessitating tax increases or leading to higher public debt levels'.[19]

If higher government deficits are more likely, this could result in greater uncertainty about sovereign creditworthiness, leading to higher costs of government funding. In the bond markets, the term premium (the extra return that investors demand to compensate for the risks of lending to governments further into the future) remains exceptionally low (Exhibit 10.17). According to data from the New York Fed, this premium remains negative and particularly low relative to history.[20] There is a clear risk that this premium may rise over time, adding to the cost of capital that governments, companies and investors will face in the Post-Modern Cycle.

The increases in spending are likely to come from several directions. Defence is one. This is a topic that I examine further in Chapter 12.

---

[18] International Monetary Fund (2022). Global Debt Database.

[19] Dunz, N. and Power, S. (2021). *Climate-Related Risks for Ministries of Finance: An Overview*. Washington, DC: The Coalition of Finance Ministers for Climate Action.

[20] Based on a model by Tobias Adrian, Richard Crump and Emanuel Moench (2013). Adrian, T., Crump, R. K. and Moench, E. (2013). Pricing the term structure with linear regressions. FRB of New York Staff Report No. 340. Available at SSRN: https://ssrn.com/abstract=1362586 or http://dx.doi.org/10.2139/ssrn.1362586.

Exhibit 10.17 Treasury term premia remain particularly low relative to history: Adrian, Crump and Moench (ACM) 10-year yield model-implied term premium

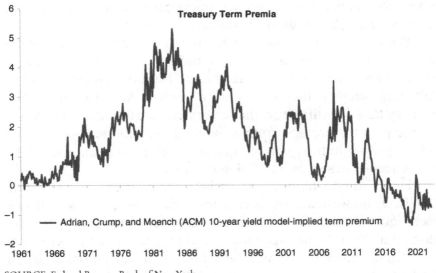

SOURCE: Federal Reserve Bank of New York

The Rise in Regulation and Industrial Policy

In 2022, the United States passed three laws – the CHIPS and Science Act, the Infrastructure Investment and Jobs Act (IIJA) and the Inflation Reduction Act (IRA) – all of which were viewed as evidence of a new trend towards state intervention and industrial policy. Increased state intervention is widely considered critical to provide the clarity needed to achieve policies around net zero carbon pledges, as well as making supply chains more resilient. But this approach is very different from the one that prevailed over much of the past quarter of a century. In his attempt to roll back state intervention, for example, US President Ronald Reagan argued in 1986 that 'the most terrifying words in the English language are: I'm from the government and I'm here to help'. In the Post-Modern Cycle, the effects of the pandemic and the war in Ukraine have changed attitudes about government involvement. The climate crisis and the vulnerability of supply chains laid bare during Covid-19, amplified by changing geopolitics, make the current backdrop very different. These factors will help to reduce uncertainty in some sectors but increase the risk premium around state intervention in others.

The three laws passed in 2022 are often said to signal that the Biden administration has embraced industrial policy as a new economic framework for the United States. National Security Advisor Jake Sullivan describes a vision of a modern American industrial strategy that 'identifies specific sectors that are foundational to economic growth, strategic from a national security perspective, and where private industry on its own isn't poised to make the investment needed to secure our national ambitions'.[21]

The United Nations Industrial Development Organization (UNIDO) published a research paper that uses machine learning techniques to classify industrial policies based on policy descriptions that include actions aimed at 'changing the composition of economic behaviour' – their definition of industrial policy. Their findings showed that, while in the 2010s around 20% of all policies in the Global Trade Advisory (GTA – a database of trade regulations) could be defined as 'industrial policy', this number had increased to 50% by 2019. The same paper reported that 60% of industrial policies are targeted at specific firms.[22]

The rise in protectionism implies that a progressively larger share of global trade has been affected by trade distortions (Exhibit 10.18). Data from the Global Trade Alert database shows that, by 2017, more than 50% of exports from G20 countries were subject to harmful trade measures, up from 20% in 2009.[23]

[21] The White House (2023b). Remarks by National Security Advisor Jake Sullivan on Renewing American Economic Leadership at the Brookings Institution. Available at https://www.whitehouse.gov/briefing-room/speeches-remarks/2023/04/27/remarks-by-national-security-advisor-jake-sullivan-on-renewing-american-economic-leadership-at-the-brookings-institution/.
[22] Juhász, R., Lane, N., Oehlsen, E. and Pérez, V. C. (2023). Trends in Global Industrial Policy. Industrial Analytics Platform.
[23] Gunnella, V. and Quaglietti, L. (2019). The economic implications of rising protectionism: A Euro area and global perspective. ECB Economic Bulletin No. 3.

Exhibit 10.18   The number of trade interventions has increased sharply over recent years

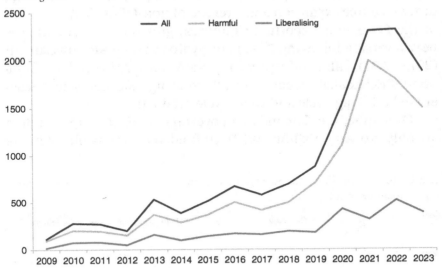

SOURCE: Global Trade Alert

Business leaders expect greater protectionism. A report by European research group The Conference Board found that almost 80% of CEOs believe an increasing number of sectors will be considered 'national security priorities' in the next 5 years.[24] The same group found that four out of five CEOs expect an acceleration in the division of the world into competing economic blocs over the next 5 years.[25]

Energy Transition Spending to Increase

Meanwhile, the commitments to decarbonisation, as well as renewed urgency to find energy security (particularly in Europe), are likely to drive more spending. Goldman Sachs analysis highlights

---

[24] Hollinger, P. (2022, May 24). European business leaders fear rising protectionism. *Financial Times.*
[25] Rowsell, J. (2022, August 19). What's behind the rise in trade protectionism? *Supply Management.*

that, between 2004 (post-technology bubble) and 2014, there was a period of energy exploration and mega-projects build-up that drove resource expansion and a revival of non-OPEC (Organization of the Petroleum Exporting Countries) growth.[26] The situation is now reversing following 7 years of hydrocarbon under-investment (2015–2021), falling oil reserve life (−50% since 2014) and declining non-OPEC ex-shale production, all requiring a steeper capex recovery in both long-cycle and short-cycle production.

Over time, the demands on governments to step up spending are only growing (Exhibit 10.19). Unfunded future liabilities in the

Exhibit 10.19   The demands on governments to step up spending are increasing: government debt as a percentage of GDP.

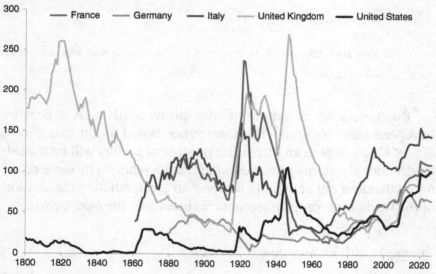

NOTE: US data from IMF before 1939. For all other countries, data from IMF for the entire period.
SOURCE: IMF

[26] Della Vigna, M., Bocharnikova, Y., Mehta, N., Choudhary, U., Bhandari, N., Modak, A., *et al.* (2023). Top projects 2023: Back to growth. Goldman Sachs Global Investment Research. Available at https://publishing.gs.com/content/research/en/reports/2023/06/27/bcd4ad94-6106-4bb8-9133-fa35a6bfa730.html.

form of pensions, insufficient spending on care for the elderly and mental health, and increased priorities for defence spending will likely continue.

Political and geopolitical perspectives are supporting this shift. Just as the 1970s saw an era of national champions (firms receiving special government support for security and political reasons) in the airline, banking and auto industries, so we are moving into an era of regional champions in energy security, chip manufacturing and battery technology. While the consequences are not yet clear, it is likely that the high burden of government debt will require a combination of higher taxes, higher inflation (which is a form of tax) or lower spending over time. This is another reason why investors should focus on companies with strong balance sheets and relatively stable cash flows as investors attach more value to the ability of companies to sustain good, compounded returns over a longer period, even in the event of higher taxes or interest rates.

The implications for investors are that rising levels of government debt probably mean the reversal of the trend towards lower corporate taxes. It also means that inflation and interest rates may well average at a higher level over the next decade or so, which would be helpful for governments in paying down their debt. These factors could reverse some of the support for the higher profit shares enjoyed over recent decades. Smolyansky (2023) estimates that lower interest expenses and corporate tax rates mechanically explain over 40% of the real growth in US corporate profits from 1989 to 2019.[27] Ultimately, it may also mean higher bond yields as governments compete for global savings. All this points to lower aggregate returns for investors and, therefore, underlines the benefits of diversification and more careful selection of companies within an overall stock market index.

---

[27] Smolyansky, M. (2023). End of an Era: The Coming Long-Run Slowdown in Corporate Profit Growth and Stock Returns. Available at: www.federalreserve.gov/econres/feds/end-of-an-era-the-coming-long-run-slowdown-in-corporate-profit-growth-and-stock-returns.htm.

6. A Rise in Capital and Infrastructure Spending

One of the most important implications of the post-financial-crisis era was the growth of the virtual economy and the decline in the relative fortunes of the 'old' economy. The consequence was a huge amount of money that flowed into the digital economy but, mostly, this happened at the expense of the 'real' economy. Capital spending in infrastructure has declined across the major markets since the start of this decade (Exhibit 10.20; see also Chapter 12).

Lower inflation reduced the incentive to invest, at least in physical capacity, and the average age of assets has risen to around 5 years older than in the 1970s/80s (Exhibit 10.21).

Capital-light industries outperformed dramatically in the decade after the financial crisis. I discuss the implications of the prospects for higher infrastructure spending in Chapter 12. Of course, this does not mean that there will not be more spending on technology as well

Exhibit 10.20   European firms are investing less than their US counterparts in future growth: growth investment ratio (growth capex + R&D/CFO)

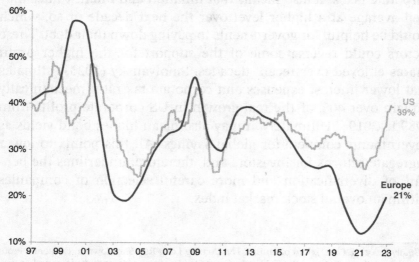

SOURCE: Goldman Sachs Global Investment Research

Exhibit 10.21   The average age of assets has risen and is around 5 years older than in the 1970s/80s: US average age – private fixed assets (years)

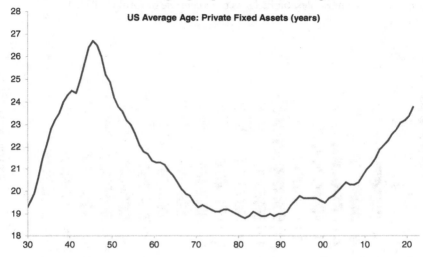

SOURCE: Goldman Sachs Global Investment Research

(a topic I cover in Chapter 11). Spending on technology solutions is likely to remain very strong – and the incentive may be even higher in areas related to energy efficiency and labour substitution. However, the shifts in the energy mix that will be required to achieve the ambition to decarbonise by 2050 will be highly capital intensive. Primary energy capex has fallen 18% over the past decade, and Goldman Sachs equity analysts expect it to grow 50% between 2022 and 2027 to $1.9 trillion (from $1.3 trillion in 2022; Exhibit 10.22).[28]

With the shift in emphasis to ESG investing, and decarbonisation in particular, the focus has transitioned in recent years to energy sustainability. However, so far it has been insufficient to offset the collapse in investment in the traditional energy space, given the smaller

---

[28] Della Vigna, M., Bocharnikova, Y., Mehta, N., Choudhary, U., Bhandari, N., Modak, A., *et al.* (2023). Top projects 2023: Back to growth. Goldman Sachs Global Investment Research. Available at https://publishing.gs.com/content/research/en/reports/2023/06/27/bcd4ad94-6106-4bb8-9133-fa35a6bfa730.html.

Exhibit 10.22   Primary energy capex could grow by roughly 50% between 2022 and 2027: energy supply capex split by fuel and power supply ($ billion, LHS) and clean energy (renewables, biofuels) as a percentage of total (%, RHS)

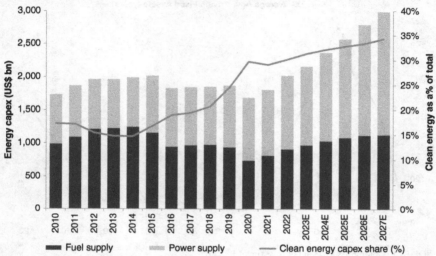

SOURCE: IEA WEI (historical data), Goldman Sachs Global Investment Research

scale and higher capital intensity per unit of energy output. Goldman Sachs equity analysts estimate that the average capex intensity of low-carbon energy developments is around twice that of hydrocarbons. This further enhances the need for energy investment as an incremental $1.5 trillion per annum capex is required by 2032.[29]

These conditions suggest that investors should look for 'enablers', or companies that can provide solutions to corporate problems to reduce costs and increase productivity. They should also look for beneficiaries of the move towards greater government spending and higher capex. Many of the companies that are most sensitive to these themes have derated in recent months and offer reasonable value and attractive growth opportunities.

---

[29] Della Vigna, M., Clarke, Z., Shahab, B., Mehta, N., Bhandari, N., Amorim, B., *et al.* (2022). Top projects 2022: The return of the energy investment cycle. Goldman Sachs Global Investment Research. Available at https://publishing.gs.com/content/research/en/reports/2022/04/19/ae5c2010-d7ef-400c-b8e7-1cf25650ef17.html.

7. Changing Demographics

In addition to factors that are shifting the investment environment, demographic changes of significant proportions are emerging. Rich developed economies are ageing at a rapid rate.

The speed of ageing is fastest in Japan and South Korea: an expected 15% of the population will be aged over 80 by 2050 in Japan (almost the same as in South Korea). In 2017, the dependency ratio across the G20 was over six people of working age (15–64) for every person aged 65 years. This ratio is set to halve, to three people of working age by 2050. In the richest countries, the ratio is expected to fall to just above 2:1 (Exhibits 10.23 and 10.24).[30]

Exhibit 10.23 Working-age population growth is expected to be negative in the Euro area and Japan: 15–64 cohort population growth, United Nations forecast

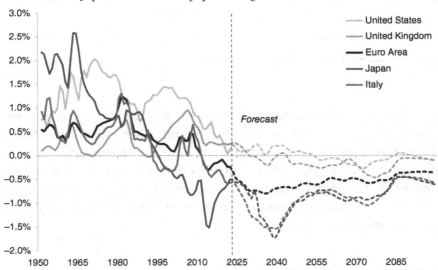

SOURCE: Goldman Sachs Global Investment Research

---

[30] International Labour Organization and Organization for Economic Co-operation and Development (2019). New job opportunities in an ageing society. Paper presented at the 1st Meeting of the G20 Employment Working Group, 25–27 February 2019, Tokyo, Japan.

Exhibit 10.24 Working-age population growth is expected to turn negative in China and other emerging markets: 15–64 cohort population growth, United Nations forecast

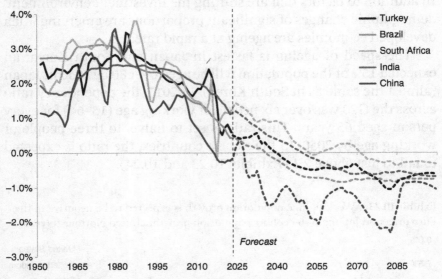

SOURCE: Goldman Sachs Global Investment Research

This will put increased burdens on already stretched government budgets as care for the elderly and other mainly unfunded liabilities coincide with a smaller working population and tax base. On the positive side, this is likely to be an additional factor that increases investment in mechanisation; and other technologies, such as AI, could improve job prospects and quality of employment in the care sector.

Ageing Populations and Deficits

The implications for government deficits and funding are profound. According to the OECD, public spending on pensions and healthcare will increase dramatically over the next few decades. Without meaningful structural reforms or cuts in pension entitlements, 'large increases in tax revenue would be needed to stabilise public debt according to the projections derived from the OECD long-term model'.[31]

Ageing Populations and New Markets

An ageing population will also create opportunities, as products and services increasingly address this under-served market. Seniors globally will be the wealthiest group by 2030 and are expected to spend $15 trillion a year (in 2011 purchasing power), up from $8.7 trillion in 2020.[32]

The shift in spending patterns as a result of demographics has brought with it another significant opportunity: owing to the numbers involved, the purchasing power of seniors is growing more strongly in Asia. China is on course to see a trebling of the spend among seniors, from $750 billion per annum to $2.1 trillion by 2030, and India is likely to see the most striking jump in spend, from around $100 billion per annum currently to around $1 trillion by 2030.

Emerging markets (EMs), and Africa in particular, could benefit from significant growth opportunities. Currently, the population of Africa is around 1.4 billion, but it is projected to rise to nearly 4 billion by the end of this century. This means that, while Africa's population currently makes up around 18% of the world total, this share would rise to 38% by 2100, while Asia's population is predicted to decline from around 60% of the world total today to 45% by 2100. Taken together, by the end of the century, 80% of the world's population will live in Africa or Asia.[33]

---

[31] Crowe, D., Haas, J., Millot, V., Rawdanowicz, Ł. and Turban, S. (2022). Population ageing and government revenue: Expected trends and policy considerations to boost revenue. OECD Economics Department Working Paper No. 1737.

[32] Fengler, W. (2021). The silver economy is coming of age: A look at the growing spending power of seniors. Available at https://www.brookings.edu/articles/the-silver-economy-is-coming-of-age-a-look-at-the-growing-spending-power-of-seniors/.

[33] Roser, M. and Rodés-Guirao, L. (2019). Future population growth. Available at https://ourworldindata.org/population-growth Our World in Data.

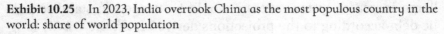

Exhibit 10.25   In 2023, India overtook China as the most populous country in the world: share of world population

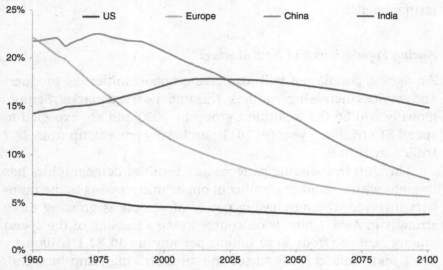

SOURCE: UN Department of Economics and Social Affairs, Goldman Sachs Global Investment Research

India's acceleration past China as the most populated country is also a significant change and creates huge potential opportunities for investors in the region (Exhibit 10.25).

Although ageing is most advanced in developed economies, many EM economies are also on track to experience a decline in the labour participation rate in the future. This highlights the difficulty of funding liabilities for countries, even when they may be faster-growing and have larger populations. It also underscores the significance of AI and other technology solutions in the future to help deal with these issues. Even as populations are ageing fastest in developed economies, the labour participation rate is slowing in emerging economies (Exhibit 10.26).[34]

---

[34] For a detailed discussion on the issues around demographics, see Roy, A. (2022). *Demographics Unravelled: How Demographics Affect and Influence Every Aspect of Economics, Finance and Policy*. Chichester: Wiley.

Exhibit 10.26   Many emerging economies are expected to experience a decline in the labour participation rate in the future: change in working-age population growth rate between 2005 and 2030

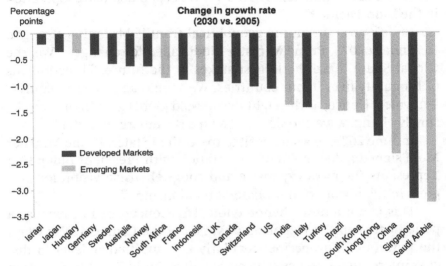

SOURCE: Goldman Sachs Global Investment Research

8. An Increase in Geopolitical Tensions and the Multipolar World

In the Modern era – the long cycle between 1982 and 2000 – declines in global risk premia followed the collapse of the Berlin Wall and the end of the Soviet Union. The impact on global risk appetite was meaningful. The boost to confidence was documented in *The End of History* by Francis Fukuyama, who argued that liberal democracy had resulted in 'the end-point of mankind's ideological evolution and the universalisation of Western liberal democracy as the final form of human government'.[35] In recent years, the geopolitical balances have been shifting. In a speech at Davos in 2022, German

---

[35] Fukuyama, F. (1992). *The End of History and the Last Man*. New York: Free Press.

Chancellor Olaf Scholtz described the emergence of a new 'multipolarity'. New alliances are forming: NATO is expanding to include Finland and Sweden, and AUKUS will deepen defence cooperation in the Indo-Pacific.[36]

India's position on the geopolitical front is becoming stronger. In January 2023, Prime Minister Modi called for changes: 'We, the Global South, have the largest stakes in the future. Three-fourths of humanity lives in our countries. We should also have an equivalent voice. Hence, as the eight-decade-old global governance model slowly changes, we should try to shape the emerging order.'

In June 2023, in a state visit to the United States, Prime Minister Modi signed a document of cooperation with President Biden that 'represents the most expansive and comprehensive vision for progress in the history of our bilateral relationship'.[37]

This is not a new phenomenon. The Concert of Europe was a period between the Napoleonic Wars and the Crimean War when the powers of Europe met regularly at a multipolar level to discuss international issues. The period after World War I is also often regarded as a period of multipolarity. However, many neo-realists see such systems as more prone to conflict and more unstable than bipolarity, or even primacy in international relations. The 'long-cycle model' in international relations, for example, argues that multipolarity is the least stable system and that unipolarity is the most stable and least conflict-prone arrangement.[38]

While these developments are difficult to price in financial markets, they are likely to mean a higher risk premium over time and, therefore, a higher cost of capital.

---

[36] AUKUS is an acronym for the trilateral security pact between Australia, the United Kingdom, and the United States.

[37] The White House (2023a). Joint Statement from the United States and India. Available at https://www.whitehouse.gov/briefing-room/statements-releases/2023/06/22/joint-statement-from-the-united-states-and-india/.

[38] The arguments about systems of stability are tested empirically in a study of polarity and warfare between global powers between 1494 and 1983. The study argues that global warfare has been least likely in periods of unipolarity and near unipolarity, slightly more prevalent in bipolar years and much more likely in multipolar periods. Thompson, W. R. (1986). Polarity, the long cycle, and global power warfare. *Journal of Conflict Resolution*, **30**(4), pp. 587–615.

Chapter 11

The Post-Modern Cycle and Technology

An electrical signal in the brain moves at 1/100,000th the speed of the signal in a silicon chip!

—Bill Gates

The excitement around the Fourth Industrial Revolution and the commercialisation of the internet initially generated one of the biggest financial bubbles in history. The bubble reached a peak at the turn of the century, before experiencing a spectacular collapse. Like many bubbles built around new technologies throughout history, it was not without foundation. Investors correctly recognised that a major new cycle of innovations would have a profound impact on growth and profitability in the future. The problem was that the scale and timing of the likely returns were overstated at the time, and many of the eventual winners did not yet exist.

As with previous similar bubbles, the eventual collapse wiped out many of the new entrants, but the technologies that drove the bubble survived; the technology sector, after a period

251

of significant de-rating, re-emerged as the main driver of performance and profits in the post-financial-crisis period. With the recent focus on new technologies, particularly around artificial intelligence (AI), the significance of technology for stock markets and economies is likely to remain crucial in the Post-Modern Cycle.

While tech stocks have been the main driver of equity market returns since the financial crisis of 2007/08, their performance has come in four distinct phases:

1. **2010–2019.** Outperformance driven by stronger earnings, the widespread adoption of smartphones, the impact of zero interest rates and the problems facing 'value' sectors.
2. **2020–2022.** During the Covid-19 pandemic, the explosion of demand for technology and related services (at a time when other consumption was restricted) led to a significant outperformance of technology companies.
3. **2022–2023.** As inflation and rising interest rates began to emerge in 2022, technology companies experienced a sharp pullback in performance, particularly in non-profitable tech companies, as they buckled under the weight of a higher cost of capital and negative impact on their 'long-duration' cash flows. Many had also overextended, buoyed by the cheap cost of capital, and needed to reduce spending as funding costs increased.
4. **2023–present.** Since the start of 2023, the technology sector has begun to outperform again, driven by the large US technology companies, viewed as potential winners from the emerging technologies around AI.

So, while the outperformance of the technology sector over the past 15 years as a whole has reflected bouts of optimism and valuations re-rating, it has mainly relied on strong underlying fundamentals. The sector has outgrown and out-earned other parts of the equity market (Exhibit 11.1), enjoying sustainably higher return on equity (Exhibit 11.2).

Exhibit 11.1   The technology sector has outgrown and out-earned other parts of the equity market: 12-month trailing EPS ($). Indexed to 100 in January 2009

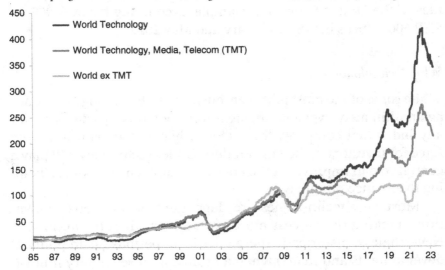

SOURCE: Goldman Sachs Global Investment Research

Exhibit 11.2   Technology sees a sustainably higher return on equity

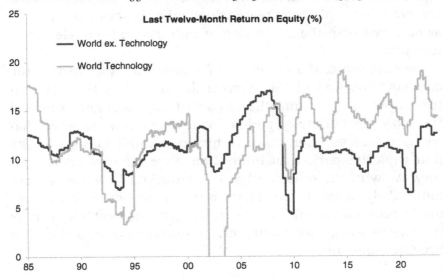

SOURCE: Goldman Sachs Global Investment Research

By the summer of 2023, this had resulted in market returns becoming increasingly concentrated again, with just 15 companies in the United States, for example, accounting for over 90% of S&P 500 returns between January and May 2023.

Why Technology Wins

While some of the most recent enthusiasm for technology may once again ultimately overstate the near-term potential, particularly for any individual company, the sector is likely to remain a driving force for investors in the Post-Modern Cycle. Technology will play a central role in improving efficiencies in non-tech companies, helping to enhance productivity.

Most new technologies are dependent on previous innovations, making the process more evolutionary than revolutionary. Nevertheless, historically there have been periods (as in political developments and in art) when a profusion of secondary innovations and ideas occurs in a relatively concentrated period. These phases create a step-change in innovation and, with it, rapid changes in the structure of the economy, stock market and society, providing a platform upon which other innovations emerge, as occurred with the innovation of railways and the telephone, for example.

In that sense, the explosion of innovations spawned by the commercialisation of the internet at the end of the last century (now evolving into the impact of AI) resembles some of the more revolutionary periods of technological advance that we have seen at other points in history. Exhibit 11.3 shows the four explosive periods of innovation since the eighteenth century. As with the other cycles of innovation, however, we are more likely to see an acceleration in the impact of technology on the economy and financial markets over the next few years as positive network effects and more productive uses of technology become dominant.

Exhibit 11.3   The history of industrial revolutions

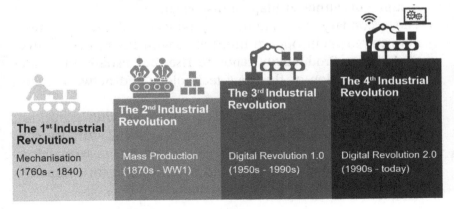

SOURCE: Goldman Sachs Global Investment Research

Characteristics of Technology Revolutions

Looking at history, we can make several interesting observations about how these periods evolve that help to contextualise the speed of change we are experiencing across economies and society today. Although it is difficult to generalise, some of the common characteristics are:

- A breakthrough technology emerges and reaches commercial scale.
- New companies and capital flood into the space.
- Speculation builds and valuations of companies rise, often resulting in a bubble.
- The bubble bursts, but the technology tends to re-emerge as a principal driver in the economy and stock market.
- The technology/industry becomes dominated by a few large players.
- Secondary innovations emerge, creating new companies and products that are enabled by the initial technology and its increased adoption.

- Other industries are disrupted by the innovations, forcing incumbents either to adapt or disappear.
- The secondary innovations in products and services create new employment opportunities and, with them, new sources of demand. Productivity tends to rise, but usually only after the full adoption of this new technology and network effects are realised.
- The speed of innovation is often associated with significant changes in broader society, seen in shifting social attitudes, consumer behaviour, government policy and business practices. These create new challenges and opportunities for companies adjusting to meet the changing demands.

Exuberance, Speculation and Bubbles

As we saw with the scaling and commercialisation of the internet and, more recently, with AI, the emergence of a significant new technology often results in growing investor exuberance, the injection of significant capital and a rapid expansion in the number of new entrants to the industry. As the understanding and acceptance of the technology grows, investor interest deepens and speculation increases.

From an investor perspective, the success and eventual impact of an innovation cannot be known at the outset, and it is even more challenging to predict which competitor is likely to succeed over the long run, leading investors to invest across multiple companies as options on their future success. Consequently, the total valuation of companies exposed to the theme as it first becomes commercial often overstates the aggregate returns that can be generated, and a bubble emerges; the bursting of the bubble is often triggered by a prominent company failure or a sharp shift in the cost of capital.

There are plenty of historical examples to illustrate this process. A recent study found that, in a sample of 51 major tech innovations introduced between 1825 and 2000, bubbles in equity prices were evident in 73% of cases.[1] The innovation of canals for transportation was an important component of the First Industrial Revolution. The first canals built generated strong returns for investors, attracting new inflows of capital that pushed up prices, and during the 1790s a bubble developed in canal stocks on the London Stock Exchange. The boom in canal stocks reached a peak in 1793. By the 1800s, the return on capital in canals had fallen from a pre-bubble peak of 50% to just 5%, and a quarter of a century later only 25% of canals were still able to pay a dividend. Nevertheless, the canal infrastructure became instrumental in reorganising industries and factories, which, in turn, spawned the growth of many new industries, businesses and products.

A similar exuberance surrounded the growth of railways in the nineteenth century, which were to become equally transformative in terms of economic growth, business organisation and societal change. Rampant speculation built up in railway stocks in the United Kingdom, and by the 1840s a bubble had formed as money flooded into the sector in search of high growth and returns. Following significant price rises, railway shares had fallen by an average of 85% from their peak by the 1850s, and the total value of these shares had dropped to less than half the capital spent on them.[2] As with the canals, the legacy of the infrastructure became pivotal to growth in other industries.

The twentieth century brought sequential waves of new technologies. The periods after World Wars I and II (WWI and WWII) saw massive demand for consumer products that attracted waves of investment as new market entrants emerged. As broadcast radio took off, for example, demand for radios increased rapidly. Between 1923 and 1930, 60% of US families purchased a radio, which resulted in a proliferation of radio stations. In 1920 US broadcast radio was

---

[1] Chancellor, E., and Kramer, C. (2000). *Devil Take the Hindmost: A History of Financial Speculation*. New York: Plume Books.
[2] Odlyzko, A. (2000). Collective hallucinations and inefficient markets: The British railway mania of the 1840s. Available at SSRN: https://ssrn.com/abstract=1537338 or http://dx.doi.org/10.2139/ssrn.1537338.

dominated by KDKA but, by 1922, 600 radio stations had opened across the United States and, as with the adoption of television technology, this increased the scope for advertising and the adoption of other products as they came to market. The value of shares in the Radio Corporation of America (RCA), for example, rose from $5 to $500 in the 1920s but collapsed by 98% between 1929 and 1932, and most radio manufacturers failed.

The personal computer (PC) revolution fuelled a similar boom in both the number of companies and the valuations of new entrants in the market. While IBM facilitated the widespread commercialisation of the PC, hundreds of companies entered the market in the 1980s. In 1983, however, several companies in the sector announced losses, including Atari, Texas Instruments and Coleco. A collapse in PC share prices followed, and many PC manufacturers went out of business, including Commodore, Columbia Data Systems and Eagle Computer. While many of the surviving businesses took many years to recover, the industry matured and became dominated by just a few companies.

This pattern was repeated during the internet bubble of the late 1990s. Speculation grew rapidly as investors began to see the potential of the internet. When search engine company Yahoo! had its initial public offering, its stock rose from $13 to $33 in a single day. Qualcomm shares rose in value by over 2,600%, 13 major large-cap stocks increased in value by over 1,000% and another seven large-cap stocks each rose by over 900% in 1999. The Nasdaq index increased fivefold over the period between 1995 and 2000. In just a month after its peak in 2000, the Nasdaq had fallen 34% as hundreds of companies lost 80% or more of their value. The Nasdaq itself had fallen by nearly 80% by the time it troughed in October 2002.

As a rule, excitement around the potential from new technologies attracts new entrants and competitors, as well as increased speculation as interest in the narrative grows and investors fear missing out. Ultimately, valuations will tend to adjust downwards, a shake-out of the industry results in fewer competitors, and the industry tends to recover, often leading the next cycle. This pattern was true for the technology sector after the tech bubble burst, and it is likely that the latest innovations, particularly around AI, will be similar and make major contributions to the return prospects for investors in the Post-Modern Cycle.

The read-across to the AI revolution is that the companies that are spending the money on AI tools and the compute power may not be the biggest winners from the new technologies over time, as we saw with the experience of the development of the internet. For example, companies that can use the tools to improve healthcare and education services may end up big winners, together with other companies that can adopt AI solutions to significantly restructure businesses to reduce costs. Innovators in new business growth areas, such as data and fact-checking, as well as new products that leverage AI, may ultimately thrive.

The Dominance Effects

Radical new technologies tend to attract significant capital and competition, and many companies eventually collapse, but this does not mean that the technology itself fails. It is more common for the initial technology to succeed as take-up and market grow, and dominant companies innovate to broaden the scope and reach of the technology. The adoption speed of technologies has tended to accelerate over time as real incomes have increased and geographical reach has grown more rapidly.

As a rule, the pattern of changing market structure tends to be similar in different waves of innovation; initially, the space is typically dominated by a few winners that become increasingly powerful as the network effect generates a virtuous cycle of growing market share and as they build increased 'moats' that sustain their dominant position. These dominant positions are ultimately vulnerable either to regulation (anti-trust) or slow adaption to innovations.

The Emergence of Secondary Technologies

While the market for a technology innovation can become dominated by a few very large companies for a long time, the initial transformative technology becomes a conduit that kickstarts a whole range of other innovations and, with this, new companies and market opportunities.

For example, while coal and steam were the foundations of the First Industrial Revolution, a range of other developments quickly followed. Mass migration to cities and the movement away from agriculture resulted in demand for new consumer products. Mechanised looms transformed the textile industry and domestic products such as soaps began to be manufactured in factories rather than at home. This generated new markets and became the catalyst for the building of consumer brands, advertising and marketing. During the railway boom, the steam engine spawned the development of the railways, and the network effect and connectivity then allowed other technologies to develop.

Similarly, during the Second Industrial Revolution, the harnessing of gas and oil to create electricity was one of the key driving inventions. But this, in turn, enabled the mass production of steel, the development of the internal combustion engine and the automobile. The start of the modern assembly line in factories became a further innovation, transforming the production and distribution of a range of new products. Similarly, the network impact of the railway boom and the telegraph fostered a host of new market opportunities and companies.

With the computer age of the Third Industrial Revolution came the rapid acceleration of service industries. The first transistorised consumer products started to appear in 1952, opening new markets as consumers were willing and able to pay a premium for low power consumption and portability. By the mid-1950s, prototype silicon devices were developed in Northern California. Plastics and lighter materials also generated significant new growth markets, while the growth of multinational companies opened new market opportunities.

Exhibit 11.4 The adoption speed of technologies has tended to accelerate over time: share of US households using specific technologies, 1860–2019

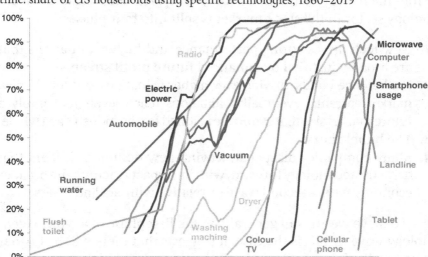

SOURCE: Our World in Data

Furthermore, the adoption speed of technologies has tended to accelerate (Exhibit 11.4).

This pattern has been evident over the past two decades. The rapid roll-out and adoption of the internet and related technologies has enabled the development and penetration of the smartphone. This, in turn, spawned an industry of companies based on the 'apps' used on these phones (think of the revolution in taxi and food delivery services, for example) and the 'internet of things' (a world of connected appliances and devices).

So, while the leading tech companies of the 2020s will most likely remain dominant in their respective markets, rapid innovation, particularly around machine learning and AI, will likely create a new wave of tech superstars. It is probable that AI and robotics will not only create innovative leading companies but also raise the prospect of major restructuring gains in non-technology sectors.

So, where are we in the lifecycle of new technologies currently? From the history mentioned above, the typical lifecycle of the technology sector in the stock market is split into four phases:

1. New tech drives strong performance and higher valuations that are broadly justified by enhanced future profit streams.
2. Exuberance builds, driving ever-higher valuations and lots of new market entrants; eventually valuations reach levels that imply a future market size that cannot be justified for the industry as a whole.
3. The bubble bursts.
4. Many companies disappear, leaving new dominant leaders that drive the technology forward, with its impact reaching the broader economy with a second wave of relative winners and losers.

I believe we are still generally in the first phase of a typical technology wave. If this is the case, it suggests that there will be further emergence of new entrants in the space and still higher valuations in this part of the market. There is a risk that the current exuberance may lead to a bubble, or to a point where incumbent valuations rise excessively relative to their future growth potential, but I do not think we are at this point yet.

In the Post-Modern Cycle, it is likely to be the digitisation of industries outside of the technology industry itself that will create more opportunities for investors over time. Developments in GreenTech, MedTech, EdTech, AI and robotics should generate a host of new growth opportunities for companies outside of the technology sector, reshaping traditional business models in areas such as banking, retail, entertainment, education, transportation and healthcare.

Can Technology Remain the Biggest Sector?

The technology sector has already been dominant in terms of market capitalisation (at least in the United States) fairly consistently since the software revolution of the 1980s, interrupted only by a brief period of financials' dominance before the financial crisis. However, the history of the sector composition of the S&P 500 as a benchmark suggests that a dominant sector can remain so for extended periods. Over time, different waves of technology resulted in different phases of sector dominance; as stock markets have become more diversified, the biggest sector has tended to account for a smaller share of the aggregate market. Nevertheless, the technology sector will probably remain the biggest sector in the global market, and many new companies are likely to enter the sector as confidence builds and IPOs re-emerge (Exhibit 11.5).

We can split the long sweep of history in the US equity market into four main periods of leadership.

1. 1800–1850s: Financials

Over this period, banks were the biggest sector. Starting with almost 100% of the equity market, the stock market developed and broadened out. By the 1850s, the sector's weight had more than halved.

Exhibit 11.5 Only a few sectors have been the biggest in the market over time, reflecting developments in the economy: market share of the largest sector in the United States (%)

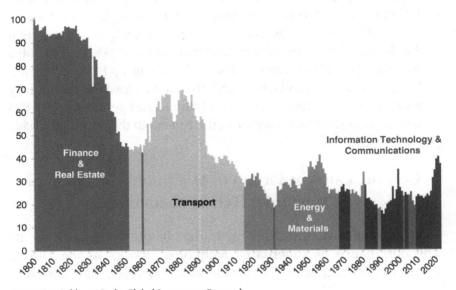

SOURCE: Goldman Sachs Global Investment Research

2. 1850s–1910s: Transport

As banks started to finance the thriving railroad system in the United States (and elsewhere for that matter), transport stocks took over as the largest in the index. In their boom years, transport stocks reached close to 70% of the index in the United States before fading to around one-third of the market capitalisation by WWI.

3. 1920s–1970s: Energy

With the huge growth of industry, powered by oil rather than steam and coal, energy stocks took over as the biggest sector. This remained the main sector group until the 1990s, although interspersed with brief periods of leadership from the emerging technology sector (in the first wave it was led by mainframes and, subsequently, by software).

4. 1980s–Present: Technology

Technology has generally been one of the biggest sectors in the United States (although not in all other countries) since the emergence of mainframe computing in the 1970s (briefly beaten by the banks sector in the run-up to the financial crisis). Of course, the leaders in the technology space have changed over this period. IBM was the biggest company as mainframes drove the data revolution in the mid-1980s; Microsoft became the biggest company as software became the main driver of technology in the 1990s; then Apple took over as the biggest company in the 2000s, and remains so today. There have been cycles, with the run-up to the tech bubble in 2000 and the collapse of tech thereafter. However, technology soon returned as the biggest sector (after a brief period when banks took over as the biggest sector in the run-up to the financial crisis).

Can the Current Group of Dominant Technology Companies Remain Leaders?

Will the next wave of technology leaders be the same or different? The dominance of super-large technology stocks in the United States and other markets is considerable. However, this pattern of market dominance is not unique to the current revolution in technology: several companies in the past have come to dominate their respective industries on the back of a major innovation or technology cycle. The evolution of the technology sector throughout history tends to show how, ultimately, it can be a 'winner takes all' market:

- Standard Oil, for example, controlled over 90% of oil production in the United States by 1900, and 85% of sales.
- Bell Telecom had reached 90% of US households by 1969. Just before it relinquished control of the Bell Operating Companies and was split into different companies in 1982, it reached 5.5% of the market.
- Between 1955 and 1973, General Motors' earnings were more than 10% of the S&P 500. At its peak, General Motors had a 50% market share in the United States and was the world's largest auto maker from 1931 through to 2007.
- As mainframe computers developed in the 1970s, there was a significant concentration of market share: IBM had over a 60% market share in mainframe computers in 1981.
- As software took over as the main driver of technology, there was yet another shift in domination. By 2000, Microsoft had a 97% share in operating systems, given its dominance in the PC and laptop markets.

The largest company in the index has historically belonged to the dominant sector at any time. Typically, it has also tended to maintain its size relative to the market until either regulation (anti-trust) intervenes to reduce market dominance or the incumbent company loses out to a more nimble new entrant with a more cutting-edge technology (Exhibit 11.6).

Nevertheless, historically it is common for new companies to emerge that dominate new products and technologies over time, particularly in the United States. For example, just over 10% of the Fortune 500 companies have remained on the list since 1955.

Based on this history, it would appear reasonable to assume the Fortune 500 list in 60 years from now will include very few of

Exhibit 11.6   The largest company in the index has historically belonged to the dominant sector: percentage of S&P 500 market cap and percentage of S&P net income before 1974

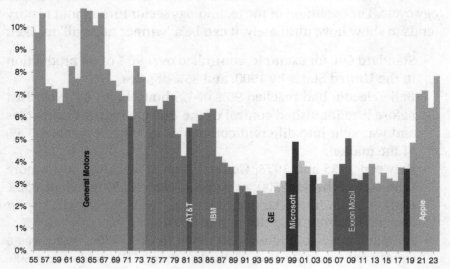

SOURCE: Goldman Sachs Global Investment Research

the current dominant companies – at least in their current form and structure. A plethora of new companies will be formed in emerging industries we cannot even imagine today. As Exhibit 11.7 shows, none of the 10 largest companies in the S&P 500 in 1985 were still in the top 10 in 2020, and only one from the list in 2000 remained in the top 10 in 2020.

While history has shown that dominant companies can continue to be leaders in their industry for a long time, many companies have been dominant but failed to remain so. In large part, this resulted from disruption caused by an innovation, or the failure to develop a new technology, often for fear of cannibalising an existing market-dominant position.

Nevertheless, I see three reasons why dominant tech companies may stay bigger for longer in the current cycle than we might have seen in historical technology cycles.

Exhibit 11.7   The 10 largest S&P 500 companies through time: by market cap as of 31 December

1985	1990		1995		2000	
IBM	IBM	2.9%	General Electric	2.6%	General Electric	4.1%
Exxon Mobil	Exxon Mobil	2.9%	AT & T	2.2%	Exxon Mobil	2.6%
General Electric	General Electric	2.3%	Exxon Mobil	2.2%	Pfizer	2.5%
AT&T	Philip Morris	2.2%	Coca-Cola	2.0%	Cisco Systems	2.4%
General Motors	Royal Dutch Shell	1.9%	Merck & Co	1.8%	Citigroup	2.2%
Amoco	Bristol-Myers Squibb	1.6%	Philip Morris	1.7%	Walmart	2.0%
Royal Dutch Shell	Merck & Co	1.6%	Royal Dutch Shell	1.6%	Microsoft	2.0%
Du Pont	Walmart	1.6%	Procter & Gamble	1.2%	American International Group	2.0%
AT & T	AT & T	1.5%	Johnson & Johnson	1.2%	Merck & Co	1.8%
Chevron	Coca-Cola	1.4%	IBM	1.1%	Intel	1.7%

2005		2010		2015		2020	
General Electric	3.3%	Exxon Mobil	3.2%	Apple	3.3%	Apple	6.7%
Exxon Mobil	3.1%	Apple	2.6%	Alphabet	2.5%	Microsoft	5.3%
Citigroup	2.2%	Microsoft	1.8%	Microsoft	2.5%	Amazon	4.4%
Microsoft	2.1%	General Electric	1.7%	Exxon Mobil	1.8%	Alphabet	3.3%
Procter & Gamble	1.7%	Chevron	1.6%	General Electric	1.6%	Meta Platforms	2.1%
Bank of America	1.6%	IBM	1.6%	Johnson & Johnson	1.6%	Tesla	1.7%
Johnson & Johnson	1.6%	Procter & Gamble	1.6%	Amazon	1.6%	Berkshire Hathaway	1.4%
American International	1.6%	AT&T	1.5%	Wells Fargo	1.5%	Johnson & Johnson	1.3%
Pfizer	1.5%	Johnson & Johnson	1.5%	Berkshire Hathaway	1.5%	JPMorgan Chase	1.2%
Philip Morris	1.4%	JPMorgan Chase	1.4%	JPMorgan Chase	1.5%	Visa	1.2%

SOURCE: Goldman Sachs Global Investment Research

First, the tech sector is deflationary. As long as that is the case, there is no real incentive for politicians to attack it. In this way, from a policy perspective, the tech sector may be different from others, such as banks, supermarkets or energy companies, where politicians often argue that the benefits (e.g., higher interest rates for savers, lower food and energy prices) are not being passed on to consumers. This does not make technology companies immune from regulation, but is more likely to come from issues around privacy and use of data, or the impact on mental health, than on pricing.

Second, technology is increasingly seen as a matter of national security. Technology, including cyber security, chips and, increasingly, AI, is considered a critical part of national infrastructure and strategic defence. This has become more important as geopolitical tensions rise across the world.

Third, the technology sector invests hugely in R&D. Given that the current incumbent winners are so cash-generative, they have an ability to maintain this investment, strengthening their market 'moat' and potential future growth.

Why Newer Technologies May Enhance Productivity

The impact of technology innovations on productivity is important because it can affect overall economic activity and, by implication, the value of the whole stock market. After years of slow growth, there are some signs of an improvement in productivity (Exhibit 11.8). Some academics argue that this could be related in part to one-off effects around the pandemic, but in part also due to a J-curve effect.[3] This is when radical new technologies, such as the internet or AI, require that significant complementary investments be made before their impact can be fully utilised and measured.

There are also good reasons to believe that productivity has been under-measured over the past couple of decades as the growth

---

[3] Brynjolfsson, E., Rock, D. and Syverson, C. (2021). The Productivity J-Curve: How intangibles complement general purpose technologies. *American Economic Journal: Macroeconomics*, **13**(1), pp. 333–372.

Exhibit 11.8   Newer technologies have enhanced productivity: GDP per capita adjusted for price changes over time (inflation) and price differences between countries: measured in international dollars in 2011 prices (logarithmic scale)

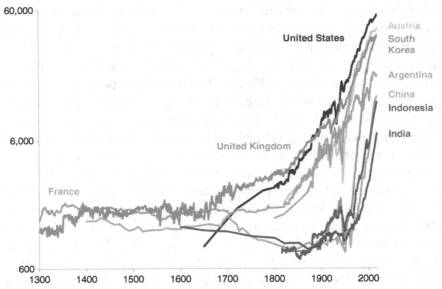

SOURCE: Our World in Data

of 'free' goods in the economy has been insufficiently measured. Goldman Sachs economists point out that it would require over 10 devices and $3,000 to replicate the most basic functions of today's smartphones, and that missing growth from 'free' digital goods such as Google Maps, camera phones and Snapchat may be underestimating activity.[4] In an experimental setting, Erik Brynjolfsson *et al.* asked consumers to choose between forgoing access to social media or paying a monetary penalty.[5] The dollar values

[4] Hatzius, J., Phillips, A., Mericle, D., Hill, S., Struyven, D., Choi, D., *et al.* (2019). Productivity Paradox v2.0: The price of free goods. Goldman Sachs Global Investment Research. Available at https://publishing.gs.com/content/research/en/reports/2019/07/15/d359dbb5-88ce-4cfb-8fdd-e7687bf2b4e1.html.

[5] Brynjolfsson, E., Collis, A. and Eggers, F. (2019). Using massive online choice experiments to measure changes in well-being. *Proceedings of the National Academy of Sciences*, **116**(15), pp. 7250–7255.

assessed by the median participant imply trillions of unmeasured consumer surplus.

There is compelling evidence from history that previous waves of technology have resulted in slower growth in productivity and economic activity than is generally believed. For example, while James Watt marketed a steam engine in 1774, it took until 1812 for the first commercially successful steam locomotive to appear, and it was not until the 1830s that British output per capita clearly accelerated because the impact of the technologies was subject to network effects. Coal transport eventually provided a major boost to growth and productivity but could not be fully adopted until transport networks were in place. Equally, the large, fixed costs of investment could only be recouped when enough users had switched to the new power source. At the same time, the use of steam power required the construction of factories and the building of canals to facilitate the transportation of raw materials and finished products. In the same way, a transfer of transportation away from the internal combustion engine to electrification may be technically possible but will require an integrated power supply system and electric charging points before it can be fully adopted.

A similar pattern can be observed in the electrical age of the 1880s. The innovations in electricity did not yield substantial productivity gains until the 1920s, when the possibilities of factory redesign were realised.[6] Concerns about the lack of productivity growth and, therefore, the mis-valuation of companies associated with technology were also widespread in the 1980s. In 1987, Nobel Economics Laureate Robert Solow argued that 'you can see the computer age everywhere except in the productivity statistics'.[7] These concerns faded when many economies saw a dramatic improvement in productivity in the 1990s.

---

[6] Crafts, N. (2004). Productivity growth in the Industrial Revolution: A new growth accounting perspective. *The Journal of Economic History*, **64**(2), pp. 521–535.
[7] Roach, S. S. (2015). Why is technology not boosting productivity? Available at https://www.weforum.org/agenda/2015/06/why-is-technology-not-boosting-productivity.

It is possible that a similar effect may be seen after the information technology revolution.[8] In this context, it makes sense that the digital revolution has not yet boosted productivity.[9]

Weak Productivity in the Internet World

Productivity growth was disappointing during the last cycle. Some have argued that this is a paradox, and that it illustrates the limited impact of such technologies and that stock prices must therefore be overvaluing their potential. But there may be good reasons to be more optimistic about the prospects for productivity growth in the Post-Modern Cycle.

First, the continuation of moves towards e-commerce and other higher-productivity areas should yield benefits. Second, the digitisation of the workplace and the increased trend towards hybrid (office/home) work may boost productivity by reducing time spent commuting and travelling. Third, the shift towards a higher cost of capital is likely to accelerate the process of 'creative destruction' in technology, with less profitable companies shutting down (as we have seen in previous waves of technology throughout history). Fourth, and perhaps most importantly, while technology in the post-financial-crisis era focused on 'nice to have' products rather than 'need to have' solutions to problems, the next cycle is likely to be driven by solution-focused technologies.

From 'Nice to Have' to 'Need to Have'

Some of the most significant growth areas over the past 15 years have been in social media, the building of platform companies and the development of apps to facilitate easier transactions. For example,

---

[8] David, P. A. and Wright, G. (1999). General purpose technologies and surges in productivity: Historical reflections on the future of the ICT revolution. Paper presented at the International Symposium on Economic Challenges of the 21st Century in Historical Perspective, Oxford, 2–4 July.
[9] Mühleisen, M. (2018). The long and short of the digital revolution. *Finance and Development*, 55(2), art. A002.

the total number of mobile apps globally has now reached a massive 8.9 million, according to a new report from RiskIQ.[10] Of course, not all of these were developed by new companies: apps have been developed to access existing services. For example, many apps link companies to a digital platform to enable their customers to order an existing product, such as takeaway food. While these are no doubt useful, in many cases the underlying product purchased has not changed. Indeed, the home delivery mechanism (often a bicycle) is arguably no more sophisticated than it was a century ago. Furthermore, according to estimates from Statista, over 60% of all apps downloaded in 2022 were games – not something that tends to boost productivity.[11] The scale of adoption of new technologies is so great that some companies have started to limit the number of emails their employees receive at certain times, to relieve stress and enhance productivity.[12]

As we move through the Post-Modern Cycle, new major challenges will increase the focus on technology as a solution. In particular, the focus on energy efficiency and decarbonisation should increase investment in technology companies that can enhance efficiency (as opposed to selling consumer products).

At the same time, ageing populations and the significant decline in labour participation should incentivise companies to spend more on mechanisation and the substitution of labour for technology.

Productivity and the Impact of AI

Perhaps the most important wave of technological innovations is emerging in the areas of AI and robotics. The speed of take-up of new language-based systems has been extraordinary. According to a

[10] RiskIQ (2021). 2020 Mobile App Threat Landscape Report: Tumultuous year bred new threats, but the app ecosystem got safer. Available at https://www.riskiq.com/wp-content/uploads/2021/01/RiskIQ-2020-Mobile-App-Threat-Landscape-Report.pdf.
[11] Armstrong, M. (2023). Games dominate global app revenue. Available at https://www.statista.com/chart/29389/global-app-revenue-by-segment/.
[12] Clark, P. (2023, June 3). The dismal truth about email. *Financial Times*.

summary by Statista, the speed of downloads of ChatGPT hit one million after just 5 days – it took 10 times longer for Netflix to achieve the same milestone.

These innovations have two potential impacts. First, on the destruction or displacement of many existing roles and, second, on generating higher productivity and growth and, in turn, potentially boosting real incomes after many years of stagnation. If this becomes a reality, the rise in real incomes will likely spawn a whole host of new sub-industries and job opportunities.

On the point about job destruction, the prospects appear alarming at first sight. Economists at Goldman Sachs argue that AI could substitute up to a quarter of current work, or possibly 300 million full-time current jobs, due to automation. That said, we should not become too worried. Worker displacement from automation has usually been offset by the creation of new jobs or industries that are hard to imagine at the time (think of the explosion in the fitness industry or eating out, for example). Most importantly, they argue that the combination of labour-saving costs and higher productivity of the workers who remain in their current roles raises the prospect of a productivity boom that could substantially enhance economic growth – particularly if, in decades to come, the prospect of near-free renewable energy becomes a reality. They estimate that in the United States alone, productivity growth could rise by just under 1.5% per year over a 10-year period following widespread adoption. Thus, AI could eventually boost global GDP by 7%.[13]

Supporting this, a recent study shows that, since the advent of deep learning approaches to technology in the 2010s, the training compute (i.e., the number of computations used to train AI models) has doubled approximately every 6 months.[14] This is less than

---

[13] Hatzius, J., Briggs, J., Kodnani, D. and Pierdomenico, G. (2023). The potentially large effects of artificial intelligence on economic growth (Briggs/Kodnani). Goldman Sachs Global Investment Research. Available at https://publishing.gs.com/content/research/en/reports/2023/03/27/d64e052b-0f6e-45d7-967b-d7be35fabd16.html.
[14] Sevilla, J., Heim, L., Ho, A., Besiroglu, T., Hobbhahn, M. and Villalobos, P. (2022). Compute trends across three eras of machine learning. arXiv:2202.05924.

one-third the doubling time implied by Moore's law, which had prevailed for the previous 60 years.[15]

A recent working paper by the U.S. National Bureau of Economic Research (NBER) studied the introduction of an AI-based conversational assistant using data from 5,179 customer support agents.[16] They found that access to the tool boosted productivity (measured by issues resolved per hour) by 14% on average. They also found that the greatest positive impact was on new or low-skilled workers – partly because the tool is designed to disseminate the knowledge of more experienced employees to newer workers, enabling them to develop more quickly. Moreover, the AI assistant improved customer sentiment and helped to boost employee retention. This is an example of how many productivity benefits from technologies related to AI may also serve non-technology companies, as they can utilise AI tools to boost productivity and efficiency. I turn to prospects for the old economy in the next chapter.

The PEARLs Framework for AI and Technology

So, is there a way to think about winners and losers in the context of rapid technology innovations? One approach to thinking about this is to have a framework that focuses on the way to innovate, respond and utilise new technologies. At Goldman Sachs we have developed a PEARLs framework, made up of:

PIONEERS – the early innovators.
ENABLERS – companies that help to facilitate the innovators to commercialise the new technologies.
ADAPTORS – companies in other industries that change their business models to commercialise the new technologies.

---

[15] Moore's law suggests that the number of transistors on a microchip doubles roughly every two years and, with it, the speed and capability of computers.
[16] Brynjolfsson, E., Li, D. and Raymond, L. (2023). Generative AI at work. NBER Working Paper No. 31161.

REFORMERS – the new entrants that reshape and disrupt other industries by leveraging the technologies to make them more scalable.

LAGGARDS – companies that are slow to change to the new innovations and are either overtaken or competed away.

The Pioneers

The creators tend to benefit first in terms of price appreciation. They are the innovators of the new technology or the companies spending most on developing it and are, generally, the easiest to spot. As we have seen, these companies have enjoyed the greatest outperformance so far, although they remain less highly valued, with stronger cash flows than has generally been the case in past cycles.

However, while the pioneers may be the easiest to identify early on, they are not always the biggest beneficiaries. Often new entrants emerge that are more nimble and can usurp a dominant incumbent, even if the incumbent remains successful. This was clearly the case, for example, in the internet search engine space. However, secondary innovations often emanate from the original technology, frequently from latter pioneers. These can create significant growth as a whole new product area, or even industry, emerges. While these are, of course, very difficult to spot in the early days of the technology, they can become some of the biggest winners. An example with the internet was the emergence of the smartphone and social media companies.

The Enablers

The companies that help facilitate a technology change are vital to its success in commercialising the opportunity. In the current AI wave this includes many of the chip companies essential to the widespread deployment of AI. Like the pioneers, these enablers are usually easy to spot as the technology scales and becomes commercially viable. However, the longer-term investment implications for these companies are not always straightforward. In the case of the internet revolution, for example, the commercial and scalable use of the internet could not have happened without the telecom companies. These enabled the roll-out of the infrastructure and were the ones investing in the networks; it was assumed that by owning the 'pipes' they would reap many of the rewards which, ultimately, other companies (and consumers) benefited from. However, as they aggressively competed for licences to buy spectrum and bore most of the costs of the infrastructure, they failed to realise an adequate return on investment to justify their inflated valuations at the time.

As Exhibits 11.9 and 11.10 show, these telecom companies appreciated as much as the technology sector over this period and became as expensive, but most failed to earn an adequate return on the investment.

Many of the beneficiaries were ultimately not the enablers of the technology but the companies that innovated or adapted to

Exhibit 11.9   US Telecom companies appreciated as much as the technology sector during the 2000s

SOURCE: Goldman Sachs Global Investment Research

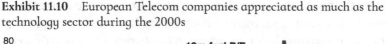

Exhibit 11.10 European Telecom companies appreciated as much as the technology sector during the 2000s

SOURCE: Goldman Sachs Global Investment Research

leverage the new technologies as they emerged: for example, innovators in the platform business world that applied new technologies to disrupt existing businesses and gain market share (e.g., ride and taxi apps), or innovators in new app-based businesses that could not exist prior to the internet networks being rolled out.

However, other enablers, such as semi-conductor companies, performed well, and we think can do so in the case of AI. The difference reflects, in large part, the barriers to entry. Most critical is whether the large capital investment often required by these companies can yield an adequate return on investment to justify their valuations.

The Adaptors

The adaptors are companies outside the tech industry that adapt to the impact of the new technology and change their business models. The relative success or otherwise of these companies is also unclear.

Companies that can use AI tools to improve healthcare and education services, for example, may end up being big winners, together with other companies that can adopt AI solutions to significantly restructure businesses to reduce costs. Innovators in new business growth areas, such as data and fact-checking, might ultimately thrive. Finally, many of the benefits may accrue to consumers in the form of cheaper new services. If all companies in a mature sector adopt a new technology that makes them more efficient, then competitive pressures often mean that the biggest winner is the consumer and, ultimately, companies that build business models to benefit from increased leisure time and higher disposable incomes.

In the end, much will depend on the extent of competition and the quality of the implementation. The majority of companies in most industries moved to adopt PCs, for example, and away from mainframes in the 1980s and 1990s. While these changes increased productivity and reduced costs, this happened across all competitors together. The main beneficiaries here were consumers, and this has largely been true in the case of the internet revolution. Most companies outside the technology sector have 'gone on-line', generating greater efficiency and better reach. But since this is true of nearly all companies, competition has led to most of these benefits going to consumers in the form of better services and lower prices. Nonetheless, many industries have seen a dominant winner that has become dominant either because it had additional scale at the outset, or its execution was much better. In the retail space, as an example, most companies have a web presence but, in several countries, a few dominant players have been more successful at developing omni-channel sales and have outperformed over time.

The Reformers

The reformers are typically new market entrants unencumbered by legacy costs. Such companies can disrupt a mature non-technology industry by utilising the innovations to create a new business model that is more scalable than those of existing competitors. Examples would include Amazon in the retail space, car-sharing apps and online banks. These companies become increasingly valuable as they reshape the dominant business model and margin dynamics in an industry, and can increase market share at the expense of the incumbents and enjoy strong revenue growth.

The Laggards

These are the companies that are often assumed to be invisible, perhaps because they have a dominant incumbent position in an industry but, for whatever reason, are slow to change and keep up with new innovations. Because these incumbents often have high valuations, they are most at risk from de-rating as they are taken over by more flexible, innovative, competitors. History has many examples of high-profile companies that seemed to have an unassailable lead in their industry but experienced a dramatic demise as they were overtaken by more nimble companies with a better, newer technology.

Kodak is a good example. It is said to have invented the first digital camera in 1975 but its engineers failed to obtain approval to launch the product because management was concerned it would negatively impact the film market. Kodak filed for bankruptcy in 2012 (Exhibit 11.11). A similar fate befell **Polaroid**. By the 1960s and early 1970s, Polaroid had a monopoly in the instant photography market. It also enjoyed sales of about 20% of the total film market and 15% of the market for cameras in the United States. While it did invest in digital technology, it failed to cope with the flood of new entrants into the market and believed that printed copies would always dominate (Exhibit 11.12).

Xerox was the first company to invent a PC, but management thought it would be too expensive to commercialise and believed that the future of the company was in copy machines, where it had a 95% market share in the 1970s.

Exhibit 11.11   Kodak invented the first digital camera in 1975 but filed for bankruptcy in 2012: stock price indexed to its maximum

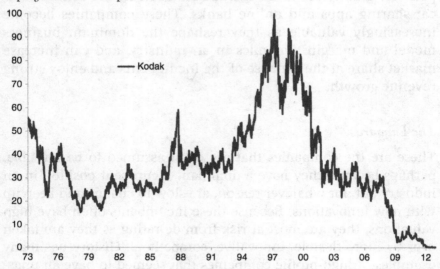

SOURCE: Goldman Sachs Global Investment Research

Exhibit 11.12   Polaroid had a monopoly in the instant photography market: stock price indexed to its maximum

SOURCE: Goldman Sachs Global Investment Research

Blockbuster Video was a successful video rental business that navigated the change from VHS to DVD, but not the change to streaming. In 2000, Netflix proposed a partnership with Blockbuster with the idea that Blockbuster would advertise the Netflix brand in their stores and Netflix would run Blockbuster online, but the proposal was turned down. Blockbuster filed for bankruptcy in 2010.

Nokia at one point had over 40% of the world mobile handset market, accounting for 70% of the Finnish stock market and around 4% of Finland's GDP. The company failed to keep up with smartphone technology and eventually sold its handset business to Microsoft in 2013. It then purchased Alcatel-Lucent as it pivoted towards telecommunication infrastructure (Exhibit 11.13).

Dell failed to keep up with changing technology and consumer demands. Innovation shifted from the enterprise to consumers, and the dominant computing platforms shifted from the desktop to smartphones and tablets. A proliferation of cloud-based offerings

Exhibit 11.13   Nokia lagged with smartphone technology: stock price indexed to its maximum

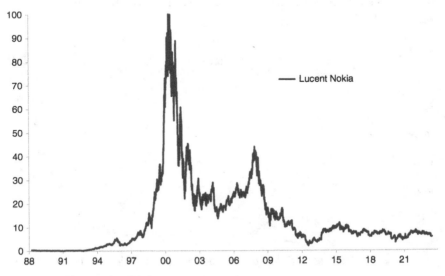

SOURCE: Goldman Sachs Global Investment Research

reduced the amount of hardware most companies required, so Dell fell behind companies such as Apple, Amazon and Microsoft.

Nevertheless, some dominant companies that collapse in market value as new entrants and technologies emerge do learn to adapt and shift their businesses. For example, in March 2000, Cisco became the most valuable company in the world with a market cap of over $500 billion, driven by its dominant position in internet protocol, but it eventually saw its share price collapse. Cisco evolved to stay relevant and shifted its business towards services such as online video and data. Similar adjustments occurred with companies such as Microsoft (Exhibit 11.14) and Ericsson.

There have already been significant re-ratings of a few companies that can be viewed as 'early winners' – companies that are either the pioneers in the space or the enablers. These are likely to continue to perform as the technology scales. Ultimately, the second-wave pioneers that innovate and create new products based on

Exhibit 11.14 Microsoft underperformed after the tech bubble and then recovered sharply: price performance return since IPO (1× = 100% gain)

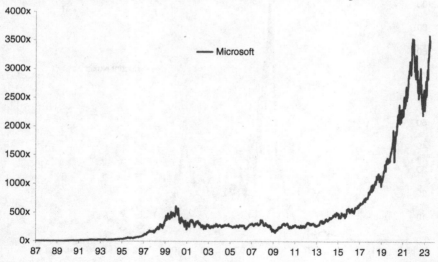

SOURCE: Goldman Sachs Global Investment Research

the original technology are also likely to offer exciting investment opportunities. In time, the bigger opportunities may be found in identifying the new reformers that reshape industries by leveraging what AI has to offer. Best-in-class adaptors with industry-leading execution are likely to provide an attractive investment opportunity. However, as many companies adapt to AI, increasing benefits should feed through to consumers. Companies that can tap into this opportunity might also benefit more that the market is currently discounting.

Chapter 12

The Post-Modern Cycle: Opportunities in the 'Old Economy'

Globally, the need for infrastructure investment is forecast to reach $94 trillion by 2040, and a further $3.5 trillion will be required to meet the United Nations' Sustainable Development Goals for electricity and water.

—Global Infrastructure Hub

E ach era has its unique problems and, in many cases, opportunities. As we enter the Post-Modern Cycle, humanity faces a series of major challenges. Changing geopolitical alliances, the future of work, ageing populations and the environment are likely to be prominent issues for the foreseeable future.

From an investment perspective, the end goal looks exciting. A successful transition to a zero-carbon world would not only generate significant improvements in health but, clearly, would hold the prospect of marginal units of energy to be consumed at close to zero cost (both financially and in terms of the planet's resources).

The International Energy Agency (IEA) estimates that global energy demand will be 8% lower in 2050 than today, despite the expectation that the global economy will be twice as large and the world's population boosted by 2 billion. The combination of more efficient use of energy, improved resource efficiency and behavioural changes should help offset increases in energy demand. Equally, although the ascent of artificial intelligence (AI) may be daunting and highly disruptive, it offers the potential for higher productivity and significant advances in many industries.

Opportunities in the 'Old Economy'

As discussed in Chapter 8, one of the most dramatic developments of the post-financial-crisis period in equity markets was the outperformance of the technology sector. This largely reflected superior earnings growth and returns on equity at a time when many traditional industries were suffering from overcapacity and low returns. The boom in spending on the digital revolution has, to a large extent, been at the expense of investment in the physical world. As Exhibit 12.1 shows, the ratio of capex spending to corporate sales has declined dramatically since the financial crisis in most economies.

The commodity complex offered limited investment prospects because many commodity prices fell sharply as a consequence of relatively weak global demand and some oversupply (Exhibit 12.2).

The backdrop of extremely low interest rates supported this trend as it helped to fund new businesses in the technology sector with ample liquidity and a low cost of capital. Companies that were unprofitable and consumed large start-up costs found it easy to raise capital. Their long duration (long period of expected payback until profitability) was not an obstacle because the low level of interest rates meant that the opportunity cost of the cash (or the return that the cash could otherwise generate) was very low.

Exhibit 12.1   The ratio of capex spending to corporate sales has declined dramatically since the financial crisis in most economies: capex-to-sales ratio (%)

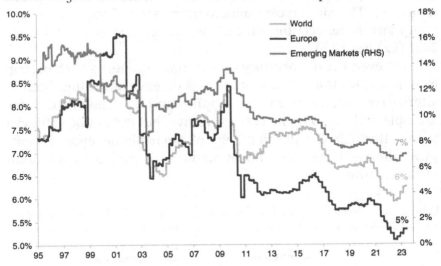

SOURCE: Goldman Sachs Global Investment Research

Exhibit 12.2   The energy and commodity complex offered limited investment prospects: refined copper supply versus copper demand (kiloton level)

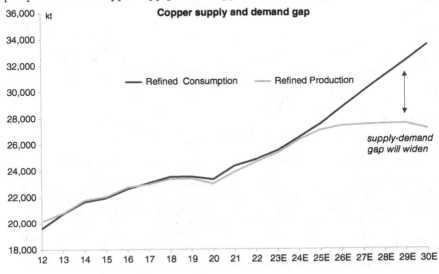

SOURCE: Goldman Sachs Global Investment Research

For a decade or more, businesses in capital-light industries dramatically outperformed those in more traditional capital-heavy industries. The more recent underperformance of the capital-light group largely reflects the shift higher in the cost of capital since 2021 (Exhibit 12.3).

However, the opportunity set for capex spending is changing. New priorities that include increased defence spending, finding alternative sources of energy supplies and decarbonisation, for example, will not only be very expensive, but cannot be achieved purely through the development of smartphone apps or software; they will need significant amounts of capital spending on infrastructure.

Exhibit 12.3 Recently, capital-light businesses have outperformed those that employ heavy capital: world capital versus non-capital-intensive industries ($ price return)

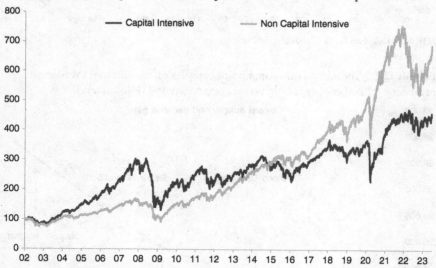

NOTE: Capital-intensive – telecom service providers, autos and parts, leisure goods, construction and materials, general industrials, industrial transport, industrial materials, industrial metal, mine, oil, gas, coal, alternative energy, electricity, gas, water. Non-capital-intensive – software and computer services, technical hardware, medical equipment services, pharmaceuticals and biotechnology, consumer services, household goods, home contents, personal goods, retailers, beverages, food producers, tobacco, drug/grocery stores.

SOURCE: Goldman Sachs Global Investment Research

Defence Spending

Global spending on defence has trended downwards since the 1970s (Exhibit 12.4). According to the International Monetary Fund, global military spend (estimated by unweighted country averages) has fallen from 3.4% of gross domestic product (GDP) during the Cold War period of 1970–1990, to less than 2% in the years after the financial crisis (2010–2019).

However, the pattern is now changing. According to the Stockholm International Peace Research Institute (SIPRI), global defence spending increased to $2 trillion in 2021. The war in Ukraine is likely to boost this even further.[1]

Exhibit 12.4   Global spending on defence has trended downwards since the 1970s: world military spending (as a share of GDP)

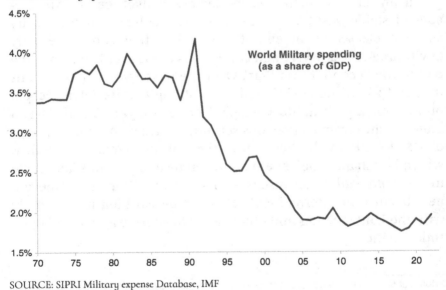

SOURCE: SIPRI Military expense Database, IMF

---

[1] Marksteiner, A. (2022). Explainer: The proposed hike in German military spending. Available at https://sipri.org/commentary/blog/2022/explainer-proposed-hike-german-military-spending.

Heightened geopolitical risk and the war in Ukraine have shifted many governments towards increased spending on defence. The German government has reset its post-Cold War foreign and security policy with the suspension of the constitutional debt brake, and created a €100 billion special fund to modernise its armed forces in the coming years. Germany has also stated that it would increase defence spend directed to North Atlantic Treaty Organization (NATO) to 2% of GDP, implying an increase of around 30% in the budget, from €53 billion in 2021 to about €70 billion. This is a step-change in the approach to defence spending, which has remained at 1.0–1.5% of GDP in Germany since the early 1990s.[2]

In the United States, President Biden signed a $768 billion defence policy bill that represented a 5% increase in military spending; this was nearly $50 billion larger than his original request, as both Democrats and Republicans believed Biden's proposal was insufficient to counter military advances by China and Russia.

Japan has also increased its defence budget, ending six decades of stable post-World War II security policy. A new security strategy released at the end of 2022 argues that 'Japan's security environment is as severe and complex as it has ever been since the end of the Second World War'. Over the next 5 years, Japan plans to spend ¥43 trillion ($313 billion) to strengthen its defence capabilities, raising its military expenditure to roughly 2% of GDP, a material shift from its previous self-imposed cap on military spend of 1% of GDP. In another sign of the shifting geopolitical reality, which is reshaping defence spending and supply chains, an article in the *Financial Times* discussed Japan's ambitions to 'achieve a new balance in international relations' by working more closely with the United States and other Allies to achieve a 'free and open Indo-Pacific'.[3]

---

[2] House of Commons Library (2022). Defence spending pledges by NATO members since Russia invaded Ukraine. Available at https://commonslibrary.parliament.uk/defence-spending-pledges-by-nato-members-since-russia-invaded-ukraine/.
[3] Inagaki, K. (2022, December 16). Japan scraps pacifist postwar defence strategy to counter China threat. *Financial Times*.

Infrastructure Spending

Another important driver for a revival of capital spending in the real economy will come from the urgent need to upgrade ageing infrastructure, while also building new infrastructure to meet the demands of a growing population. This raises the question of who will pay and how the cost of investment can be made attractive enough to make investing in new technologies commercially viable. But the need is certainly there.

According to the Global Infrastructure Hub and Oxford Economics, an increase in the global population by almost 2 billion by 2040, and a nearly 50% increase in urban populations (as migration to cities increases), will provide a massive boost to infrastructure spending.[4] They estimate that the scale of this spending is likely to reach $94 trillion by 2040 to keep pace with economic and demographic changes. They also estimate that the amount would rise to $97 trillion if the United Nations' Sustainable Development Goals were met (including clean water, sanitation and electricity), as they would require global spending as a share of GDP to rise from the current 3% to 3.7%.

Other estimates point to a similar scale of investment. According to a report by McKinsey Global Institute, $57 trillion will need to be spent on building and maintaining global infrastructure between now and 2030, more than the total value of the world's infrastructure assets today.[5] These investments are required simply to replace existing ageing infrastructure, and they reflect the challenges of a larger global population in emerging economies.

At a meeting of the China Central Financial and Economic Affairs Commission (CFEAC) on 26 April 2022, President Xi Jinping called for infrastructure construction to be comprehensively

---

[4] Global Infrastructure Hub (2017). Global infrastructure investment need to reach USD97 trillion by 2040. Available at https://www.gihub.org/media/global-infrastructure-investment-need-to-reach-usd97-trillion-by-2040/.
[5] McKinsey Global Institute (2013). McKinsey: 57 trillion dollar for global infrastructure. Available at https://www.consultancy.uk/news/153/mckinsey-57-trillion-dollar-for-global-infrastructure.

strengthened, and for the development of a modern infrastructure system. He noted that the state of China's infrastructure still falls short of what is needed for national development, and called for infrastructure investment to be stepped up. In Europe, too, infrastructure is a key pillar of the European Recovery Fund, a comprehensive fiscal package put in place to help rebuild Europe's economy after the Covid pandemic. According to the European Union, the combination of NextGenerationEU – the temporary instrument designed to boost the recovery – and long-term spending plans focused on areas such as climate change and digital transformation has triggered 'the largest fiscal package ever financed in Europe, worth over €800 billion'.[6]

Green Spending

Perhaps the most remarkable change that will be required in investment spending will come from the requirements of decarbonisation. The scale of this challenge in terms of building infrastructure is enormous. According to the International Energy Agency (IEA), 'This calls for nothing less than a complete transformation of how we produce, transport'.[7]

According to the Energy Transition Commission, the capital investment required to meet a net-zero carbon emissions target for the global economy would, alone, amount to $3.5 trillion between 2020 and 2050, three times the current pace of annual spend of around $1 trillion. The Commission estimates that roughly 70% of this is required for low-carbon power generation, transition and distribution. Part of this investment would be offset by reduced investment in fossil fuels, which, they estimate, would cut the annual net cost to around $3 trillion per annum over the next 30 years.[8]

---

[6] European Commission (2021). Recovery plan for Europe. https://commission.europa.eu/strategy-and-policy/recovery-plan-europe_en.

[7] International Energy Agency (2021). Net Zero by 2050: A Roadmap for the Global Energy Sector.

[8] Energy Transitions Commission (2023). Financing the transition: Making money flow for net zero. Available at https://www.energy-transitions.org/publications/financing-the-transition-etc/.

The number of countries announcing pledges to achieve net-zero emissions over the coming decades continues to grow. However, in a recent report, the IEA explained that government pledges – even if fully achieved – fall short of what is required to bring global energy-related carbon dioxide emissions to net zero by 2050, which would help prevent global surface temperatures from rising 1.5°C above pre-industrial levels.[9] According to the report, energy groups would need to stop all new oil and gas exploration projects from this year to keep global warming in check. An unprecedented increase in spending on low-carbon technologies would also be required – around $5 trillion in energy investments per year by 2030, up from around $2 trillion today.

The report also provides details on an overhaul of energy supply and demand, whereby coal, oil and gas demand would fall respectively by 90%, 75% and 50% by 2050. Solar would become the single biggest energy source, meeting 20% of global energy demand.

Improvements in energy efficiency mean that global energy demand in 2050 should be around 8% lower than it is today, even though the world economy is likely to be more than twice as big. Electricity use will grow, accounting for around half of total energy consumption by 2050.

The good news is that, according to the United Nations, it would not cost much more to ensure that the new infrastructure projects that are embarked upon globally are compatible with climate goals. The critical issue, however, is that the upfront costs will be higher, although they can largely be offset by efficiency gains and fuel savings over the lifetime of the project. According to the United Nations, the Global South will account for roughly two-thirds of global infrastructure investments (around $4 trillion per year) and will require international financing support. Again, the advantage is that, despite the daunting costs, the new infrastructure projects can 'lead in building sustainable infrastructure that "leapfrogs" the inefficient, sprawling and polluting systems of the past'.[10]

---

[9] International Energy Agency (2021). Net Zero by 2050: A Roadmap for the Global Energy Sector.
[10] The New Climate Economy (2016). The Sustainable Infrastructure Imperative: Financing for Better Growth and Development.

While the scale of these requirements may appear overwhelming, the projects are feasible with the correct incentives and investment. Bear in mind that we have already seen a transformation in energy provision over the past decade. The US shale revolution started in 2008 and over the following decade turned the United States into the world's largest oil and gas producer. Shale production is close to reaching a peak. Since the United States can no longer rely on shale as a competitive advantage over the next decade, the incentive to invest in a new energy revolution has increased and led to a focus on policy incentives.

Oil analysts at Goldman Sachs estimate that renewable technologies can deliver twice the scale of energy produced by shale and unlock as much as 43 million barrels of oil equivalent per day through 'green electrons' (70%, mostly solar and wind) and 'green molecules' (30%, mostly hydrogen and bioenergy) by 2032, and that this can drive $3 trillion of infrastructure investment over the coming decade.[11]

Government Policy and Spending

Capital spending to update existing infrastructure and meet the needs of decarbonisation is one thing, but the question of who pays for it is another. That said, the combination of government plans to reach net zero and the emergence of environmental, social and governance (ESG) investment mandates (a focus on environmental, social and governance factors) among investors is at least moving capital in the right direction.

While much of the required investment is likely to come from the private sector, incentives are needed to jump-start this investment. History suggests that higher levels of investment will bring

---

[11] Della Vigna, M. (2023). The third American energy revolution. Goldman Sachs Global Investment Research. Available at https://publishing.gs.com/content/research/en/reports/2023/03/22/4b92c394-2af6-4119-b469-0117d9946b71.html.

down the cost of new investment and technologies as they reach scale, thereby accelerating a virtuous cycle.

The most recent developments are encouraging. The US CHIPS and Science Act, signed in 2022, will 'make historic investments that will poise US workers, communities and business to win the race for the 21st century. It will strengthen American manufacturing, supply chains and national security'.[12] Increasingly, the focus is on national security and the resilience of supply chains in the wake of the pandemic and in the light of growing geopolitical tensions. The 2002 Inflation Reduction Act (IRA) in the United States is the most ambitious and significant policy intervention to date. The U.S. Congressional Budget Office (CBO) has estimated that the budgetary impact from the Bill's Energy and Climate provisions would total $391 billion over the 2022–2031 period. This includes about $265 billion in tax credits to incentivise investments in renewable energy and low-emission fuels. Importantly, the incentive structure is shaped in a way that makes most cleantech industries profitable at a large scale. This should include both renewable electrons (such as solar, wind, energy storage and electric vehicles) and renewable molecules (such as bioenergy, clean hydrogen and carbon capture). It also aims to make it more attractive for individuals to make greener choices in transportation and improve the efficiency of homes.

Goldman Sachs analysts estimate that the IRA could cost the government around $1.2 trillion through to 2032, three times the CBO estimate. Importantly, however, this could then unlock around $3 trillion of infrastructure investments out to 2032, 2.5 times the scale of the investment.

Given the protectionist implications of the Act in the form of the provisions for manufacturing in the United States, Europe has responded with its own version – the Green Deal Net Zero Industry Act. Just as countries competed over a long period

---

[12] The White House (2022, August 9). FACT SHEET: CHIPS and Science Act will lower costs, create jobs, strengthen supply chains, and counter China.

to reduce corporate taxes to help attract investment, they are now competing with subsidies and tax breaks to do the same in emerging technologies that are likely to spur the transition to a net-zero economy.

The European version focuses on three central areas. First, faster investment in renewables through an easing of permission processes. Second, a 'Made in Europe' focus, to offset the risk of migration of European manufacturing to the United States, attracted by the US IRA. This is taking the form of the European Commission suggesting that at least 40% of clean energy equipment should be manufactured locally, coupled with a Critical Raw Materials Act to address the sourcing of critical materials. Third, the support of €375 billion in funds (through grants, tax credits, direct investments and loans), which has already been approved (but not yet deployed under the Recovery Act proposed to support recovery from the Covid pandemic). In essence, this package matches the size and scope of the US IRA plan, so that the combined initiatives could release up to €6 trillion in capital. Indeed, by 2050, renewable energy could reach 80–90% as a share of total power generation for the EU, with the rest met via batteries, hydrogen and carbon capture and storage (CCS).

This would mark a significant change from recent years when, overall, Europe has suffered from a lack of investment (although the trend has been towards a significant increase in renewables-related investment in recent years). As Exhibit 12.5 shows, while overall capital expenditure in the United States and Europe has been fairly flat, capex in a basket of European renewables companies has bucked the trend. An aggregation of global renewables-related companies shows a similar trend of higher investment (see Exhibit 12.6).[13]

---

[13] Jaisson, G., Oppenheimer, P., Bell, S., Peytavin, L. and Ferrario, A. (2021). Renewables and other companies investing for the future. Goldman Sachs Global Investment Research. Available at https://publishing.gs.com/content/research/en/reports/2021/06/08/08d49f00-f091-4c9b-ab64-b0a398023f33.html.

Exhibit 12.5   While overall spending on capex in the United States and Europe has been fairly flat, European renewables companies are investing at a much faster pace: capital expenditure indexed to 100 in 2015

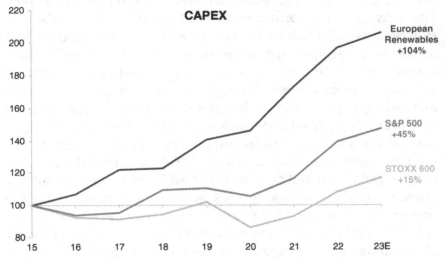

SOURCE: Goldman Sachs Global Investment Research

Exhibit 12.6   The same is true for global renewables companies: capex and R&D expenditure for basket of global renewable companies (€ bn)

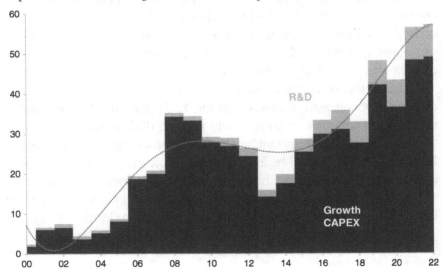

SOURCE: Goldman Sachs Global Investment Research

Commodities Spending

Another area likely to attract investment is the commodity market. This may seem counterintuitive, given the plans to decarbonise. However, overall demand for energy will rise over the transition period to a decarbonised economy, and this will require more demand for existing energy sources before sufficient capacity is available to meet demand through renewable sources. Commodity markets tend to move in long-term super cycles. For example, analysis by Bilge Erten and Jose Antonio Ocampo argues that there have been several super cycles since the nineteenth century.[14]

The Global Financial Crisis of 2008/9 interrupted the super cycle as global demand collapsed. The S&P GSCI, a benchmark for investment in the commodity markets and a measure of commodity performance over time, fell more than 60% over the following decade. The combination of the collapse in prices and ultra-low rates of return on capital, coupled with the growth in ESG policies, has starved the industry of capital. This resulted in a reduced supply of commodities, which created the conditions for rapid price increases as global demand recovered in the aftermath of the Covid pandemic.

While there are good reasons to invest less in carbon-intensive commodities, ironically, the transition away from an economy built on hydrocarbons to a net-zero-carbon economy cannot happen without many raw materials. Copper remains essential for electric vehicles, heating, wind and solar energy, as well as for energy storage.

In addition, so-called 'green demand' for copper has second-round effects on power grid demand (Exhibit 12.7). To build the renewable energy infrastructure, countries will need to digitise the power grids so that renewable energy can be used and transported most efficiently. Digital power grids will be able to monitor electrical loads for supply and demand in real time, but they are more copper-intensive. Consequently, rising demand for green investment is likely to require increased demand for copper; similarly for lithium (Exhibit 12.8).

---

[14] Erten, B. and Ocampo, J. A. (2013). Super cycles of commodity prices since the mid-nineteenth century. *World Development*, 44, pp. 14–30.

Exhibit 12.7   Green demand will represent 47% of additional copper demand for the rest of the decade

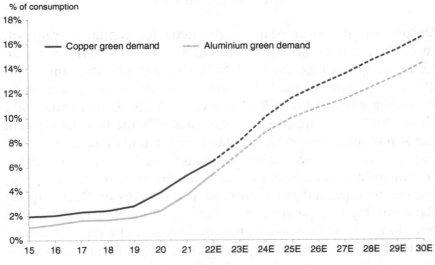

SOURCE: Goldman Sachs Global Investment Research

Exhibit 12.8   Green demand will constitute roughly 90% of lithium demand by 2030

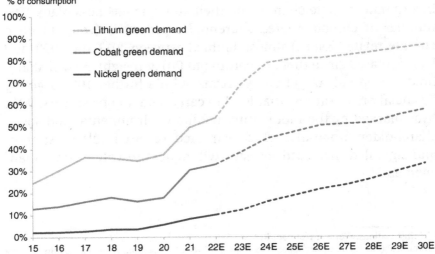

SOURCE: Goldman Sachs Global Investment Research

How Investment Markets Can Help Fund the Capex Boom

Despite the daunting scale of the need for capital investment, recent years have seen an acceleration in such investment. In terms of green investment, UNCTAD estimates that the value of sustainability-themed investment products in global capital markets increased to $3.2 trillion in 2020, or more than 80% since 2019. The number of sustainability-themed investment funds had increased to almost 4,000 by the middle of 2020, a 30% increase compared with 2019. Meanwhile, social bonds and mixed-sustainability bonds have increased fivefold over the same period, boosted by supranational entities such as the African Development Bank and the European Union. These investment products should help to fund the increase in required investment via a variety of vehicles: sustainable funds, green bonds, social bonds and mixed-sustainability bonds.[15] Flows into ESG funds have also risen globally, as shown in Exhibit 12.9.

Over the past decade, for example, investors have taken an increasingly active role in encouraging corporate management to incorporate climate change into their strategic business plans. The number of climate-related shareholder proposals (votes to push climate-related issues) almost doubled between 2011 and 2020, and has increased since then. According to Proxy Insight, 50% of shareholder proposals target energy firms, with a further 10% targeting financial organisations that lend to carbon energy producers; 2021 'was marked by the momentum behind environmental and social shareholder proposals, which garnered record levels of support and signalled increased investor willingness to vote against management'.[16]

---

[15] United Nations. World Investment Report 2021.
[16] Smith, J. (2022a). Four key takeaways from the 2022 proxy season. Available at https://www.ey.com/en_us/board-matters/four-key-takeaways-from-the-2022-proxy-season.

Exhibit 12.9   Flows into ESG funds have risen globally: cumulative flows into ESG and non-ESG funds ($ billion monthly). Areas are overlapping

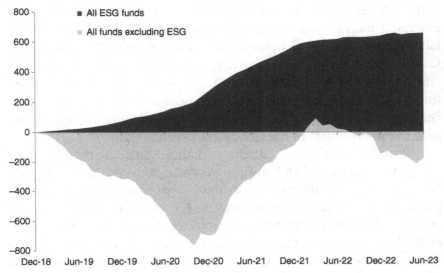

SOURCE: Goldman Sachs Global Investment Research

The result has been an effective rise in the cost of capital for traditional carbon energy producers which, in turn, is driving changes in the industry, with many traditional energy firms now investing in new cleaner energy generation.[17]

The Future of Jobs

The future of the job market is highly uncertain. AI is likely to have a major impact, as we discussed in Chapter 11. The combination of ageing populations in large parts of the developed world and rising populations in parts of the Global South, together with the need to fund decarbonisation, will pose major challenges. But it will also create

---

[17] Nathan, A., Galbraith, G. L. and Grimberg, J. (2020). Investing in climate change. Goldman Sachs Global Investment Research. Available at https://publishing.gs.com/content/research/en/reports/2021/12/13/97ad6bdf-a7c0-4716-80f9-3ee5240036df.html.

opportunities in both the 'new' and the 'old' sectors of the economy. As AI replaces many job functions that exist today, others will emerge. Although ageing is most advanced in developed economies, many emerging market economies will also experience a decline in the labour participation rate in the future. This highlights the difficulty of funding liabilities for countries even when they may be faster-growing and have larger populations. It also underscores the significant role that AI and other technology solutions could play in the future to help deal with these issues, and how, with these advances, many of the growth opportunities in the labour market will change.

According to the U.S. Bureau of Labor Statistics, the US economy is projected to add 8.3 million new jobs between 2021 and 2031. Many of these are likely to be in traditional areas of the economy, particularly related to the care sector. For example, the healthcare sector and 'social assistance' are projected to add 2.6 million jobs, more than any other sector, with the fastest growth in areas related to family services, driven in large part by the ageing of the baby-boom population and the higher prevalence of chronic health conditions.[18]

At the same time, investment in the capital infrastructure required to make the green revolution a reality will also pay dividends in terms of employment. Clean energy companies have already created significant clean energy jobs for electricians, construction workers, mechanics and others.[19]

In a recent analysis commissioned by the BlueGreen Alliance from the Political Economy Research Institute (PERI) and the University of Massachusetts Amherst, the US Inflation Reduction Act, through over 100 climate, energy and environmental investments, will create more than 9 million new jobs over the next decade in the United States alone.[20]

---

[18] U.S. Bureau of Labor Statistics (2018). Employment projections: 2018–2028 summary. Available at https://www.bls.gov/news.release/archives/ecopro_09042019.pdf.

[19] Climate Power (2023). Clean energy boom: The 142,016 (and counting) new clean energy jobs across the United States. Available at https://climatepower.us/wp-content/uploads/sites/23/2023/04/Clean-Energy-Boom-Report-%E2%80%94-April-2023.pdf.

[20] BlueGreen Alliance (2022). 9 Million jobs from climate action: The Inflation Reduction Act. Available at https://www.bluegreenalliance.org/site/9-million-good-jobs-from-climate-action-the-inflation-reduction-act/.

So, although AI, robotics and other technologies are likely to displace labour, they are likely to generate new opportunities in the traditional sectors. Additionally, many of the new roles will be in service-related jobs that do not currently exist. According to a report in 2018 by Dell Technologies, authored by the Institute for the Future (IFTF) and a panel of technology, business and academic experts, 85% of the jobs that will exist in 2030 have not yet been invented.[21] While the timing may be aggressive, the idea that new jobs will come along that can harness technologies and new approaches to traditional industries and create new job opportunities is important.

Don't Forget the Power of Nostalgia

One final thought on the 'Old Economy'. While technology is likely to play an even larger role in economies and markets in the Post-Modern Cycle, the more technologised we become, the more value there is in what we leave behind. This may seem to be a curious perspective, but history tells us that technologies that displace things often pave the way for new markets that value the very things that appear to have been rendered obsolete. This is particularly the case in a world that increasingly forces us towards social isolation and digital communication. Marketing experts have increasingly tapped into the trend of 'nostalgia marketing', which seems to have a particular appeal to so-called millennials.[22]

This trend is happening across a range of industries and generating significant growth for new and existing companies. The focus on

---

[21] Dell Technologies (2018). Realizing 2030: A divided vision of the future. Realizing 2030: A divided vision of the future. Available at https://www.delltechnologies.com/content/dam/delltechnologies/assets/perspectives/2030/pdf/Realizing-2030-A-Divided-Vision-of-the-Future-Research.pdf.

[22] Friedman, L. (2016). Why nostalgia marketing works so well with millennials, and how your brand can benefit. Available at https://www.forbes.com/sites/laurenfriedman/2016/08/02/why-nostalgia-marketing-works-so-well-with-millennials-and-how-your-brand-can-benefit/.

sustainability and interest in the past together create new consumer markets. According to research conducted by GlobalData for ThredUP, a US second-hand store, the resale clothes market is growing at 11 times the rate of traditional retail. This global market is expected to nearly double to $350bn by 2027.[23] The trend is accelerating; ThredUP noted that 118 million customers attempted to resell clothing for the first time in 2021, compared with just 36.2 million first-time sellers in 2020. Meanwhile, according to a report by Statistica, as of 2021, 42% of millennials and Gen Z respondents stated that they were likely to shop for second-hand items.[24] Fashion magazines such as *Vogue* and *Harper's Bazaar* have also spotted the trend.[25,26]

As other examples of companies that are tapping into this phenomenon: Sony recently brought back the Walkman; the film *Top Gun* was a box office success in 2022 (while the first version was a hit in 1986); Kate Bush had a chart topper with her 1985 song *Running Up the Hill*, from the series *Stranger Things* – her first UK number 1 hit since *Wuthering Heights* in 1978; ABBA reignited their 1970s success with *ABBA Voyage*, their first studio album in 40 years, and opened a show of the same name in London. The show is a virtual experience using avatars of the four band members from their 1970s heyday. It has been a huge hit, with over a million visitors to the 'concert' in the first year. It is a good example of how technological innovation is also levered to tap into the nostalgia market.[27]

Fear of disruption has often been overestimated. For example, when the railways dominated technology in the nineteenth century, there were concerns that horses would no longer be required.

---

[23] ThredUP Resale Report (2023). Available at https://www.thredup.com/resale.
[24] Smith, P. (2022b). Female consumer willingness to buy secondhand apparel by age worldwide 2019. Available at https://www.statista.com/statistics/828034/willingness-to-buy-secondhand-items-by-age-worldwide/.
[25] de Klerk, A. (2021, June 23). Secondhand clothing market set to be twice the size of fast fashion by 2030. *Harper's BAZAAR*.
[26] Farra, E. (2020, November 21). 2020 was a big year for old clothes: How vintage, secondhand, and upcycling took off. *Vogue*.
[27] Kielty, M. K. (2023, April 19). ABBA doesn't know how 'Voyage' show has succeeded. *Ultimate Classic Rock*.

As it turned out, railways created increased demand for horses because loads still had to be transported to and from railway stations.[28] This 'last mile problem' has parallels with today, as mobility and delivery solutions are required to satisfy consumer demand as it migrates to the internet.

Technology can drive spin-offs that are not so high-tech. App-based businesses were able to scale up traditional retail stores and address a much greater market. The growth in social media and internet shopping has also led to a growing problem of cyber security and safety, creating new markets for companies offering solutions. So, solving problems that new technologies create is a good place to look for new opportunities to emerge.

For instance, food is increasingly purchased through the internet, but it is often delivered by motorbikes, bicycles and cars (older technologies); the same is true for online purchases of consumer products. This, in turn, creates new companies that can use technology platforms to solve these logistical problems more efficiently.

On Your Bike

A similar trend has emerged in cities with respect to cycle and scooter sharing. Few would have predicted the steady growth in the bicycle market a decade ago; the global bicycle market was valued at over $64 billion in 2022 and is expected to grow at a compound rate of 9.7% from 2023 to 2030.[29]

Perhaps even more striking is how the bicycle is outselling the car. Analysis of 30 European countries by the Confederation of the European Bicycle Industry (CONEBI) and the European Cyclists Federation (ECF) suggests that, at the current trajectory,

---

[28] Odlyzko, A. (2000). Collective hallucinations and inefficient markets: The British railway mania of the 1840s. Available at SSRN: https://ssrn.com/abstract=1537338 or http://dx.doi.org/10.2139/ssrn.1537338.

[29] Grand View Research (2023a). Bicycle Market Size, Share and Trends Analysis Report, 2023–2030.

10 million more bikes will be sold per year in Europe by 2030, representing a rise of 47% compared with 2019. On this basis, the 30 million bikes sold annually in Europe would be more than double the annual sales of cars.[30] Cargo bikes are also selling fast as a solution to congested cities for delivery companies – although many are now electric, this is the delivery mechanism that was used in the Victorian period for many companies (Exhibit 12.10).[31]

Exhibit 12.10   A twentieth-century advertisement for a Hirondelle Saint Etienne delivery tricycle: print from *La Manufacture Française D'Armes et Cycles de Saint-Étienne*, a French mail-order catalogue

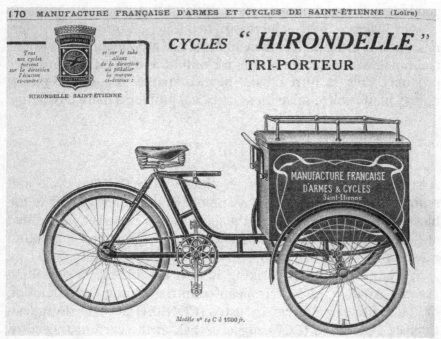

SOURCE: Photo by Art Media/Print Collector/Getty Images. https://www.gettyimages.com/detail/news-photo/hirondelle-saint-etienne-delivery-tricycle-advertisement-news-photo/463927375

---

[30] Sutton, M. (2020, December 2). Annual bike sales to run at more than double new car registrations by 2030. *Cycling Industry News*.
[31] Market Prospects (2022). The rising popularity of cargo bikes. Available at https://www.market-prospects.com/index.php/articles/popularity-of-cargo-bikes.

The growing value of nostalgia marketing has good precedents. When digital watches emerged in the 1970s, it was widely expected that mechanical watches would disappear. These fears were misplaced, as traditional watchmakers rebranded themselves and benefited from the trend for quality and nostalgia. The value of Swiss mechanical watches today is around 14 billion Swiss francs, and they continue to adapt despite the advent of quartz, digital and smart watches.[32]

A similar pattern emerged with cinema. The advent of video technology in the 1980s, and then DVDs in 1997, raised expectations that cinemas would shut down given the convenience of being able to watch films at home. Again, as it turned out, cinema reinvented itself and has become a fast-growing sector in the entertainment industry. Global cinema ticket sales are projected to reach over $15 billion in 2023, rising to over $18 billion by 2027.[33] Film studios have adapted by combining theatre businesses with streaming to generate new sources of revenue.

Even vinyl records are making a comeback among the younger generation, attracted by their retro appeal, with over four million chart-eligible albums sold in the United Kingdom alone in 2018.[34] According to the Recording Industry Association of America, for the first time since 1986, revenues from vinyl records in the United States are larger than from CDs.[35] Vinyl sales grew 28.7% by value year-over-year to $626 million in 2020 (although this still only accounts for 5.2% of total revenues by value). Revenues from CDs declined 23% to $483 million, continuing a long-term decline, providing an interesting example of how new technologies that displace obsolete technologies can themselves end up being displaced.

As evidence of the rapidly changing – and often unpredictable – nature of the 'high street', HMV records are set to reopen a flagship

[32] Shahbandeh, M. (2021). Swiss watch industry – statistics & facts. Available at https://www.statista.com/topics/7813/swiss-watch-industry/.

[33] Statista (2023). Cinema tickets – worldwide. Available at https://www.statista.com/outlook/dmo/eservices/event-tickets/cinema-tickets/worldwide.

[34] Asprou, E. (2019, October 22). Vinyl records to outsell CDs in 2019 for the first time in 40 years. Classic FM.

[35] Friedlander, P. (2021). Year-end 2020 RIAA revenues statistics. Available at https://www.riaa.com/wp-content/uploads/2021/02/2020-Year-End-Music-Industry-Revenue-Report.pdf.

store in London.[36] The business of selling the past is growing rapidly. In 2018, 'nostalgia' was the most common internet search related to fashion, according to Google.[37]

In the twenty-first century, in a highly digitalised world where almost everyone is connected to the internet and the cutting edge of technology threatens to displace jobs and companies, it is meaningful that the biggest company in Europe is LVMH. This is a company that sells the value of heritage in historic brands. It was formed in 1987 through the merger of two old companies: Louis Vuitton (founded in 1854) and Moet Hennessey, which itself was a merger in 1971 between Moet & Chandon, the champagne producer (founded in 1743) and Hennessey, producer of cognac (founded in 1765). According to its website, the company develops the brands that 'perfectly encapsulate all that they have embodied for our customers for centuries'. At the time of writing, the business of selling historic luxury brands has made its CEO and Chairman, Bernard Arnault, the second-richest person in the world (just behind Elon Musk), with an estimated personal net worth of more than $200 billion.[38]

As the ubiquity of technology increases and individuals increase their reliance on technology as they communicate via networks, the value they place on 'authenticity' and human connectivity – which can evoke a nostalgic image of a simpler, pre-digital life – is likely to grow. This is true across many different product categories, including food. According to Grand View Research, for example, the market for so-called 'artisanal' bakery products was valued globally at $95.13 billion in 2022 and is likely to grow at a compound rate of 5.7% from 2023 to 2030.[39]

Companies that help anchor consumers in the 'comfort' of the past in a fast-changing and uncertain world are likely to prosper in the Post-Modern Cycle.

---

[36] Foster, A. (2023, April 28). HMV's flagship Oxford Street store to reopen. BBC News.
[37] Fashion Technology Accelerator (2022). Second-hand business growth: Vintage today. Available at https://www.ftaccelerator.it/blog/second-hand-business-vintage/.
[38] Forbes Wealth Team (2023). The top ten richest people in the world. The top ten richest people in the world. Available at https://www.forbes.com/sites/forbeswealthteam/article/the-top-ten-richest-people-in-the-world/.
[39] Grand View Research (2023b). Artisanal Bakery Products Market Size, Share and Trends Analysis Report, 2023–2030.

Chapter 13
Summary and Conclusions

The past is always tense and the future, perfect.

—Zadie Smith

Cycles

The history of markets shows patterns of both cycles and longer-term trends, or super cycles. In *The Long Good Buy: Analysing Cycles in Markets*, I looked at the cycles throughout history and pointed to some important indicators that can help investors to identify repeated patterns and possible triggers for inflection points in markets. In this book, I have focused more on the longer-term trends. Most cycles evolve within these longer-term trends.

Cycles tend to repeat themselves in equity markets despite very different economic and political environments. The cycles of the past 70 years can typically be split into four distinct phases, each driven by distinct factors (for example, expectations of changes in future growth rates or in valuations).

1. **The Despair phase.** The period when the market moves from its peak to its trough, also known as the bear market. Prices fall on average by around 35% over 14 months.

2. **The Hope phase.** This is typically a short period (on average nine months in the United States), when the market rebounds from its trough valuation, or the P/E multiple expansion. This occurs in anticipation of a forthcoming recovery in the economic cycle, as well as future profit growth, and leads to a rise in the trailing P/E multiple. Prices rise by an average annualised 67% over nine months.

3. **The Growth phase.** This is usually the longest period (on average 49 months in the United States), when earnings growth is generated, and drives return. Prices rise by an average annualised 7% over 45 months.

4. **The Optimism phase.** This is the final part of the cycle, when investors become increasingly confident, or perhaps even complacent, and where valuations tend to rise again and outstrip earnings growth, thereby setting the stage for the next market correction. Psychology plays an important part in this phase of rising valuations. Prices rise by an average annualised 34% over 21 months.

Thus, the Despair phase is the part of the cycle that investors should focus on avoiding. But there are different types of bear market.

- **Structural bear markets** – triggered by structural imbalances and financial bubbles. Very often there is a price shock, such as deflation, and a banking crisis that follows. Structural bear markets on average see falls of 57%, last 42 months and take 111 months to return to their starting point in nominal terms (116 months in real terms).
- **Cyclical bear markets** – typically triggered by rising interest rates, impending recessions and falls in profits. They are a function of the economic cycle. Cyclical bear markets on average see falls of 31%, last 26 months and take 48 months to return to their starting point in nominal terms (61 months in real terms).
- **Event-driven bear markets** – triggered by a one-off shock that either does not lead to a domestic recession or temporarily

knocks a cycle off course. Common triggers are wars, an oil price shock, an emerging markets crisis or technical market dislocations. The principal driver of the bear market is a rise in risk premia rather than a rise in interest rates at the outset. Event-driven bear markets on average see falls of 29%, last eight months and recover within 13 months in nominal terms (55 months in real terms).

Super Cycles

Short-term cycles are important, but long-term trends, or super cycles, tend to have a dominant impact on investor returns. In this book, I discussed the very long-term trends in some of the key fundamentals that impact financial markets. These include economic activity, inflation and interest rates, government debt and inequality. In terms of financial markets themselves, the combination of these and other factors, such as social attitudes, policy and geopolitics, can substantially affect returns for investors.

Loosely speaking, for risky assets such as equities, some of these long-trending periods can be described as 'Fat and Flat' – relatively long periods during which cycles oscillate around relatively flat returns. Others are secular bull markets – long periods in which cycles continue to operate but within an upward-trending trajectory.

Generally, the periods that are 'Fat and Flat' can still generate meaningful opportunities for investors, but alpha (differences within the market) matters more than beta (movements at the index level). Often, these 'Fat and Flat' periods require investors to rely less on valuation expansion as a driver of returns and more on the ability of companies to compound returns over time through a combination of dividend payments and reinvestment.

In developed economies there were five major super cycles between the end of World War II and 2020. Each has had different drivers and return profiles, which are a function of the confluence of economic, political and social drivers.

- **1949–1968: total returns 1,109%, annualised returns 14%.** This was a period of strong economic growth, institution building and lower geopolitical risk premia. A baby boom and rapid technological change resulted in a powerful consumer boom.
- **1968–1982: total real returns −39%, annualised returns −4%.** This was a period dominated by high interest rates and inflation, labour unrest, a collapse in global trade and rising government deficits.
- **1982–2000: total real returns 1,356%, annualised returns 16%.** This was the period I call the Modern Cycle because it was much longer, with less volatility, than the traditional cycles that preceded it. This era was dominated by disinflation and a falling cost of capital. Supply-side reforms in economies boosted margins. The end of the Soviet Union reduced risk premia and ushered in an era of globalisation.
- **2000-2009: total real returns −58%, annualised −9%.** This was an era dominated by bubbles. The collapse of the technology bubble of 2000 dominated the first part of the super cycle. Falling interest rates provided the conditions for the US housing bubble and its eventual collapse. The financial crisis that followed resulted in a deep structural bear market.
- **2009–2020: total real returns 417%, annualised 16%.** This was an era dominated by zero interest rates and quantitative easing (QE). Rising valuations and the dominance of the US equity market and technology drove a large wedge between Growth and Value.

The Covid-19 pandemic triggered a brief event-driven bear market, and US equities fell 34% in total real terms. But the combination of interest rate cuts (where still possible), more QE, huge fiscal support and successful Covid vaccines resulted in a powerful rebound. In 2021, the S&P 500 rose by 27% (or 29% including dividends), ranking in the 85th percentile of all annual returns since 1962. While technology once again dominated (as consumers were limited to online shopping during lockdowns), the emergence of inflation and higher interest rates ushered in a new 'Fat and Flat' market range.

The Post-Modern Cycle

The emerging Post-Modern Cycle is being shaped by a combination of different drivers:

1. **A rise in the cost of capital.** This cycle is likely to experience higher yields, both nominal and real (adjusted for inflation).
2. **A slowdown in trend growth.** A combination of slower population growth and productivity is reducing the long-term trend rate of growth.
3. **A shift from globalisation to regionalisation.** We are emerging into an era of greater regionalisation driven by technology. Cheaper and less labour-intensive production is making onshoring or near-shoring more viable. Decarbonisation is placing an emphasis on more locally sourced production, while growing geopolitical tensions and increased protectionist trade policies are creating a different set of commercial incentives.
4. **A rise in the cost of labour and commodities.** Whereas the last 20 years were characterised by cheap and plentiful energy and labour, we are emerging from the pandemic into an environment of tighter labour and commodity markets.
5. **An increase in government spending and debt.** We are entering a period of increased regulation, bigger government (higher government shares of gross domestic product, GDP), higher taxes, higher interest expenses for corporates, and potentially lower profit shares of GDP.
6. **A rise in capital and infrastructure spending.** Over the next decade, demands to simplify supply chains from a security and environmental, social and governance perspective, coupled with increased spending on defence and decarbonisation, are likely to push capex higher.
7. **Changing demographics.** Ageing populations in many developed economies have led to rising dependency ratios and increased cost burdens for governments. This, in turn, is driving higher government borrowing and a higher tax burden.

As we move into the Post-Modern Cycle, new major challenges will increase the focus on technology as a solution. In particular, the focus on energy efficiency and decarbonisation should increase investment in technology companies that can enhance efficiency (as opposed to selling consumer products in particular).

At the same time, ageing populations, and the significant decline in labour participation, should incentivise companies to spend more on mechanisation and the substitution of labour for technology.

The emergence of artificial intelligence (AI) as a dominant technology will have far-reaching implications. First, on the destruction or displacement of many existing roles in the workplace. Second, on generating higher productivity and growth and, in turn, real incomes after many years of stagnation. If this becomes a reality, the rise in real incomes will likely spawn a whole host of new sub-industries and job opportunities.

This Post-Modern Cycle is also likely to generate significant opportunities in the 'Old Economy' of mature industries. The opportunity set for capital expenditure is changing. New priorities that include increased defence spending, finding alternative sources of energy supplies and decarbonisation, for example, will not only be very expensive, but also cannot be achieved purely through the development of smartphone apps or software; they need significant amounts of capital spending on infrastructure that effectively retools modern economies. Furthermore, many traditional labour-intensive, high-fixed-cost industries will likely be major beneficiaries of AI as they boost efficiency and reduce costs.

In an increasingly digital, if not virtual, world, consumers will likely value tradition. Nostalgia is already a large market and is likely to grow. High technology and tradition can coexist. The biggest company in the United States is a technology company, whereas in Europe the biggest company manufactures handmade high-end leather goods and fashion. Bifurcation and selectivity will be key for investors, just as innovation and adaption will be key for companies.

References

Chapter 1: An Introduction to Cycles and Secular Trends

Akerlof, G. A. and Shiller, R. J. (2010). *Animal Spirits: How Human Psychology Drives the Economy, and Why It Matters for Global Capitalism*. Princeton, NJ: Princeton University Press.

Aristotle (1944). *Aristotle in 23 Volumes,* Book V, section 1311b, translated by H. Rackham. London: Heinemann (Cambridge, MA: Harvard University Press).

Baddeley, M. (2010). Herding, social influence and economic decision-making: Socio-psychological and neuroscientific analyses. *Philosophical Transactions of The Royal Society,* Series B, **365**, pp. 281–290.

Basu, D. (2016). Long waves of capitalist development: An empirical investigation. University of Massachusetts Amherst, Department of Economics Working Paper No. 2016-15.

Borio, C. (2013). On time, stocks and flows: Understanding the global macroeconomic challenges. *National Institute Economic Review*, **225**(1), pp. 3–13.

Borio, C. (2014). The financial cycle and macroeconomics: What have we learnt? *Journal of Banking & Finance*, **45**, pp. 182–198.

Borio, C., Disyatat, P. and Juselius, M. (2013). Rethinking potential output: Embedding information about the financial cycle. BIS Working Paper No. 404.

Bruno, V. and Shin, H. S. (2015). Cross-border banking and global liquidity. *Review of Economic Studies*, **82**(2), pp. 535–564.

Dhaoui, A., Bourouis, S. and Boyacioglu, M. A. (2013). The impact of investor psychology on stock markets: Evidence from France. *Journal of Academic Research in Economics*, **5**(1), pp. 35–59.

Eckstein, O. and Sinai, A. (1986). The mechanisms of the business cycle in the postwar era. In R. J. Gordon (ed.), *The American Business Cycle: Continuity and Change*. Chicago, IL: University of Chicago Press, pp. 39–122.

Evans, R. (2014, May 23). How (not) to invest like Sir Isaac Newton. *The Telegraph*.

Fama, E. F. (1970). Efficient capital markets: A review of theory and empirical work. *The Journal of Finance*, **25**(2), pp. 383–417.

Filardo, A., Lombardi, M. and Raczko, M. (2019). Measuring financial cycle time. Bank of England Staff Working Paper No. 776.

Fisher, I. (1933). The debt-deflation theory of great depressions. *Econometrica*, **1**(4), pp. 337–357.

Kahneman, D. and Tversky, A. (1979). Prospect theory: An analysis of decision under risk. *Econometrica*, **47**(2), pp. 263–292.

Keynes, J. M. (1936). *The General Theory of Employment, Interest, and Money*. London: Palgrave Macmillan.

Kindleberger, C. (1996). *Manias, Panics and Crashes*, 3rd ed. New York: Basic Books.

Klingberg, F. J. (1952). The historical alternation of moods in American foreign policy. *World Politics*, **4**(2), pp. 239–273.

Loewenstein, G., Scott, R. and Cohen, J. D. (2008). Neuroeconomics. *Annual Review of Psychology*, **59**, pp. 647–672.

Mackay, C. (1852). *Extraordinary Popular Delusions and the Madness of Crowds*, 2nd ed. London: Office of the National Illustrated Library.

Malmendier, U. and Nagel, S. (2016). Learning from inflation experiences. *The Quarterly Journal of Economics*, **131**(1), pp. 53–87.

Minsky, H. P. (1975). *John Maynard Keynes*. New York: Columbia University Press.

Minsky, H. P. (1986). *Stabilizing an Unstable Economy: A Twentieth Century Fund Report*. New Haven, CT: Yale University Press.

Minsky, H. P. (1992). The Financial Instability Hypothesis. Jerome Levy Economics Institute Working Paper No. 74. Available at SSRN: https://ssrn .com/abstract=161024 or http://dx.doi.org/10.2139/ssrn.161024.

Odlyzko, A. (2010). Collective hallucinations and inefficient markets: The British railway mania of the 1840s. Available at SSRN: https://ssrn.com/abstract=1537338 or http://dx.doi.org/10.2139/ssrn.1537338.

Rose, R. and Urwin, D. W. (1970). Persistence and change in Western party systems since 1945. *Political Studies*, **18**(3), pp. 287–319.

Schlesinger, A. M. (1999). *The Cycles of American History*. Boston, MA: Houghton Mifflin.

Shaw, E. S. (1947). Burns and Mitchell on business cycles. *Journal of Political Economy*, **55**(4), pp. 281–298.

Shiller, R. J. (1981). Do stock prices move too much to be justified by subsequent changes in dividends? *The American Economic Review*, **71**(3), pp. 421–436.

Shiller, R. J. (2000). *Irrational Exuberance*. Princeton, NJ: Princeton University Press.

Soros, G. (2014). Fallibility, reflexivity, and the human uncertainty principle. *Journal of Economic Methodology*, **20**(4), pp. 309–329.

Thompson, K. W., Modelski, G. and Thompson, W. R. (1990). Long cycles in world politics. *The American Historical Review*, **95**(2), pp. 456–457.

Wilde, O. (1889). *The Decay of Lying: A Dialogue*. London: Kegan Paul, Trench & Co.

Zullow, H. M. (1991). Pessimistic ruminations in popular songs and news magazines predict economic recession via decreased consumer optimism and spending. *Journal of Economic Psychology*, **12**(3), pp. 501–526.

Chapter 2: Equity Cycles and Their Drivers

Oppenheimer, P., Jaisson, G., Bell, S. and Peytavin, L. (2022). Bear repair: The bumpy road to recovery. Goldman Sachs Global Investment Research, Global Strategy Paper. Available at https://publishing.gs.com/content/research/en/reports/2022/09/07/8ebbd20c-9099-4940-bff2-ed9c31aebfd9.html.

Chapter 3: Super Cycles and Their Drivers

Alfani, G. (2021). Economic inequality in preindustrial times: Europe and beyond. *Journal of Economic Literature*, **59**(1), pp. 3–44.

Álvarez-Nogal, C. and De La Escosura, L. P. (2013). The rise and fall of Spain (1270–1850). *The Economic History Review*, **66**(1), pp. 1–37.

Basu, D. (2016). Long waves of capitalist development: An empirical investigation. University of Massachusetts Amherst, Department of Economics Working Paper No. 2016-15.

Bernanke, B. S. (2005). The global saving glut and the U.S. current account deficit. Speech at the Sandridge Lecture, Virginia Association of Economics, Richmond, VA, March 10.

Bernanke, B. S. (2010). Causes of the recent financial and economic crisis. Testimony before the Financial Crisis Inquiry Commission, Washington, D.C.

Bernanke, B. S., Bertaut, C. C., DeMarco, L. P. and Kamin, S. (2011). International capital flows and the returns to safe assets in the United States, 2003–2007. International Finance Discussion Paper No. 1014.

Bolt, J. and van Zanden, J. L. (2020). The Maddison Project. Maddison-Project Working Paper No. WP-15.

Broadberry, S. (2013). Accounting for the Great Divergence: Recent findings from historical national accounting. London School of Economics and CAGE, Economic History Working Paper No. 184.

Broadberry, S., Campbell, B., Klein, A., Overton, M., and van Leeuwen, B. (2011). *British Economic Growth, 1270–1870: An Output-Based Approach*. Cambridge: Cambridge University Press.

Bryan, M. (2013). The Great Inflation. Available at https://www.federalreservehistory.org/essays/great-inflation.

Costa, L. F., Palma, N., and Reis, J. (2013). The great escape? The contribution of the empire to Portugal's economic growth, 1500–1800. *European Review of Economic History*, **19**(1), pp. 1–22.

Drehmann, M., Borio, C. and Tsatsaronis, K. (2012). Characterising the financial cycle: Don't lose sight of the medium term! BIS Working Paper No. 380.

Fouquet, R. and Broadberry, S. (2015). Seven centuries of European economic growth and decline. *Journal of Economic Perspectives*, **29**(4), pp. 227–244.

King, S. D. (2023). *We Need to Talk About Inflation: 14 Urgent Lessons from the Last 2,000 Years*. New Haven, CT: Yale University Press.

Lindert, P. H. (1986). Unequal English wealth since 1670. *Journal of Political Economy*, **94**(6), pp. 1127–1162.

Lunsford, K. G. and West, K. (2017). Some evidence on secular drivers of US safe real rates. Federal Reserve Bank of Cleveland Working Paper No. 17-23.

MacFarlane, H. and Mortimer-Lee, P. (1994). Inflation over 300 years. Bank of England.

Maddison, A. (2001). *The World Economy: A Millennial Perspective*. Paris: OECD.

Malanima, P. (2011). The long decline of a leading economy: GDP in central and northern Italy, 1300–1913. *European Review of Economic History*, **15**(2), pp. 169–219.

McCombie, J. S. L. and Maddison, A. (1983). Phases of capitalist development. *The Economic Journal*, **93**(370), pp. 428–429.

Owen, J. (2012). Old Coppernose – quantitative easing, the medieval way. Royal Mint.

Piketty, T. (2014). *Capital in the Twenty-First Century*. Translated by A. Goldhammer. Cambridge, MA: The Belknap Press of Harvard University Press.

Piketty, T. (2020). *Capital and Ideology*. Translated by A. Goldhammer. Cambridge, MA: Harvard University Press.

Poghosyan, T. (2015). How do public debt cycles interact with financial cycles? IMF Working Paper No. 15(248).

Ritter, J. R. and Warr, R. S. (2002). The decline of inflation and the bull market of 1982–1999. *The Journal of Financial and Quantitative Analysis*, **37**(1), pp. 29–61.

Roser, M. (2013). Economic growth. Available at https://ourworldindata.org/economic-growth.

Schmelzing, P. (2020). Eight centuries of global real interest rates, R-G, and the 'suprasecular' decline, 1311–2018. Bank of England Staff Working Paper No. 845.

Schön, L. and Krantz, O. (2012). The Swedish economy in the early modern period: Constructing historical national accounts. *European Review of Economic History*, **16**(4), pp. 529–549.

Schön, L. and Krantz, O. (2015). New Swedish historical national accounts since the 16th century in constant and current prices. Department of Economic History, Lund University. Lund Papers in Economic History No. 140.

Shirras, G. F. and Craig, J. H. (1945). Sir Isaac Newton and the currency. *The Economic Journal*, **55**(218/219), pp. 217–241.

Stockhammer, E. and Gouzoulis, G. (2022). Debt–GDP cycles in historical perspective: The case of the USA (1889–2014). *Industrial and Corporate Change*, **32**(2), pp. 317–335.

Summers, L. H. (2014). U.S. economic prospects: Secular stagnation, hysteresis, and the zero lower bound. *Business Economics*, **49**(2), pp. 65–73.

Szreter, S. (2021). The history of inequality: The deep-acting ideological and institutional influences. IFS Deaton Review of Inequalities.

Thomas, R. and Dimsdale, N. (2017). A Millennium of UK Macroeconomic Data. Bank of England OBRA Dataset.

van Zanden, J. L. and van Leeuwen, B. (2012). Persistent but not consistent: The growth of national income in Holland 1347–1807. *Explorations in Economic History*, **49**(2), pp. 119–130.

Chapter 4: 1949–1968: Post-World War II Boom

Anstey, V. (1943). *World Economic Survey, 1941–42* [Book Review]. *Economica*, **10**(38), pp. 212–214.

Crafts, N. (2020). Rebuilding after the Second World War: What lessons for today? Warwick Economics Department, CAGE Research Centre.

Crafts, N. F. R. (1995). The golden age of economic growth in Western Europe, 1950–1973. *The Economic History Review*, **48**(3), pp. 429–447.

Eduqas (2018). *Austerity, Affluence and Discontent: Britain, 1951–1979* [GCSE History Resource].

Federal Reserve Bank of Boston (1984). *The International Monetary System: Forty Years After Bretton Woods*. Boston, MA: Federal Reserve Bank of Boston.

Frankel, R. S. (2021). When were credit cards invented: The history of credit cards. Available at https://www.forbes.com/advisor/credit-cards/history-of-credit-cards/.

Glyn, A., Hughes, A., Lipietz, A. and Singh, A. (1988). The rise and fall of the golden age. United Nations University WIDER Working Paper No. 43/1988.

Goss, J. (2022). *Design, 1950–75*. Essay – The Metropolitan Museum of Art.

International Monetary Fund (2020). The end of the Bretton Woods System (1972–81). Available at https://www.imf.org/external/about/histend.htm.

Kim, W. (2022). Television and American consumerism. *Journal of Public Economics*, **208**, art. 104609.

Miller, A., Berlo, J. C., Wolf, B. J. and Roberts, J. L. (2018). *American Encounters: Art, History, and Cultural Identity*. Washington, D.C.: Washington University Libraries.

Notestein, F. W. (1983). Frank Notestein on population growth and economic development. *Population and Development Review*, **9**(2), pp. 345–360.

Powell, J. H. (2020). New economic challenges and the Fed's monetary policy review. Speech (via webcast) at Navigating the Decade Ahead: Implications for Monetary Policy, an economic policy symposium sponsored by the Federal Reserve Bank of Kansas City, Jackson Hole, WY, 27th August.

Reinhart, C. M., Kirkegaard, J. F. and Sbrancia, M. B. (2011). Financial repression redux. Available at https://www.imf.org/external/pubs/ft/fandd/2011/06/pdf/reinhart.pdf.

Rose, J. (2021). Yield curve control in the United States, 1942 to 1951. Available at https://www.chicagofed.org/publications/economic-perspectives/2021/2.

Statista (2023). Average annual growth in the economic output of Western European countries during the Golden Age from 1950 to 1970. Available at https://www.statista.com/statistics/730758/western-europe-economic-manufacturing-output-growth-golden-age/.

The Economic Times (2008, July 1). General Motors's stock skids to 1950s level.

The National WWII Museum (2013). *Thanks to Penicillin . . . He Will Come Home! The Challenge of Mass Production* [Lesson Plan from the Education Department].

United Nations (2017). Post-war reconstruction and development in the Golden Age of Capitalism. *World Economic and Social Survey 2017*, pp. 23–48.

Vonyó, T. (2008). Post-war reconstruction and the Golden Age of economic growth. *European Review of Economic History*, **12**(2), pp. 221–241.

Whiteley, N. (1987). Toward a throw-away culture. Consumerism, 'style obsolescence' and cultural theory in the 1950s and 1960s. *Oxford Art Journal*, **10**(2), pp. 3–27.

Chapter 5: 1968–1982: Inflation and Low Returns

Boughton, J. M. (2002). Globalization and the silent revolution of the 1980s. *Finance & Development*, **39**(1), pp. 40–43.

Bryan, M. (2013). The Great Inflation. Available at https://www.federal reservehistory.org/essays/great-inflation.

Church, M. (1976, November 29). Catching up with punk. *The Times*.

Fletcher, N. (2018). "If only I could get a job somewhere": The emergence of British punk. Young Historians Conference, 19. Available at https://pdx scholar.library.pdx.edu/younghistorians/2018/oralpres/19.

Hodgson, J. D. and Moore, G. H. (1972). *Analysis of Work Stoppages, 1970*. U.S. Department of Labor, Bulletin 1727.

Irwin, D. A. (1994). The new protectionism in industrial countries: Beyond the Uruguay Round. IMF Policy Discussion Paper No. 1994/005.

Lydon, J., Matlock, G., Cook, P. T. and Jones, S. P. (1976). *No Future*.

Maddison Database (2010). https://www.rug.nl/ggdc/historicaldevelopment/ maddison/releases/maddison-database-2010?lang=en.

Meltzer, A. H. (1991). US policy in the Bretton Woods era. *Federal Reserve Bank of St. Louis Review*, **73**(3), pp. 54–83.

Schwenk, A. E. (2003). Compensation in the 1970s. *Compensation and Working Conditions*, **6**(3), pp. 29–32.

Siegel, J. J. (2014). *Stocks for the Long Run: The Definitive Guide to Financial Market Returns & Long-Term Investment Strategies*. New York: McGraw-Hill Education.

United Nations Department of Economic and Social Affairs (2017). World Economic and Social Survey 2017: Reflecting on Seventy Years of Development Policy Analysis. New York: United Nations.

Chapter 6: 1982–2000: The Modern Cycle

Bernanke, B. (2004). The Great Moderation: Remarks before the Meetings of the Eastern Economic Association, Washington, D.C.

Boughton, J. M. (2002). Globalization and the silent revolution of the 1980s. *Finance & Development,* **39**(1), pp. 40–43.

Boughton, J. M. (2012). *Tearing Down Walls: The International Monetary Fund, 1990–1999.* Washington, D.C.: International Monetary Fund.

Brookings (2001). The long and large decline in U.S. output volatility. Available at https://www.brookings.edu/articles/the-long-and-large-decline-in-u-s-output-volatility/.

Corsetti, G., Pesenti, P. and Roubini, N. (1998a). What caused the Asian currency and financial crisis? Part I: A macroeconomic overview. NBER Working Paper No. 6833.

Corsetti, G., Pesenti, P. and Roubini, N. (1998b). What caused the Asian currency and financial crisis? Part II: The policy debate. NBER Working paper No. 6834.

Côté, D. and Graham, C. (2004). Convergence of government bond yields in the euro zone: The role of policy harmonization. Bank of Canada Working Paper No. 2004-23.

Crafts, F. R. N. (2004). The world economy in the 1990s: A long run perspective. Department of Economic History, London School of Economics, Working Paper No. 87/04.

Cutts, R. L. (1990). Power from the ground up: Japan's land bubble. *Harvard Business Review,* **May/Jun**. https://hbr.org/1990/05/power-from-the-ground-up-japans-land-bubble.

Dabrowski, M. (2022). Thirty years of economic transition in the former Soviet Union: Macroeconomic dimension. *Russian Journal of Economics,* **8**(2), pp. 95–121.

Danielsson, J., Valenzuela, M. and Zer, I. (2016). Learning from history: Volatility and financial crises. FEDS Working Paper No. 2016-93.

Encyclopaedia Britannica (1987). President Ronald Reagan speaking at the Berlin Wall, 1987. https://www.britannica.com/story/mr-gorbachev-tear-down-this-wall-reagans-berlin-speech.

Feldstein, M. (1994). American economic policy in the 1980s: A personal view. In M. Feldstein (ed.), *American Economic Policy in the 1980s.* Chicago, IL: University of Chicago Press, pp. 1–80.

Fox, J. (2017). The mostly forgotten tax increases of 1982–1993. Available at https://www.bloomberg.com/view/articles/2017-12-15/the-mostly-forgotten-tax-increases-of-1982-1993.

Hodkinson, S. (2019). *Safe as Houses: Private Greed, Political Negligence and Housing Policy After Grenfell*. Manchester: Manchester University Press.

Hoj, J., Kato, T. and Pilat, D. (1995). Deregulation and privatisation in the service sector. OECD Economic Studies No. 25.

International Monetary Fund. Money Matters: An IMF Exhibit – The Importance of Global Cooperation. Debt and Transition (1981–1989), Part 4 of 7. Available at https://www.imf.org/external/np/exr/center/mm/eng/dt_sub_3.htm.

Johnston, E. (2009, January 6). Lessons from when the bubble burst. *The Japan Times*.

Laffer, A. (2004). The Laffer Curve: Past, present, and future. Available at https://www.heritage.org/taxes/report/the-laffer-curve-past-present-and-future.

Lankes, H., Stern, N., Blumenthal, M. and Weigl, J. (1999). Capital flows to Eastern Europe. In M. Feldstein (ed.), *International Capital Flows*. Chicago, IL: University of Chicago Press, pp. 57–110.

Miller, M., Weller, P. and Zhang, L. (2002). Moral hazard and the US stock market: Analysing the 'Greenspan Put'. *The Economic Journal*, **112**(478), pp. C171–C186.

Okina, K., Shirakawa, M. and Shiratsuka, S. (2001). The asset price bubble and monetary policy: Experience of Japan's economy in the late 1980s and its lessons. *Monetary and Economic Studies*, **19**(S1), pp. 395–450.

Parry, T. R. (1997). The October '87 crash ten years later. FRBSF Economic Letter, Federal Reserve Bank of San Francisco.

Pera, A (1989). Deregulation and privatisation in an economy-wide context. *OECD Journal: Economic Studies*, **12**, pp. 159–204.

Piketty, T. (2014). *Capital in the Twenty-First Century*. Translated by A. Goldhammer. Cambridge, MA: The Belknap Press of Harvard University Press.

Ritter, J. R. and Warr, R. S. (2002). The decline of inflation and the bull market of 1982–1999. *The Journal of Financial and Quantitative Analysis*, **37**(1), pp. 29–61.

Stock, J. H. and Watson, M. W. (2002). Has the business cycle changed and why? *NBER Macroeconomics Annual*, **17**, pp. 159–218.

Syed, M. and Walsh, J. P. (2012). The tiger and the dragon. *Finance & Development*, **49**(3), pp. 36–39.

The Economist (1997, April 3). Freedom in the air.

The Economist (2002, June 27). Coming home to roost.

Turner, G. (2003). *Solutions to a Liquidity Trap: Japan's Bear Market and What It Means for the West*. London: GFC Economics.

Wessel, D. (2018). For the Fed, is it 1998 all over again? Available at https://www.brookings.edu/articles/for-the-fed-is-it-1998-all-over-again/.

Williamson, J. (1998). Globalization: The concept, causes, and consequences. Keynote address to the Congress of the Sri Lankan Association for the Advancement of Science, Colombo, Sri Lanka, 15th December.

Chapter 7: 2000–2009: Bubbles and Troubles

Berkshire Hathaway (2022). Annual Report.

Cohen, B. H. and Remolona, E. M. (2001). Overview: Financial markets prove resilient. *BIS Quarterly Review*, **Dec**, pp. 1–12.

Gompers, P. A. and Lerner, J. (2004). *The Venture Capital Cycle*, 2nd ed. Cambridge, MA: MIT Press.

Gordon, J. N. (1999). Deutsche Telekom, German corporate governance, and the transition costs of capitalism. Columbia Law School, Center for Law and Economic Studies, Working Paper No. 140.

Hayes, A. (2023). Dotcom bubble definition. Available at https://www.investopedia.com/terms/d/dotcom-bubble.asp.

Makinen, G. (2002). *The Economic Effects of 9/11: A Retrospective Assessment*. Congressional Research Service Report RL31617.

Mason, P. (2011, October 7). Thinking outside the 1930s box. BBC News.

McCullough, B. (2018). A revealing look at the dot-com bubble of 2000 — and how it shapes our lives today. Available at https://ideas.ted.com/an-eye-opening-look-at-the-dot-com-bubble-of-2000-and-how-it-shapes-our-lives-today/.

Norris, F. (2000, January 3). The year in the markets; 1999: Extraordinary winners and more losers. *New York Times*.

Oppenheimer, P. C. (2020). *The Long Good Buy*. Chichester: Wiley.

Perez, C. (2009). The double bubble at the turn of the century: Technological roots and structural implications. *Cambridge Journal of Economics*, **33**(4), pp. 779–805.

Pezzuto, I. (2012). Miraculous financial engineering or toxic finance? The genesis of the U.S. subprime mortgage loans crisis and its consequences on the global financial markets and real economy. *Journal of Governance and Regulation*, **1**(3), pp. 113–124.

Romer, C. and Romer, D. (2017). New evidence on the aftermath of financial crises in advanced countries. *American Economic Review*, **107**(10), pp. 3072–3118.

Skeel, D. (2018). History credits Lehman Brothers' collapse for the 2008 financial crisis. Here's why that narrative is wrong. Available at https://www.brookings.edu/articles/history-credits-lehman-brothers-collapse-for-the-2008-financial-crisis-heres-why-that-narrative-is-wrong/.

The Financial Crisis Inquiry Commission (2011). The CDO machine. *Financial Crisis Inquiry Commission Report*, Chapter 8. Stanford, CA: Financial Crisis Enquiry Commission at Stanford Law.

Torres, C., Ivry, B. and Lanman, S. (2010). Fed reveals Bear Stearns assets it swallowed in firm's rescue. Available at https://www.bloomberg.com/news/articles/2010-04-01/fed-reveals-bear-stearns-assets-swallowed-to-get-jpmorgan-to-rescue-firm.

Weinberg, J. (2013). The Great Recession and its aftermath. Available at https://www.federalreservehistory.org/essays/great-recession-and-its-aftermath.

Chapter 8: 2009–2020: The Post-Financial-Crisis Cycle and Zero Interest Rates

Antolin, P., Schich, S. and Yermi, J. (2011). The economic impact of protracted low interest rates on pension funds and insurance companies. *OECD Journal: Financial Market Trends*, **2011**(1), pp. 237–256.

Balatti, M., Brooks, C., Clements, M. P. and Kappou, K. (2016). Did quantitative easing only inflate stock prices? Macroeconomic evidence from the US and UK. Available at SSRN: https://ssrn.com/abstract=2838128 or http://dx.doi.org/10.2139/ssrn.2838128.

Belke, A. H. (2013). Impact of a low interest rate environment – global liquidity spillovers and the search-for-yield. Ruhr Economic Paper No. 429.

Bernanke, B. S. (2005). The global saving glut and the U.S. current account deficit. Speech at the Sandridge Lecture, Virginia Association of Economics, Richmond, VA, March 10.

Borio, C., Piti, D. and Rungcharoenkitkul, P. (2019). What anchors for the natural rate of interest? BIS Working Paper No. 777.

Caballero, R. J. and Farhi, E. (2017). The safety trap. *The Review of Economic Studies*, **85**(1), pp. 223–274.

Christensen, J. and Krogstrup, S. (2019). How quantitative easing affects bond yields: Evidence from Switzerland. Available at https://res.org.uk/mediabriefing/how-quantitative-easing-affects-bond-yields-evidence-from-switzerland/.

Christensen, J. H. E. and Speigel, M. M. (2019). Negative interest rates and inflation expectations in Japan. *FEBSF Economic Letter*, **22**.

Cunliffe, J. (2017). The Phillips curve: Lower, flatter or in hiding? Speech given at the Oxford Economics Society. Available at https://www.bankofeng land.co.uk/speech/2017/jon-cunliffe-speech-at-oxford-economics-society.

Gagnon, J., Raskin, M., Remache, J. and Sack, B. (2011). The financial market effects of the Federal Reserve's large-scale asset purchases. *International Journal of Central Banking*, 7(1), pp. 3–43.

Gilchrist, S. and Zakrajsek, E. (2013). The impact of the Federal Reserve's large-scale asset purchase programs on corporate credit risk. NBER Working Paper No. 19337.

Lazonick, W. (2014). Profits without prosperity. *Harvard Business Review*, **Sept**. https://hbr.org/2014/09/profits-without-prosperity.

Lian, C., Ma, Y. and Wang, C. (2018). Low interest rates and risk taking: Evidence from individual investment decisions. *The Review of Financial Studies*, **32**(6), pp. 2107–2148.

OECD Business and Finance Outlook (2015). Chapter 4: Can pension funds and life insurance companies keep their promises?

Summers, L. H. (2015). Demand side secular stagnation. *American Economic Review*, **105**(5), pp. 60–65.

Chapter 9: The Pandemic and the Return of 'Fat and Flat'

Averstad, P., Beltrán, A., Brinkman, M., Maia, P., Pinshaw, G., Quigley, D., *et al.* (2023). McKinsey Global Private Markets Review: Private markets turn down the volume. Available at https://www.mckinsey.com/industries/private-equity-and-principal-investors/our-insights/mckinseys-private-markets-annual-review.

Cerclé, E., Bihan, H. and Monot, M. (2021). Understanding the expansion of central banks' balance sheets. Banque de France Eco Notepad, Post No. 209.

Deloitte Center for Financial Services (2021). The rise of newly empowered retail investors. Available at https://www2.deloitte.com/content/dam/Deloitte/us/Documents/financial-services/us-the-rise-of-newly-empowered-retail-investors-2021.pdf?ref=zoya-blog.

Franck, T. and Li, Y. (2020, March 8). 10-year Treasury yield hits new all-time low of 0.318% amid historic flight to bonds. CNBC.

Haley, B. (2022). Venture capital 2021 recap—a record breaking year. Available at https://insight.factset.com/venture-capital-2021-recap-a-record-breaking-year.

Harari, D., Keep, M. and Brien, P. (2021). Coronavirus: Effect on the economy and public finances. House of Commons Briefing Paper No. 8866.

Kaissar (2021). GameStop Furor Inflicts Lasting Pain on Hedge Funds. Bloomberg.

Koetsier, J. (2020). 97% of executives say Covid-19 sped up digital transformation. Available at https://www.forbes.com/sites/johnkoetsier/2020/09/10/97-of-executives-say-covid-19-sped-up-digital-transformation/.

Levy, A. (2021, December 24). Here are the top-performing technology stocks of 2021. CNBC.

Matthews, S. (2020). U.S. jobless rate may soar to 30%, Fed's Bullard says. Available at https://www.bloomberg.com/news/articles/2020-03-22/fed-s-bullard-says-u-s-jobless-rate-may-soar-to-30-in-2q.

Mueller-Glissmann, C., Rizzi, A., Wright, I. and Oppenheimer, P. (2021). The Balanced Bear – Part 1: Low(er) returns and latent drawdown risk. GOAL – Global Strategy Paper No. 27.

Organisation for Economic Co-operation and Development (2020). G20 GDP Growth – First quarter of 2020.

Ponciano, J. (2021). Is the stock market about to crash? Available at https://www.forbes.com/sites/jonathanponciano/2021/02/12/is-the-stock-market-about-to-crash/.

Reed, S. and Krauss, C. (2020, April 20). Too much oil: How a barrel came to be worth less than nothing. *The New York Times*.

Sandford, A. (2020, April 2). Coronavirus: Half of humanity on lockdown in 90 countries. Euronews.

Scheid, B. (2020). Top 5 tech stocks' S&P 500 dominance raises fears of bursting bubble. Available at https://www.spglobal.com/marketintelligence/en/news-insights/latest-news-headlines/top-5-tech-stocks-s-p-500-dominance-raises-fears-of-bursting-bubble-59591523.

Strauss, D. (2020, September 23). Pandemic knocks a tenth off incomes of workers worldwide. *Financial Times*.

UNESCO (2020). Education: From school closure to recovery. Available at https://www.unesco.org/en/covid-19/education-response.

United States Census Bureau (2022). Impacts of the COVID-19 pandemic on business operations. Available at https://www.census.gov/library/publications/2022/econ/2020-aces-covid-impact.html.

Waters, R. (2022, August 1). Venture capital's silent crash: When the tech boom met reality. *Financial Times*.

Chapter 10: Post-Modern Cycle

Acemoglu, D. and Autor, D. (2011). Chapter 12 – Skills, tasks and technologies: Implications for employment and earnings. *Handbook of Labor Economics*, **4**(Part B), pp. 1043–1171.

Adrian, T., Crump, R. K. and Moench, E. (2013). Pricing the term structure with linear regressions. FRB of New York Staff Report No. 340. Available at SSRN: https://ssrn.com/abstract=1362586 or http://dx.doi.org/10.2139/ssrn.1362586.

Autor, D. (2022). The labor market impacts of technological change: From unbridled enthusiasm to qualified optimism to vast uncertainty. NBER Working Paper No. w30074. Available at SSRN: https://ssrn.com/abstract=4122803 or http://dx.doi.org/10.2139/ssrn.4122803.

Bergquist, A.-K. and Söderholm, K. (2016). Sustainable energy transition: The case of the Swedish pulp and paper industry 1973–1990. *Energy Efficiency*, **9**(5), pp. 1179–1192.

Cigna, S., Gunnella, V. and Quaglietti, L. (2022). Global value chains: Measurement, trends and drivers. ECB Occasional Paper No. 2022/289.

Congressional Budget Office (2021). Budgetary effects of climate change and of potential legislative responses to it. CBO Publication No. 57019.

Crowe, D., Haas, J., Millot, V., Rawdanowicz, Ł. and Turban, S. (2022). Population ageing and government revenue: Expected trends and policy considerations to boost revenue. OECD Economics Department Working Paper No. 1737.

Daly, K. and Gedminas, T. (2022). The path to 2075 — slower global growth, but convergence remains intact. Goldman Sachs Global Investment Research, Global Economics Paper. Available at https://publishing.gs.com/content/research/en/reports/2022/12/06/af8feefc-a65c-4d5e-bcb6-51175d816ff1.html.

Della Vigna, M., Bocharnikova, Y., Mehta, N., Choudhary, U., Bhandari, N., Modak, A., *et al.* (2023). Top projects 2023: Back to growth. Goldman Sachs Global Investment Research. Available at https://publishing.gs.com/content/research/en/reports/2023/06/27/bcd4ad94-6106-4bb8-9133-fa35a6bfa730.html.

Della Vigna, M., Clarke, Z., Shahab, B., Mehta, N., Bhandari, N., Amorim, B., *et al.* (2022). Top projects 2022: The return of the energy investment cycle. Goldman Sachs Global Investment Research. Available at https://publishing.gs.com/content/research/en/reports/2022/04/19/ae5c2010-d7ef-400c-b8e7-1cf25650ef17.html.

Dunz, N. and Power, S. (2021). *Climate-Related Risks for Ministries of Finance: An Overview*. Washington, DC: The Coalition of Finance Ministers for Climate Action.

Fengler, W. (2021). The silver economy is coming of age: A look at the growing spending power of seniors. Available at https://www.brookings.edu/articles/the-silver-economy-is-coming-of-age-a-look-at-the-growing-spending-power-of-seniors/.

Fukuyama, F. (1992). *The End of History and the Last Man*. New York: Free Press.

Gunnella, V. and Quaglietti, L. (2019). The economic implications of rising protectionism: A Euro area and global perspective. ECB Economic Bulletin No. 3.

Habakkuk, H. J. (1962). *American and British Technology in the Nineteenth Century: The Search for Labour-Saving Inventions*. Cambridge: Cambridge University Press.

Hollinger, P. (2022, May 24). European business leaders fear rising protectionism. *Financial Times*.

International Labour Organization and Organization for Economic Co-operation and Development (2019). New job opportunities in an ageing society. Paper presented at the 1st Meeting of the G20 Employment Working Group, 25–27 February 2019, Tokyo, Japan.

International Monetary Fund (2022). Global Debt Database.

Juhász, R., Lane, N., Oehlsen, E. and Pérez, V. C. (2023). *Trends in Global Industrial Policy*. Industrial Analytics Platform.

Medlock, K. B. (2016). The shale revolution and its implications for the world energy market. *IEEJ Energy Journal*, **Special Issue**, pp. 89–95.

Myers, J. (2021). This is what people think about trade and globalization. World Economic Forum.

Oppenheimer, P., Jaisson, G., Bell, S., Peytavin, L. and Graziani, F. (2022). The Postmodern Cycle: Positioning for secular change. Goldman Sachs Global Investment Research, Global Strategy Paper. Available at https://publishing.gs.com/content/research/en/reports/2022/05/09/521c316d-2d20-4784-b955-57641712e9d0.html.

Organisation for Economic Co-operation and Development (2017). Towards a better globalisation: How Germany can respond to the critics. Better Policies Series.

Oxenford, M. (2018). The lasting effects of the financial crisis have yet to be felt. Chatham House Expert Comment.

President Clinton (2000). The United States on track to pay off the debt by end of the decade. Available at https://clintonwhitehouse5.archives.gov/WH/new/html/Fri_Dec_29_151111_2000.html.

PwC (2021). *The Potential Impact of Artificial Intelligence on UK Employment and the Demand for Skills*. A Report by PwC for the Department for Business, Energy and Industrial Strategy.

Roser, M. and Rodés-Guirao, L. (2019). Future population growth. Available at https://ourworldindata.org/population-growth.

Rowsell, J. (2022, August 19). What's behind the rise in trade protectionism? *Supply Management*.

Roy, A. (2022). *Demographics Unravelled: How Demographics Affect and Influence Every Aspect of Economics, Finance and Policy.* Chichester: Wiley.

Smolyansky, M. (2023). End of an Era: The Coming Long-Run Slowdown in Corporate Profit Growth and Stock Returns. Available at: https://www.federalreserve.gov/econres/feds/end-of-an-era-the-coming-long-run-slowdown-in-corporate-profit-growth-and-stock-returns.htm.

The White House (2022). The Impact of Artificial Intelligence on the Future of Workforces in the European Union and the United States of America. Available at https://www.whitehouse.gov/wp-content/uploads/2022/12/TTC-EC-CEA-AI-Report-12052022-1.pdf.

The White House (2023a). Joint Statement from the United States and India. Available at https://www.whitehouse.gov/briefing-room/statements-releases/2023/06/22/joint-statement-from-the-united-states-and-india/.

The White House (2023b). Remarks by National Security Advisor Jake Sullivan on Renewing American Economic Leadership at the Brookings Institution. Available at https://www.whitehouse.gov/briefing-room/speeches-remarks/2023/04/27/remarks-by-national-security-advisor-jake-sullivan-on-renewing-american-economic-leadership-at-the-brookings-institution/.

Thompson, W. R. (1986). Polarity, the long cycle, and global power warfare. *Journal of Conflict Resolution*, **30**(4), pp. 587–615.

United Nations (2022). *World Population Prospects 2022: Summary of Results.* New York: United Nations Department of Economic and Social Affairs.

Chapter 11: The Post-Modern Cycle and Technology

Armstrong, M. (2023). Games dominate global app revenue. Available at https://www.statista.com/chart/29389/global-app-revenue-by-segment/.

Baskin, J. S. (2013). The internet didn't kill Blockbuster, the company did it to itself. Available at https://www.forbes.com/sites/jonathansalembaskin/2013/11/08/the-internet-didnt-kill-blockbuster-the-company-did-it-to-itself/.

Brynjolfsson, E., Collis, A. and Eggers, F. (2019). Using massive online choice experiments to measure changes in well-being. *Proceedings of the National Academy of Sciences*, **116**(15), pp. 7250–7255.

Brynjolfsson, E., Li, D. and Raymond, L. (2023). Generative AI at work. NBER Working Paper No. 31161.

Brynjolfsson, E., Rock, D. and Syverson, C. (2021). The Productivity J-Curve: How intangibles complement general purpose technologies. *American Economic Journal: Macroeconomics*, **13**(1), pp. 333–372.

Chancellor, E. and Kramer, C. (2000). *Devil Take the Hindmost: A History of Financial Speculation*. New York: Plume Books.

Clark, P. (2023, June 3). The dismal truth about email. *Financial Times*.

Crafts, N. (2004). Productivity growth in the Industrial Revolution: A new growth accounting perspective. *The Journal of Economic History*, **64**(2), pp. 521–535.

David, P. A. and Wright, G. (1999). General purpose technologies and surges in productivity: Historical reflections on the future of the ICT revolution. Paper presented at the International Symposium on Economic Challenges of the 21st Century in Historical Perspective, Oxford, 2–4 July.

Hatzius, J., Briggs, J., Kodnani, D. and Pierdomenico, G. (2023). The potentially large effects of artificial intelligence on economic growth (Briggs/Kodnani). Goldman Sachs Global Investment Research. Available at https://publishing.gs.com/content/research/en/reports/2023/03/27/d64e052b-0f6e-45d7-967b-d7be35fabd16.html.

Hatzius, J., Phillips, A., Mericle, D., Hill, S., Struyven, D., Choi, D., *et al.* (2019). Productivity Paradox v2.0: The price of free goods. Goldman Sachs Global Investment Research. Available at https://publishing.gs.com/content/research/en/reports/2019/07/15/d359dbb5-88ce-4cfb-8fdd-e7687bf2b4e1.html.

Mühleisen, M. (2018). The long and short of the digital revolution. *Finance and Development*, **55**(2), art. A002.

Odlyzko, A. (2000). Collective hallucinations and inefficient markets: The British railway mania of the 1840s. Available at SSRN: https://ssrn.com/abstract=1537338 or http://dx.doi.org/10.2139/ssrn.1537338.

RiskIQ (2021). 2020 Mobile App Threat Landscape Report: Tumultuous year bred new threats, but the app ecosystem got safer. Available at https://www.riskiq.com/wp-content/uploads/2021/01/RiskIQ-2020-Mobile-App-Threat-Landscape-Report.pdf.

Roach, S. S. (2015). Why is technology not boosting productivity? Available at https://www.weforum.org/agenda/2015/06/why-is-technology-not-boosting-productivity.

Sevilla, J., Heim, L., Ho, A., Besiroglu, T., Hobbhahn, M. and Villalobos, P. (2022). Compute trends across three eras of machine learning. arXiv:2202.05924.

Smith, D. K. and Alexander, R. C. (1999). *Fumbling the Future: How Xerox Invented, then Ignored, the First Personal Computer*. Bloomington, IN: iUniverse.

Chapter 12: The Post-Modern Cycle: Opportunities in the 'Old Economy'

Asprou, E. (2019, October 22). Vinyl records to outsell CDs in 2019 for the first time in 40 years. Classic FM.

BlueGreen Alliance (2022). 9 Million jobs from climate action: The Inflation Reduction Act. Available at https://www.bluegreenalliance .org/site/9-million-good-jobs-from-climate-action-the-inflation-reduction-act/.

Climate Power (2023). Clean energy boom: The 142,016 (and counting) new clean energy jobs across the United States. Available at https://climatepower .us/wp-content/uploads/sites/23/2023/04/Clean-Energy-Boom-Report-%E2%80%94-April-2023.pdf.

de Klerk, A. (2021, June 23). Secondhand clothing market set to be twice the size of fast fashion by 2030. *Harper's BAZAAR*.

Dell Technologies (2018). Realizing 2030: A divided vision of the future. Available at https://www.delltechnologies.com/content/dam/delltechnologies/ assets/perspectives/2030/pdf/Realizing-2030-A-Divided-Vision-of-the-Future-Research.pdf.

Della Vigna, M. (2023). The third American energy revolution. Goldman Sachs Global Investment Research.

Energy Transitions Commission (2023). Financing the transition: Making money flow for net zero. Available at https://www.energy-transitions .org/publications/financing-the-transition-etc/.

Erten, B. and Ocampo, J. A. (2013). Super cycles of commodity prices since the mid-nineteenth century. *World Development*, **44**, pp. 14–30.

European Commission (2021). Recovery plan for Europe. Available at https:// commission.europa.eu/strategy-and-policy/recovery-plan-europe_en.

Farra, E. (2020, November 21). 2020 was a big year for old clothes: How vintage, secondhand, and upcycling took off. *Vogue*.

Fashion Technology Accelerator (2022). Second-hand business growth: Vintage today. Available at https://www.ftaccelerator.it/blog/second-hand-business-vintage/.

Forbes Wealth Team (2023). The top ten richest people in the world. Available at https://www.forbes.com/sites/forbeswealthteam/article/the-top-ten-richest-people-in-the-world/.

Foster, A. (2023, April 28). HMV's flagship Oxford Street store to reopen. BBC News.

References

333

Friedlander, P. (2021). Year-end 2020 RIAA revenues statistics. Available at https://www.riaa.com/wp-content/uploads/2021/02/2020-Year-End-Music-Industry-Revenue-Report.pdf.
Friedman, L. (2016). Why nostalgia marketing works so well with millennials, and how your brand can benefit. Available at https://www.forbes.com/sites/laurenfriedman/2016/08/02/why-nostalgia-marketing-works-so-well-with-millennials-and-how-your-brand-can-benefit/.
Global Infrastructure Hub (2017). Global infrastructure investment need to reach USD97 trillion by 2040. Available at https://www.gihub.org/media/global-infrastructure-investment-need-to-reach-usd97-trillion-by-2040/.
Grand View Research (2023a). Bicycle Market Size, Share and Trends Analysis Report, 2023–2030.
Grand View Research (2023b). Artisanal Bakery Products Market Size, Share and Trends Analysis Report, 2023–2030.
House of Commons Library (2022). Defence spending pledges by NATO members since Russia invaded Ukraine. Available at https://commonslibrary.parliament.uk/defence-spending-pledges-by-nato-members-since-russia-invaded-ukraine/.
Inagaki, K. (2022, December 16). Japan scraps pacifist postwar defence strategy to counter China threat. *Financial Times*.
International Energy Agency (2021). Net Zero by 2050: A Roadmap for the Global Energy Sector.
Jaisson, G., Oppenheimer, P., Bell, S., Peytavin, L. and Ferrario, A. (2021). Renewables and other companies investing for the future. Goldman Sachs Global Investment Research. Available at https://publishing.gs.com/content/research/en/reports/2021/06/08/08d49f00-f091-4c9b-ab64-b0a398023f33.html.
Kielty, M. K. (2023, April 19). ABBA doesn't know how 'Voyage' show has succeeded. *Ultimate Classic Rock*.
Market Prospects (2022). The rising popularity of cargo bikes. Available at https://www.market-prospects.com/index.php/articles/popularity-of-cargo-bikes.
Marksteiner, A. (2022). Explainer: The proposed hike in German military spending. Available at https://sipri.org/commentary/blog/2022/explainer-proposed-hike-german-military-spending.
McKinsey Global Institute (2013). McKinsey: 57 trillion dollar for global infrastructure. Available at https://www.consultancy.uk/news/153/mckinsey-57-trillion-dollar-for-global-infrastructure.
Nathan, A., Galbraith, G. L. and Grimberg, J. (2020). Investing in climate change. Goldman Sachs Global Investment Research.

Odlyzko, A. (2000). Collective hallucinations and inefficient markets: The British railway mania of the 1840s. Available at SSRN: https://ssrn.com/abstract=1537338 or http://dx.doi.org/10.2139/ssrn.1537338.

Shahbandeh, M. (2021). Swiss watch industry – statistics & facts. Available at https://www.statista.com/topics/7813/swiss-watch-industry/.

Smith, J. (2022a). Four key takeaways from the 2022 proxy season. Available at https://www.ey.com/en_us/board-matters/four-key-takeaways-from-the-2022-proxy-season.

Smith, P. (2022b). Female consumer willingness to buy secondhand apparel by age worldwide 2019. Available at https://www.statista.com/statistics/828034/willingness-to-buy-secondhand-items-by-age-worldwide/.

Statista (2023). Cinema tickets – worldwide. Available at https://www.statista.com/outlook/dmo/eservices/event-tickets/cinema-tickets/worldwide.

Sutton, M. (2020, December 2). Annual bike sales to run at more than double new car registrations by 2030. *Cycling Industry News*.

The New Climate Economy (2016). The Sustainable Infrastructure Imperative: Financing for Better Growth and Development.

The White House (2022, August 9). FACT SHEET: CHIPS and Science Act will lower costs, create jobs, strengthen supply chains, and counter China.

ThredUP Resale Report (2023). Available at https://www.thredup.com/resale.

United Nations (2023). World Investment Report 2021.

U.S. Bureau of Labor Statistics (2018). Employment projections: 2018–2028 summary. Available at https://www.bls.gov/news.release/archives/ecopro_09042019.pdf.

Suggested Reading

Anderson, R. G. (2010). The first U.S. quantitative easing: The 1930s. Federal Reserve Bank of St. Louis Economic Synopses No. 17. Available at https://files.stlouisfed.org/files/htdocs/publications/es/10/ES1017.pdf.

Armantier, O., Goldman, L., Koşar, G., Topa, G., van der Klaauw, W. and Williams, C. J. (2022, February 14). What are consumers' inflation expectations telling us today? *Liberty Street Economics*.

Arroyo Abad, L. and van Zanden, J. L. (2016). Growth under extractive institutions? Latin American per capita GDP in colonial times. *Journal of Economic History*, **76**(4), pp. 1182–1215.

Axenciuc, V. (2012). Produsul intern brut al Romaniei: 1862–2000. Institutl de Economie Nationala, 1.

Baffigi, A. (2011). Italian National Accounts, 1861–2011. Banca d'Italia Economic History Working Papers No. 18.

Barro, R. J. and Ursua, J. F. (2008). Macroeconomic crises since 1870. *Brookings Papers on Economic Activity, Economic Studies Program, The Brookings Institution*, **39**(1), pp. 255–350.

Bassino, J.-P., Broadberry, S., Fukao, K., Gupta, B. and Takashima, M. (2018). Japan and the Great Divergence, 730–1874. CEI Working Paper Series 2018-13.

Bernanke, B. S. (2015). Why are interest rates so low? Available at https://www.brookings.edu/articles/why-are-interest-rates-so-low/.

Bèrtola, L. (2016). El PIB per capita de Uruguay 1870–2016: una reconstruccion. PHES Working Paper No. 48.

Bèrtola, L. and Ocampo, J. A. (2012). *The Economic Development of Latin America Since Independence*. Oxford: Oxford University Press.

Blanchard, O. (2022). Why I worry about inflation, interest rates, and unemployment. Available at https://www.piie.com/blogs/realtime-economic-issues-watch/why-i-worry-about-inflation-interest-rates-and-unemployment.

Bolt, J. and van Zanden, J. L. (2020). Maddison style estimates of the evolution of the world economy. A new 2020 update. Maddison-Project Working Paper WP-15.

Broadbent, B. (2018). The history and future of QE. Available at https://www.bankofengland.co.uk/-/media/boe/files/speech/2018/the-history-and-future-of-qe-speech-by-ben-broadbent.pdf?la=en&hash=127499DFD9AE5D6E0F3FC73529E83FDF9766471D.

Broadberry, S. and van Leeuwen, B. (2011). *The Growth of the English Economy, 1086-1270*. London: LSE.

Broadberry, S. N., Custodis, J. and Gupta, B. (2015). India and the great divergence: An Anglo-Indian comparison of GDP per capita, 1600–1871. *Explorations in Economic History*, **55**, pp. 58–75.

Broadberry, S. N., Guan, H. and Li, D. D. (2018). China, Europe and the Great Divergence: A study in historical national accounting, 980–1850. *Journal of Economic History*, **78**(4), pp. 955–1000.

Buyst, E. (2011). Towards estimates of long term growth in the Southern Low Countries, ca. 1500–1846. Available at https://warwick.ac.uk/fac/soc/economics/seminars/seminars/conferences/venice3/programme/buyst.pdf.

Caballero, R. J. (2010). Macroeconomics after the crisis: Time to deal with the pretense-of-knowledge syndrome. *Journal of Economic Perspectives*, **24**(4), pp. 85–102.

Caballero, R. J. and Krishnamurthy, A. (2009). Global imbalances and financial fragility. *American Economic Review*, **99**(2), pp. 584–588.

Caballero, R. J., Farhi, E. and Gourinchas, P.-O. (2017). The safe assets shortage conundrum. *Journal of Economic Perspectives*, **31**(3), pp. 29–46.

Caballero, R. J., Farhi, E. and Gourinchas, P.-O. (2020). Global imbalances and policy wars at the zero lower bound. NBER Working Paper w21670.

Cha, M. S., Kim, N. N., Park, K.-J. and Park, Y. (2020). *Historical Statistics of Korea*. New York: Springer.

Clark, G. (2007a). The long march of history: Farm wages, population, and economic growth, England 1209–1869. *The Economic History Review*, **60**(1), pp. 97–135.

Clark, G. (2007b). *A Farewell to Alms: A Brief Economic History of the World*. Princeton, NJ: Princeton University Press.

Clark, G. (2014). The price history of English agriculture, 1209–1914. In *Research in Economic History*. Bingley: Emerald Publishing, pp. 41–123.

Crafts, N. F. R. and Harley, C. K. (1992). Output growth and the British Industrial Revolution: A restatement of the Crafts–Harley view. *The Economic History Review*, **45**(4), pp. 703–730.

De Corso, G. (2013). Venezuelan economic growth from the conservative oligarchy to the Bolivarian Revolution: 1830–2012. *Revista de Historia Económica – Journal of Iberian and Latin American Economic History*, **31**(3), pp. 321–357.

Del Negro, M., Giannone, D., Giannoni, M. P. and Tambalotti, A. (2019). Global trends in interest rates. *Journal of International Economics*, **118**, pp. 248–262.

DeLong, B. J. (2002). Productivity growth in the 2000s. *NBER Macroeconomics Annual*, **17**, pp. 113–145.

Diffie, B. W. and Boxer, C. R. (1962). Four centuries of Portuguese expansion, 1415–1825: A succinct survey. *The William and Mary Quarterly*, **19**(4), p. 640.

Dumenil, G., Glick, M. A. and Lévy, D. (2000). Long-term trends in profitability: The recovery of World War II. Jerome Levy Economics Institute Working Paper No. 10.

Eloranta, J., Voutilainen, M. and Nummela, I. (2016). Estimating Finnish economic growth before 1860.

Fatas, A. (2000). Do business cycles cast long shadows? Short-run persistence and economic growth. *Journal of Economic Growth*, **5**(2), pp. 147–162.

Federal Reserve Bank of New York (2002). Economic Policy Review – Financial Innovation and Monetary Transmission.

Feinstein, C. H. (1991). A new look at the cost of living 1870–1914. In J. Foreman-Peck (ed.), *New Perspectives on the Late Victorian Economy: Essays in Quantitative Economic History, 1860–1914*. Cambridge: Cambridge University Press, pp. 151–179.

Feinstein, C. H. (1998). Pessimism perpetuated: Real wages and the standard of living in Britain during and after the Industrial Revolution. *The Journal of Economic History*, **58**(3), pp. 625–658.

Fiorentini, G., Galesi, A., Pérez-Quirós, G. and Sentana, E. (2018). The rise and fall of the natural interest rate. Banco de Espana Working Paper No. 1822.

Fourie, J. and Van Zanden, J. L. (2013). GDP in the Dutch Cape Colony: The national accounts of a slave-based society. *South African Journal of Economics*, **81**(4), pp. 467–490.

Fukao, K., Bassino, J.-P., Makino, T., Paprzycki, R., Settsu, T., Takashima, M. and Tokui, J. (2015). *Regional Inequality and Industrial Structure in Japan: 1874–2008*. Tokyo: Maruzen.

Fukao, K., Ma, D. and Yuan, T. (2007). Real GDP in pre-war East Asia: A 1934–36 benchmark purchasing power parity comparison with the U.S. *Review of Income and Wealth*, **53**(3), pp. 503–537.

Gamber, E. N. (2020). The historical decline in real interest rates and its implications for CBO's projections. Congressional Budget Office Working Paper 2020-09.

Garcia, A. S. (2005). Las cuentas nacionales de Cuba, 1960–2005. Available at https://digital.csic.es/bitstream/10261/29002/4/PIB%201690-2010.pdf.

Gerbaudo, P. (2021, February 13). Big government is back. *Foreign Policy*.

Girod, S. J. G. (2016). Part 1: The end of globalization? Available at https://www.imd.org/research-knowledge/strategy/articles/part-1-the-end-of-globalization/.

Goodhart, C. and Pradhan, M. (2020). The great demographic reversal. *Economic Affairs*, **40**(3), pp. 436–445.

Gourinchas, P. O. and Rey, H. (2016). Real interest rates, imbalances and the curse of regional safe asset providers at the zero lower bound. NBER Working Paper w22618.

Gregory, P. R. (1982). *Russian National Income, 1885–1913*. Cambridge: Cambridge University Press.

Grytten, O. H. (2015). Norwegian gross domestic product by industry 1830–1930. Norges Bank Working Paper 19/2015.

Haberler, G., Harris, S. E., Leontief, W. W. and Mason, E. S. (1951). Professor Joseph A. Schumpeter. *The Review of Economics and Statistics*, **33**(2), pp. 89–90.

Hansen, A. H. (1951). Schumpeter's contribution to business cycle theory. *The Review of Economics and Statistics*, **33**(2), pp. 129–132.

Herranz-Loncán, A. and Peres-Cajías, J. (2016). Bolivian GDP per capita since the mid-nineteenth century. *Cliometrica*, **10**, pp. 99–128.

Hills, S., Thomas, R. and Dimsdale, N. (2010). The UK recession in context – what do three centuries of data tell us? *Bank of England Quarterly Bulletin*, **Q4**, pp. 277–291.

Høj, J., Kato, T. and Pilat, D. (1995). Deregulation and privatisation in the service sector. OECD Economic Studies No. 25.

Hördahl, P., Sobrun, J. and Turner, P. (2016). Low long-term interest rates as a global phenomenon. BIS Working Paper No. 574.

International Monetary Fund (2000). IMF World Economic Outlook (WEO), Asset Prices and the Business Cycle.

Ivanov, M. (2006). Bulgarian national income between 1892 and 1924. Bulgarian National Discussion Papers DP/54/2006.

Jongrim, H., Kose, M. A. and Ohnsorge, F. (2022, July 1). Today's global economy is eerily similar to the 1970s, but governments can still escape a stagflation episode. *Brookings*.

Keynes, J. M. (1930). Economic possibilities for our grandchildren. In *Essays in Persuasion*. London: Palgrave Macmillan, pp. 358–373.

Kim, C.-J. and Nelson, C. R. (1999). Has the U.S. economy become more stable? A Bayesian approach based on a Markov-switching model of the business cycle. *The Review of Economics and Statistics*, **81**(4), pp. 608–616.

King, S. D. (2018). *Grave New World: The End of Globalization, the Return of History*. New Haven, CT: Yale University Press.

Kostelenos, G., Petmezas, S., Vasiliou, D., Kounaris, E. and Sfakianakis, M. (2007). *Gross Domestic Product 1830–1939*. Sources of Economic History of Modern Greece: Quantitative Data and Statistical Series 1830–1939. Historical Archives of the National Bank of Greece, Athens.

Krantz, O. (2017). Swedish GDP 1300–1560: A tentative estimate. Lund Papers in Economic History: General Issues No. 152.

Laubach, T. and Williams, J. C. (2016). Measuring the natural rate of interest redux. *Business Economics*, **51**(2), pp. 57–67.

Lindert, P. H. (2004). *Growing Public: Social Spending and Economic Growth Since the Eighteenth Century*. Cambridge: Cambridge University Press.

Lisack, N., Sajedi, R. and Thwaites, G. (2021). Population ageing and the macroeconomy. Banque de france Working Paper WP #745.

Maddison, A. (1995). *Monitoring the World Economy 1820–1992*. Paris: OECD.

Maddison, A. (2001). *The World Economy*. Paris: OECD.

Maddison, A. (2003). *The World Economy: Historical Statistics*. Paris: OECD.

Maddison, A. (2007). Contours of the World Economy, 1–2030 AD: Essays in Macro-economic History. Oxford: Oxford University Press.

Malinowski, M. and van Zanden, J. L. (2017). National income and its distribution in preindustrial Poland in a global perspective. *Cliometrica*, **11**(3), pp. 375–404.

Markevich, A. and Harrison, M. (2011). Great War, Civil War, and recovery: Russia's national income, 1913 to 1928. *The Journal of Economic History*, **71**(3), pp. 672–703.

McCusker, J. J. (2006). *Historical Statistics of the United States*, Millennial Edition Online: Colonial Statistics. Cambridge: Cambridge University Press.

Meister, D. (2011, February 2). Ronald Reagan, enemy of the American worker. *Truthout*.

Milanovic, B. (2006). An estimate of average income and inequality in Byzantium around year 1000. *Review of Income and Wealth*, **52**(3), pp. 449–470.

Milner, H. (1987). Resisting the protectionist temptation: Industry and the making of trade policy in France and the United States during the 1970s. *International Organization*, **41**(4), pp. 639–665.

Mitchell, B. R. (1988). *British Historical Statistics*. Cambridge: Cambridge University Press.

Nazrin Shah, S. (2017). *Charting the Economy: Early 20th Century Malaya and Contemporary Malaysian Contrasts*. Oxford: Oxford University Press.

Neufeld, D. (2020, February 4). Visualizing the 700-year fall of interest rates. *Visual Capitalist*.

O'Sullivan, M. (2022, December 15). Return of the state – will big government come back as recession hits? *Forbes*.

Palma, N. (2019). Money and modernization in early modern England. University of Manchester and CEPR. EHES Working Paper No. 147.

Palma, N. and Reis, J. (2019). From convergence to divergence: Portuguese economic growth, 1527–1850. *The Journal of Economic History*, **79**(2), pp. 477–506.

Pamuk, S. (2006). Estimating economic growth in the Middle East since 1820. *The Journal of Economic History*, **66**(3), pp. 809–828.

Pamuk, Ş. (2009). Estimating GDP per capita for the Ottoman Empire in a European comparative framework, 1500–1820. XVth World Economic History Congress.

Pamuk, Ş. and Shatzmiller, M. (2011). Real wages and GDP per capita in the Medieval Islamic Middle East in comparative perspective, 700–1500. IXth Conference of the European Historical Economics Society.

Pfister, U. (2011). Economic growth in Germany, 1500–1850. Quantifying Long Run Economic Development Conference, University of Warwick.

Prados de la Escosura, L. (2009). Lost decades? Economic performance in post-independence Latin America. *Journal of Latin America Studies*, **41**, pp. 279–307.

Prados de la Escosura, L. (2017). *Spanish Economic Growth, 1850-2015*. London: Palgrave Macmillan.

Ramskogler, P. (2015). Tracing the origins of the financial crisis. *OECD Journal: Financial Market Trends*, **2014**(2), pp. 47–61.

Ridolfi, L. (2016). The French economy in the longue durée: A study on real wages, working days and economic performance from Louis IX to the Revolution (1250–1789). *European Review of Economic History*, **12**(4), pp. 437–438.

Roy, A. (2021). *Demographics Unravelled: How Demographics Affect and Influence Every Aspect of Economics, Finance and Policy*. Chichester: Wiley.

Scheidel, W. and Friesen, S. J. (2009). The size of the economy and the distribution of income in the Roman Empire. *Journal of Roman Studies*, **99**, pp. 61–91.

Schumpeter, J. (1927). The explanation of the business cycle. *Economica*, **21**, pp. 286–311.

Seminario, B. (2015). El Desarrallo de la Economía Peruana en la Era Moderna. Universidad de Pacifico, Lima.

Smits, J. P., Horlings, E. and van Zanden, J. L. (2000). *The Measurement of Gross National Product and Its Components 1800–1913*. Groningen Growth and Development Centre Monograph Series No. 5.

Stohr, C. (2016). Trading gains: New estimates of Swiss GDP, 1851–2008. LSE Economic History Working Paper 245/2016.

Sugimoto, I. (2011). Economic Growth of Singapore in the Twentieth Century: Historical GDP Estimates and Empirical Investigations. Economic Growth Centre Research Monograph Series No. 2.

Summers, H. L. (2014). Reflections on the new 'Secular Stagnation hypothesis'. Available at https://cepr.org/voxeu/columns/reflections-new-secular-stagnation-hypothesis.

Sutch, R. (2006). National income and product. In S. B. Carter, S. S. Gartner, M. R. Haines, *et al.* (eds), *Historical Statistics of the United States: Earliest Time to the Present*. New York: Cambridge University Press, pp. 23–25.

The Conference Board (2020). Total Economy Database.

The U.S. Census Bureau (2020). Population data.

The Victorian Web (2010). The Victorian revolution in letter writing. Available at https://victorianweb.org/technology/letters/intro.html.

The Washington Post (1982, May 24). The boom of the 1980s. *The Washington Post*.

Van Bavel, J. and Reher, D. S. (2013). The baby boom and its causes: What we know and what we need to know. *Population and Development Review*, **39**(2), pp. 257–288.

Van der Eng, P. (2010). The sources of long-term economic growth in Indonesia, 1880–2008. *Explorations in Economic History*, **47**, pp. 294–309.

Van Zanden, J. (2012). Economic growth in Java 1815–1939: The reconstruction of the historical national accounts of a colonial economy. Maddison-Project Working Paper WP-3.

Van Zanden, J. L. (2009). *The Long Road to the Industrial Revolution: The European Economy in a Global Perspective, 1000–1800*. Leiden: Brill.

Ward, M. and Devereux, J. (2012). The road not taken: Pre-revolutionary Cuban living standards in comparative perspective. *Journal of Economic History*, **72**(1), pp. 104–132.

Wike, R., Fetterolf, J., Schumacher, S. and Moncus, J. J. (2021). Citizens in
    Advanced Economies Want Significant Changes to Their Political Systems.
    Pew Research Center's Global Attitudes Project.

Wu, H. X. (2014). China's growth and productivity performance debate revis-
    ited – accounting for China's sources of growth with a new data set. The
    Conference Board Economics Program Working Paper Series, EWP#14-01.

Xu, Y., Shi, Z., van Leeuwen, B., Ni, Y., Zhang, Z. and Ma, Y. (2016). Chinese
    national income, ca. 1661–1933. *Asia-Pacific Economic History Review*,
    57(3), pp. 368–393.

Index

Page numbers followed by e refer to exhibits.

343